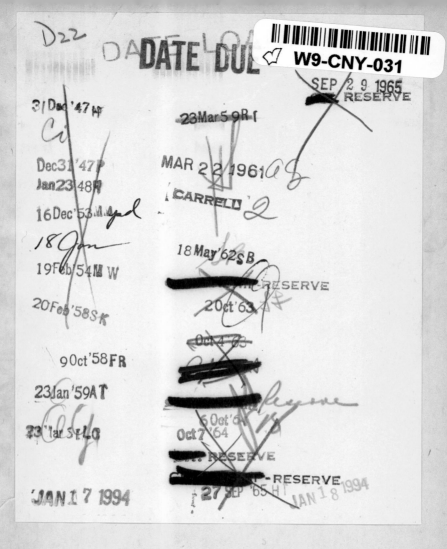

Seizure of Territory

THE STIMSON DOCTRINE
AND RELATED PRINCIPLES IN LEGAL THEORY
AND DIPLOMATIC PRACTICE

By Robert Langer

PRINCETON, NEW JERSEY
PRINCETON UNIVERSITY PRESS, 1947

Printed in the United States of America
By American Book–Stratford Press, Inc., New York

ALL human history is pervaded by the struggle of two principles: one of them expressed in the slogan, *Macht geht vor Recht;* the other in the Roman maxim, *Ex iniuria ius non oritur.* In the field of territorial change the first principle prevailed unchallenged throughout the centuries, embodied in the so-called "right of conquest." By virtue of this principle, the seizure of territory by a State which was able to overpower a weaker neighbor was legally nobody else's concern; it just had to be "accepted as a fact" by the other members of the international community. Only very late the idea began to develop that a territorial change, to be fully effective, should be based on something more than a unilateral tour de force, namely, on some form of assent on the part of third States. In this development, two stages are discernible. At first the right to change the territorial status quo by unilateral action was only challenged by States which were parties to the treaties by which that status had previously been established. At a later stage it was conceived that such changes should be a matter of concern, politically as well as legally, even to States which were neither directly nor indirectly affected by the respective transfer. This conception manifested itself in the idea, now commonly known as the Stimson Doctrine, of non-recognition of territorial changes brought about by force or the threat of force. It is the object of this book to examine whether and how far such non-recognition was raised to the rank of a legal duty under international law, and to analyze its implications in the various fields of governmental activity. To this effect the subject matter was divided into three parts. The first traces the development of the non-recognition principle, as reflected in diplomatic practice and in the drafts of international jurists. The second discusses the legal aspects of non-recognition, while the third undertakes to digest the diplomatic practice of the last decade.

Wartime conditions, of course, imposed restrictions, especially regarding the third part of the work. It was impossible to ascertain in detail the attitude of all those States which had assumed commitments of non-recognition regarding forcible seizures of territory; the practice of the most prominent Powers, however, as well as that of the League of Nations, was open to investigation. In selecting the material, the author deemed it proper also to give wide scope to the views of members of the British Parliament who opposed the recognition policies of their government. In presenting the subject matter, the author refrained as far as possible from interpolated comment, preferring to let the documents speak for themselves, and to draw his conclusions in a final part. The object of the latter is to analyze how far the non-recognition principle was able to assert itself in the turmoil of the last decade, and whether it should be maintained or even broadened in its scope of application.

*   *   *

The author wishes to express his gratitude to the members of the Faculties of Law and Political Science of Columbia University, New York, under whose auspices this work was initiated and matured: to his sponsor, Professor Joseph P. Chamberlain, whose scholarly advice, generously given with inexhaustible patience, was a constant source of inspiration; to Professor Charles C. Hyde, whose constructive criticism was instrumental in condensing and concentrating the subject matter; to Professor Philip C. Jessup, whose suggestions were essential in giving the manuscript the finishing touch; to Professor Nathaniel Peffer, whose first-hand knowledge of the "Greater Asia Co-Prosperity Sphere" helped the author a great deal to grasp the involved problems of the Far East.

The author is also indebted to Miss Florence Firner, of the John B. Moore Library of Columbia University, whose untiring assistance was invaluable in securing the voluminous source material, and to Miss Mariana Smith, secretary to Professor Chamberlain, whose coordinating genius contributed immensely to the comparatively rapid completion of this work.

New York City, September 1946   ROBERT LANGER

TABLE OF CONTENTS

PART I

Historical Survey

CHAPTER I

TERRITORIAL CHANGE IN
EUROPE, 1792–1878

UNTIL a comparatively recent period international relations were based on the conception that territorial changes effected by force or the threat of force did not require for their full validity the assent of Powers not directly affected by them, and that consequently no room was left for the granting or withholding of such assent. During the French Revolution and the Napoleonic Wars a different tendency developed. Napoleon, although asserting that France herself needed no recognition,[1] was very eager to obtain the assent, in the form of "explicit recognition," to the territorial readjustments which marked the conclusion of his various campaigns, even from such sovereigns whose possessions were neither directly nor indirectly affected by the respective changes.[2]

The British Government never formally recognized the French Republic nor the French Empire and its dependencies. It did, however, conclude with France truces and peace treaties such as the Treaty of Amiens, signed on March 27, 1802,[3] or the treaties which ended Napoleon's rule. It is rather hard not to see in these acts some sort of recognition.

The United States Government tended to consider the changes effected by the French campaigns from the angle of recognition of new governments and States rather than from that of the recognition of conquests. In contradistinction to British policies, the keynote of the American attitude with

---

[1] "La République française n'a pas besoin de reconnaissance, tout comme le soleil n'a pas besoin d'être reconnu." (Quoted by Lecharny, *La Validité Interne des Gouvernements de Fait*, 17)

[2] Art. 1 Franco-Dutch Treaty of the Hague, May 16, 1795 (4 De Clercq 236); Art. 8 Treaty of Campoformio, October 17, 1797 (*Ibid.* 335); Art. 9 Treaty of Amiens, March 27, 1802 (*Ibid.* 484); Art. 5 and 7 Treaty of Pressburg, December 26, 1805 (2 De Clercq 145); Art. 5, 14, 15, 18-20 Franco-Russian Treaty of Tilsit, July 7, 1807 (*Ibid.* 207); Art. 16 Franco-Prussian Treaty of Paris, September 8, 1808 (*Ibid.* 270)

[3] 1 De Clercq 484

regard to these changes was the acceptance of the fait accompli. This attitude was in the main based on Jefferson's philosophy as expressed in two letters to Ambassador Morris. In the first of these letters, dated November 7, 1792, Jefferson wrote:

It accords with our principles to acknowledge any government to be rightful which is formed by the will of the nation substantially declared. . . . With such a government every kind of business may be done. But there are some matters which I conceive may be transacted with a government de facto; such, as for instance, as the reforming the unfriendly restrictions on our commerce and navigations.[4]

The second letter, dated March 12, 1793, had the following text:

We certainly cannot deny to other nations that principle whereon our own government is founded; that every nation has a right to govern itself internally under what form it pleases and to change these forms at its own will; and externally to transact business with other nations through whatever organ it chooses whether that be a king, convention, assembly, president or whatever it be. The only thing essential is the will of the nation.[5]

The first case confronting the United States with the question of recognizing a territorial change connected with the French revolutionary wars arose when the United States Minister to the Netherlands, John Quincy Adams, sought instructions as to the course he should pursue in case of the conquest of that country by France. Mr. Randolph, then Secretary of State, replied:

Should the United Netherlands become a dependency of France, Mr. Adams' mission would of course be ended by the extinction of the nation itself.[6]

This instruction reveals the absence of any idea of nonrecognition of territorial changes effected by conquest. Nothing indicates that the Government of the United States changed its attitude in the later course of the Napoleonic era.

The most involved problem with which the Government of the United States had to deal in connection with the Na-

4 1 Moore, *Dig.* 120
5 *Ibid.*
6 *Ibid.* 128

poleonic territorial changes was that of Naples. The Kingdom of the Two Sicilies had been split by the Napoleonic conquest, the Bourbon King had withdrawn to Sicily, while Naples became a Napoleonic puppet kingdom under Murat, who assumed the title "King Joachim the First." The United States maintained relations with this State, and an American consul had his seat at Naples. In 1809, the Neapolitan Government invited American vessels to come to its ports, but when they arrived in greater numbers, they were seized and confiscated. After Murat's fall, the United States demanded indemnity for the seizures from the Bourbon Government, which had retransferred its seat from Sicily to Naples. The Bourbon Government took the position that the acts of "usurpers" could not be "visited upon the people subjected to their yoke, or upon the legitimate sovereigns." The true sovereign, it was argued, had never ceased to be in a state of war with the usurper of his dominions. The negotiations dragged on from 1816 until they broke down in 1825. They were resumed in 1831, and after an interesting exchange of correspondence, the controversy was finally settled in October, 1832. The King of the Two Sicilies undertook to pay to the United States the equivalent of $1,755,000 "for the depredations, sequestrations, confiscations, and destruction of the vessels and cargoes of merchants of the United States . . . inflicted by Murat during the years 1809, 1810, 1811, and 1812." [7]

The Napoleonic era was brought to an end by a general settlement, embodied in the Final Act of the Congress of Vienna, signed on June 9, 1815.[8] The original signatories were Austria, France, Great Britain, Prussia, Russia, Spain, Portugal, and Sweden. Art. 119, however, provided for the accession to the Act of "all the Powers assembled in Congress, as well as the Princes and Free Towns who have concurred in the arrangements specified, and in the acts confirmed, in this General Treaty."

The Final Act had been preceded by various separate treaties such as the Austrian-Prussian-Russian Treaties of May 3, 1815,[9] and the Treaty of May 31, 1815, between the

[7] Moore, *Arb.* 4577
[8] French text, 2 De Clercq 567, English text, 2 *BFSP* 7
[9] Below, 7

King of the Netherlands and the Powers of the Quadruple Alliance (Austria, Great Britain, Prussia, Russia).[10] These several treaties were incorporated into the Final Act in the form of annexes. Obviously with reference to them the preamble of the Final Act stated:

> The Powers who signed the Treaty concluded at Paris on May 30, 1814 . . . being now desirous to embrace in one common transaction the various results of their negotiations for the purpose of confirming them by the reciprocal ratifications. . .

The last words, beginning with "for the purpose," suggest that the draftsmen of the instrument intended to attach to the "reciprocal ratifications" some legal significance. The wording, however, is so vague that it is hard to derive from it precise conclusions of law. Doubtless Fischer Williams is right in asserting that it would be going too far to see in that action the implied claim that the assent of the recognizing parties should form a precondition of the legal validity of the transaction.[11] Nor could the words of the preamble be construed as expressing any ideas of collective guarantee or "collective security." On the other hand, it cannot be denied that the Final Act of Vienna was essentially what might be called a constitutional treaty in the sense that it embraced the territorial status of all of Europe except the areas which were under non-Christian sovereignty.

This status, however, was before long subjected to a series of modifications. The first of these changes were effected by voluntary bilateral agreements between those directly concerned, with no interference from third signatories of the Vienna Act. It was by means of such an agreement that Prussia acquired from Denmark Danish Pomerania in exchange for Lauenburg. In 1830, however, the first attempt was made to change the treaty status by force. In that year the Belgian provinces revolted against the Netherlands, to which country they had been united under the Treaty of May 31, 1815. This treaty—concluded, as the preamble

---

10 Below, 7

11 In "La Doctrine de la Reconnaissance en Droit International et ses Développements Récents," 44 *Hague Rec.* 203: "Ce serait sans doute aller trop loin que de voir dans cette action la prétention tacite que l'assentiment des parties reconnaissantes serait une condition suspensive de la validité juridique de l'opération."

said, "in order to establish a just equilibrium in Europe" [12]—had been annexed to, and partly incorporated into, the Final Act of Vienna.[13] Since a settlement by means of bilateral agreement proved impossible, the King of the Netherlands invoked the intervention of the five Great Powers who were signatories to the Vienna Act.[14] The Powers intervened, but the result of their action was no other than acquiescence in the accomplished fact, sugar-coated for the Dutch King by the following language:

> The Courts of . . . , taking into consideration the events which have occurred in the United Kingdom of the Netherlands since September, 1830, the obligation which they are under to prevent these events from disturbing the general peace, and the necessity which arises from these events of making certain modifications in the transactions of 1815. . . .[15]

The words of this preamble were significant far beyond the individual case to which they applied. For they expressed the principle of the "European Concert." Consisting of the European Great Powers, it was henceforth to be the keeper of the "Public Law of Europe," while only a very limited role was to be played by the smaller Powers whose signatures had been placed on the instrument of Vienna.

Before long another case arose in which the right even of signatory Great Powers themselves to participate in decisions involving changes in the territorial treaty status of Vienna was contested. During the Congress of Vienna the three Powers which had partitioned Poland in the eighteenth century—Austria, Prussia, and Russia—reached an agreement concerning the area of the former Republic. It was laid down in three treaties, signed on May 3, 1815.[16] As in the Belgian case, these treaties were annexed to, and partly incorporated into, the Final Act of the Congress of Vienna. Under this arrangement the greater part of ethnic Poland, henceforth known as Congress Poland, was ". . . united to the Russian Empire . . . , irrevocably attached to it by its

[12] 2 De Clercq 546 ("Afin d'établir un juste équilibre en Europe . . .")
[13] Final Act Art. 65-73, and Annex X
[14] 18 *BFSP* 728
[15] Preamble of the Treaty of London, concluded between Belgium and the five Powers on November 15, 1831 (18 *BFSP* 645)
[16] Austro-Russian Treaty (2 *BFSP* 56); Prusso-Russian Treaty (*Ibid.* 63); Austro-Prusso-Russian Treaty concerning Cracow (*Ibid.* 74)

Constitution . . ." and was to be possessed by the Russian Tsar and his successors "in perpetuity." [17] The area of Cracow was made into a "free, independent, and strictly neutral City, under the protection of Austria, Russia, and Prussia." [18] Soon after the Congress of Vienna, Tsar Alexander I granted a liberal constitution to Congress Poland. Yet under his successor, Nicholas I, a bloody insurrection broke out which was crushed after heavy fighting. On February 26, 1832, the Russian Government issued a manifesto to the effect that Congress Poland would be perpetually united to the Russian Empire and would form an integral part thereof. The British Government protested against this unilateral change of the treaty status, but acquiesced after a lengthy correspondence.[19]

About fifteen years later the Free City of Cracow was annexed to Austria under an agreement concluded between the latter, Russia, and Prussia, without even consulting the other contracting parties of the Treaty of Vienna. This time not only Great Britain, but also France protested.[20] In the end, however, both acquiesced, the British statesmen perhaps because they held that, as a British Foreign Secretary had put it in one of his instructions,

> It would be inconsistent with the power and dignity of the British Empire to insist too strongly upon points which . . . it might be inexpedient, if not impossible, to enforce by arms.[21]

It is in fact hard to deny that in those days the only alterna-

[17] Final Act Art. I
[18] *Ibid.* Art. VI
[19] 37 *BFSP* 1416 ff.
[20] For the correspondence regarding the annexation of Cracow see 24 *BFSP* 1352; Angeborg 1832; 35 *BFSP* 1042 ff. In particular an instruction dispatched by Guizot to the French envoy in Vienna on December 3, 1846 (35 *BFSP* 1093), is noteworthy for its attempt to define the concept "public law of Europe." It reads: "M. le Prince de Metternich dit . . . que les trois cours avaient créé à elles seules, le 3 mai 1815, le petit État de Cracovie, et qu'ells avaient ensuite 'présenté au Congrès de Vienne, pour enregistrement, la Convention passée entre elles.' Le Gouvernement du Roi ne saurait admettre une assertion si étrangère aux principes et même au langage des grandes transactions qui constituent le droit public européen. Les Puissances indépendantes qui traitent sur un pied de parfaite égalité, et délibérant sur des interêts communs, ne sont jamais appelées à enregistrer des déterminations et des actes adoptés sans leur participation. . . ."
[21] Palmerston's instruction to Lord Durham, St. Petersburg, dated July 3, 1832 (37 *BFSP* 1439).

tive to yielding was military action, since the idea of non-recognition was not yet born.

The most fateful changes in the treaty status of Vienna were brought about by the unification of Germany and Italy. The former involved at first no annexation of foreign territories, except in the case of Schleswig-Holstein. Italian unity, however, could only be achieved by conquest, namely, by the annexation to the Kingdom of Sardinia of the Lombardo-Venetian provinces of the Austrian Empire and of the territories of various independent Italian States (Tuscany, Naples-Sicily, etc.). Neither the Sardinian annexations nor the annexation of the Danish Duchies nor the ensuing forcible incorporation of four members of the German Confederation (Hanover, Hesse-Cassel, Nassau, and Frankfurt) into Prussia met with any serious opposition from the signatories of the Treaty of Vienna or from other Powers; acquiescence in the fait accompli was general. Exactly the same was the case when in 1871 Germany wrested Alsace and Lorraine from France.

It was the problems of southeastern Europe that gave birth to the idea that territorial changes, to be fully effective, required the assent of Powers other than those directly concerned. An early step in this direction was the collective intervention of the Powers in the Greek struggle for independence and their collective recognition of the latter.[22] The idea took further shape in the Treaty of Paris, signed on March 30, 1856,[23] which ended the Crimean war. To the said treaty not only the belligerents (Great Britain, France, Sardinia, Turkey, and Russia) affixed their signatures, but also the remaining Great Powers of Europe, Austria and Prussia. The constitutional character of the treaty is revealed in its Article 7 in which the Contracting Parties

declare the Sublime Porte admitted to participate in the advantages of the Public Law and System (Concert) of Europe. Their Majesties engage, each on his part, to respect the independence and the territorial integrity of the Ottoman Empire; guarantee in common

---

[22] See Protocol of St. Petersburg, April 4, 1826 (1 Hertslet 129); Treaty of London, July 7, 1827 (*Ibid.* 136); Treaty of Adrianople, September 14, 1829 (*Ibid.* 145); Protocol of London, February 3, 1830 (2 Hertslet 149); Treaty of London, July 5, 1832 (*Ibid.* 159); Treaty of London, July 21, 1832 (*Ibid.* 167).

[23] 46 *BFSP* 8

the strict observance of that engagement, and will, in consequence, consider any act tending to its violation as a question of general interest.

Further articles gave collective sanction to the autonomous status of Serbia, Wallachia and Moldavia, which had hitherto been based on the bilateral Russian-Turkish Treaty of Bucharest, signed in 1812,[24] and also to the transfer of southwestern Bessarabia from Russia to Moldavia. It certainly would be unwarranted to see in these provisions legal rules clearly determining the law of territorial change in the Balkan area. It may be said, however, that they reflect the idea of the "Public Law of Europe" with less vagueness than did the preamble to the Act of Vienna, and in about the same sense as Guizot's note of December 3, 1846. It is also a fact that the settlement of Paris showed more resistance to destruction by unilateral action than did the territorial setup created by the Final Act of Vienna. Thus, when Russia undertook in 1878 to change the treaty status single-handed (by the Treaty of San Stefano), her action was thwarted by other signatories to the Treaty of Paris, and only such territorial readjustments could be effected as won the recognition of the signatories, or of their successors. This recognition was embodied in a new constitutional treaty, the Act of the Congress of Berlin, concluded by Great Britain, the Austro-Hungarian Monarchy, France, Germany, Italy, Russia, and Turkey on July 13, 1878.[25] Under the provisions of this treaty, the Contracting Powers collectively undertook to erect Bulgaria into an autonomous principality, to recognize the independence of Rumania, Serbia, and Montenegro, to delimit the boundaries of these entities, and to sanction the retrocession of southwestern Bessarabia to Russia.

The territorial order thus created was to last for about one generation. It certainly cannot be claimed that the principles of recognition embodied in the Congress Act of Berlin constituted rules of international law, but within the orbit of treaty law they asserted the idea that territorial changes affecting a treaty status should not be fully effective unless

[24] 13 *BFSP* 908
[25] 69 *BFSP* 749

recognized also by signatories other than those directly concerned.[26]

[26] The law of territorial change prevailing in Europe in 1878 is summarized in Temperley's *History of the Peace Conference* (Vol. 5, p. 116) as follows: "By that time it had become a recognized principle of European international custom that in Eastern Europe the establishment of new States was a matter of general interest, requiring the formal recognition of the Great Powers who in fact, though not in law, were acting as the Concert of Europe. . . ." The statement, however, stresses that this action was confined to the East of Europe.

CHAPTER II

EUROPE, 1878–1914

I_N Europe the period from 1878 to 1908 was one of comparative quiet in which no major territorial problems had to be solved. The Hague Conventions of 1899 and 1907 were completely silent on the law of territorial change and consequently on recognition, although these issues were broached at the 1907 Conference during the discussion of plans to revise the 1899 Convention on the Pacific Settlement of International Disputes. The Brazilian delegation declared that it would like to see the Conference adopt a provision contemplating the renunciation of the right of conquest. It submitted the following draft:

> None of the Signatory Powers shall undertake to alter, by means of war, the present boundaries of its territory at the expense of any of the other Powers until arbitration has been proposed by the Power claiming the right to make the alteration and refused, or if the other Power disobeys the arbitral award. If any of these Powers violate this engagement, the change of territory brought about by arms will not be legally valid.[1]

That the suggestion was made by a Latin-American delegation may be attributed to the fact that the idea of "outlawing the right of conquest" had already for decades occupied the minds of Latin-American statesmen and scholars. The Conference, however, took no action on the Brazilian proposal.

In 1908 the Austro-Hungarian Monarchy proclaimed the annexation of Bosnia-Herzegovina,[2] and Bulgaria declared her independence.[3] These unilateral acts constituted a flagrant violation of the territorial status established by the Congress Treaty of Berlin. Again, the faits accomplis were

[1] *Protocols of the Hague Peace Conference 1907*, I 551
[2] The occupation and administration of the Turkish provinces of Bosnia-Herzegovina had been entrusted to Austria-Hungary under Art. 25 of the Treaty of Berlin in 1878.
[3] 5 Gooch-Temperley 876 ff.

finally accepted, yet for a moment the possibility of non-recognition was held out,[4] and in the final settlement the principle was asserted that territorial changes in southeastern Europe required the recognition of all the European Great Powers.[5]

During the Balkan wars of 1912 and 1913 the Powers which formed the Concert of Europe tried once again to play the same role as in 1856 and 1878. Yet their efforts failed when the Treaty of London, drafted under their auspices, miscarried,[6] and the territorial setup of the Balkans was radically changed by treaties to which only the States directly affected were parties.[7] The sole result of the collective action of the Powers, assembled in a "Conference of Ambassadors," was the creation, in July, 1913, of an "independent and sovereign" Albanian State,[8] whose frontiers, however, not even later conferences were able to delimit satisfactorily.[9] It was, of course, possible to claim that the inter-Balkanic treaties of 1913, in order to attain full legal force, required the assent of the Signatory Powers of the Act of the Congress of Berlin. Such was, in fact, the position taken

[4] See 5 Gooch-Temperley, documents No. 296, 319, 320, e.g. Sir Edward Grey's note of October 6, 1908, to Sir G. Buchanan, Sofia: "We cannot admit the right of any Power to alter an international treaty without the consent of the Contracting Powers. H. M. Gvt. cannot therefore recognize what has been done until the views of other Powers are known, especially of Turkey who is more concerned than anybody else." (Doc. 319)

[5] See the diplomatic correspondence on the abolition of Art. 25 of the Treaty of Berlin (Martens, *Nouv. Rec. Gén.*, S. 3, II 661; IV 31 ff.), and the final adhesion of the Powers (*Ibid.* 46 ff.), especially the note from Count Berchtold to Count Aehrental, dated March 15, 1909: "Dans l'opinion du Gouvernement Impérial [Russe] un arrangement direct entre l'Autriche-Hongrie et la Turquie n'exclut pas la nécessité de soumettre la question de Bosnie-Hercegovine à une conférence des Puissances Signataires du Traité de Berlin. . . ." (*Ibid.* 31), and the note from Sir Edward Grey to Count Mensdorff, dated March 16, 1909: "Since the Austro-Turkish Protocol involves an alteration of the Treaty of Berlin, it requires to be submitted to all the Signatory Powers." (*Ibid.* 32) See also 104 *BFSP* 239.

[6] Treaty of London, signed May 30, 1913, between Bulgaria, Greece, Montenegro, Serbia, Turkey (107 *BFSP* 656). See also 9/II Gooch-Temperley 1026 ff., especially 1047.)

[7] Treaty of Bucharest, signed August 10, 1913, between Bulgaria, Greece, Montenegro, Rumania, Serbia (107 *BFSP* 658); Treaty of Constantinople, signed September 29, 1913, between Bulgaria and Turkey (*Ibid.* 706); Treaty of Athens, signed November 14, 1913, between Greece and Turkey (*Ibid.* 893); Treaty of Constantinople, signed March 14, 1914, between Serbia and Turkey, providing that the Contracting Parties "considèrent le Traité de Londres . . . comme ratifié en ce qui les concerne" (108 *BFSP* 579)

[8] 9/II Gooch-Temperley 943

[9] *Ibid.* 1065; 10/I Gooch-Temperley 86 ff.; 4 Temperley 338

by the British Government. In December, 1913, the British envoys in Athens and Belgrade reported to Sir Edward Grey that the Greek and Serbian Governments had officially communicated to them the content of the new treaties.[10] Thereupon Sir Edward Grey sent to the British Missions at the Courts of the Great Powers the following instruction:

His Majesty's Government are of the opinion that these new territorial arrangements constitute a departure from the Treaty of Berlin and cannot therefore acquire formal validity without the expressed assent of the Powers signatories of that Treaty. The Powers are free to withhold that assent. . . .

His Majesty's Government consider, however, that it is in the general interest that the situation should be regularized as soon as possible, and they are therefore anxious to learn the views and intentions of the Powers on this subject.[11]

The results of the diplomatic steps taken by the British envoys upon this instruction were summarized in a circular note dispatched by Sir Edward Grey on May 6, 1914.[12] It read:

The French Government are of opinion that the Balkan States who accepted the Treaty of Berlin in 1878 are bound by its stipulations. The French Government also hold that the Powers would be justified in making their recognition of the recent territorial changes contingent upon an undertaking by the annexing States to respect those provisions of the Treaties which guarantee the rights of religious minorities.

The German Government entirely share the view of His Majesty's Government.

The Russian Government consider the Great Powers, having formally intervened in the Treaty of London of May 30, 1913, have hereby recognized the cession, under Art. 2 of the Treaty, of territories by the Sultan to the Balkan States . . . and they hold that the capitulations have ceased to exist in the newly acquired territories by the mere fact of their annexation.

The view of the Italian Government is that the regulation of the present Balkan situation requires the sanction of the Powers, but that such sanction need not be expressed in a collective form, to which they are themselves opposed. They intend to give their own sanction independently of the other Powers.

The Austro-Hungarian Government are reluctant to give their public assent to any view that might call in question the full validity of the distribution of territory made by the Treaty of Bucharest.

[10] 10/I Gooch-Temperley 287
[11] *Ibid.* 292
[12] *Ibid.* 323

From the above . . . it is clear that there is no prospect of agreement, within reasonable time, as to the procedure to be adopted in dealing with the question.

And Sir Edward Grey concluded:

In these circumstances His Majesty's Government consider that they must act on their own view, that is, they will inform the Governments of Greece, Roumania, Servia, Bulgaria, and Montenegro that His Majesty's Government, so far as they themselves are concerned, are willing to recognize the recent annexations of territories to the respective States, in so far as these annexations constitute a departure from the settlement sanctioned by the Treaty of Berlin . . . provided that the respective annexing States on their part acknowledge the binding force, in respect of the annexed territories, of those provisions of the Treaty of Berlin which ensure the equal rights of religious or national minorities.

This instruction was repeated on June 15, 1914,[13] and once more the Foreign Office emphasized its position in a note to a Jewish Committee, dated July 28, 1914.[14] Further steps were prevented by the outbreak of the First World War. After its termination, the territorial status of the Balkans was settled by the multilateral treaties of Neuilly (November 27, 1919) and Lausanne (July 24, 1923) to which the Great Powers were parties.[15]

On June 24, 1919, Clemenceau, acting on behalf of the Supreme Council, dispatched to the Polish Peace Delegation a note in order to induce them to sign a treaty for the protection of minorities.[16] In this note he wrote:

It has long been established procedure of the public law of Europe that when a State is created, or even when large accessions

[13] *Ibid.* 334

[14] "Gentlemen: I am directed by Secretary Sir Edward Grey to inform you that he has given careful considerations to your letter of 14th inst. on the subject of the rights of native Jews in Rumania.

"I am to observe, in reply, that questions arising under the Convention of Paris 1858 and the Treaty of Berlin 1878 being, as you rightly point out, matters of European concern, it is for the Signatory Powers of those instruments to deal collectively with any infractions, or alleged infractions, of their terms by particular States.

"I am, however, to add that Sir Edward Grey will bear in mind the arguments and suggestions contained in your letter when the moment arrives for H. M. Gvt. definitely to recognize the recent annexations of territories by the Balkan States." (5 Temperley 120)

[15] The Treaty of Neuilly was concluded between the Powers and Bulgaria (112 *BFSP* 781), the Treaty of Lausanne between the Powers and Turkey (28 *LNTS* 12).

[16] 5 Temperley 433

of territory are made to an established State, the joint and formal recognition by the Great Powers would be accompanied by the requirement that such a State should, in the form of a binding international convention, undertake to comply with certain principles of government.

As far as southeastern Europe was concerned, Clemenceau's statement was correct; for other European areas, however, the law was in 1914 pretty much the same as it had been in the preceding century—for the aggressor the right of conquest, for third Powers the right at best of lodging a protest, if and when such a conquest violated a treaty which bore their signature.

CHAPTER III

EASTERN EUROPE, 1914–1918

Already in the early nineteenth century it was a well-established principle of international law that a belligerent military occupant was not entitled to exercise the powers of sovereignty in enemy territory before he had definitively and validly annexed it, and that annexation could not be considered definitive and valid unless and until the subjugation of the defeated enemy had been effected so thoroughly and completely that his possible resistance might fairly and safely be regarded as a negligible potentiality.[1] In many instances, of course, this rule was disregarded, and premature annexation of occupied enemy territory proclaimed.[2]

The first serious violation of the principle during the First World War occurred when the German and Austro-Hungarian Governors General of Congress Poland—which had been occupied by the armed forces of the Central Powers in 1915—issued on November 5, 1916, manifestoes to the effect that the Polish territories wrested from Russian domination would be made into an "autonomous State endowed with a hereditary Monarchy and a constitution." [3] (The determination of the borders of the new State, however, was to remain in suspense.) The avowed aim of this step was the formation of a Polish armed force, to be recruited from among the subjects of Russian Poland. The Imperial Government of Russia hastened to protest against this violation of international law,[4] and so did the *Chambre des Députés* of the French Republic in an *ordre du jour* of November 15,

[1] Phillipson, *Termination of War and Treaties of Peace,* 21; see also below, 106, 117

[2] In 1900 Great Britain resorted to the premature annexation of the Orange Free State and the South African Republic. On November 5, 1911, King Victor Emmanuel III issued a decree of annexation placing Tripolitania and Cyrenaica under the full sovereignty of the Kingdom of Italy although the war between the latter and Turkey was still in progress. (Phillipson, *op. cit.* 22-27)

[3] 2 *Polish Doc.* 57

[4] *Ibid.* 80

1916.[5] These protests did not impress the governments of the Central Powers very strongly, yet the execution of their plans lagged due to the inherent antagonism of the German and Austro-Hungarian interests regarding Poland.

Events in the Russian sphere started to move faster when, in March, 1917, the Tsarist regime was overthrown and a Provisional Government, headed by Prince Lvov, established. On March 29, 1917,[6] the new Government issued a proclamation to the effect that it was prepared to grant to the Polish nation self-determination, and that it considered the creation of an independent Polish State, consisting of all the territories in which the Polish people formed the majority of the inhabitants, as a pledge of lasting peace in Europe.[7] This proclamation was followed on April 9, 1917, by a manifesto to the Russian people in which the Government expressed the wish to secure a durable peace on the basis of national self-determination.[8]

On November 7, 1917, the Maximalist Socialists headed by Lenin seized the reins of government in Russia. Among the first acts of the new regime of the People's Commissars was the issuance of a "Declaration of Peace" and of a "Declaration of the Rights of the Peoples of Russia." The former proclaimed the slogan of "Peace without annexations and without indemnities," and is remarkable for its endeavor to define the term "annexations." [9] The latter recognized the

[5] Ibid. 92
[6] New Style. The change of the Russian Calendar from the Old to the New Style became effective on January 1, 1918 (new style); yet for simplicity's sake all dates are rendered in the latter.
[7] 2 Polish Doc. 151
[8] Ibid. 159
[9] The Declaration of Peace, November 8, 1917:
The Workers' and Peasants' Government . . . proposes . . . to begin at once negotiations leading to a just and democratic peace.
Such a peace the government considers to be an immediate peace without annexations (i.e. without the seizure of foreign nationalities) and without indemnities. . . .
By annexation or seizure of foreign territory the Government, in accordance with the legal concepts of democracy in general and of the working classes in particular, understands any incorporation of a small and weak nationality by a large and powerful State without a clear, definite and voluntary expression of agreement and desire by the weak nationality, regardless of the time when such forcible incorporation took place, regardless also of how developed or how backward is the nation forcibly attached or forcibly detained within the frontiers of the State, and finally, regardless of whether or not this large nation is located in Europe or in distant lands beyond the seas.

equality and sovereignty of the peoples of Russia, including the right of complete secession and of the establishment of free and independent States.[10]

The first reaction to the Declaration came from the Ukrainians, when on November 20, 1917, a "Rada" (Council), meeting at Kiev, proclaimed an "autonomous Ukrainian People's Republic." [11] A few weeks later an armistice was signed between the Government of the People's Commissars and the Central Powers, and in the last days of 1917 German, Austro-Hungarian, Bulgarian, Turkish, and Soviet Russian delegates met in a peace conference at Brest-Litovsk. The negotiations had hardly started when a delegation of Ukrainians, representing the Kiev Rada, arrived and demanded admission to the conference table. On January 12, 1918, the plenipotentiaries of the Central Powers extended to them, over the protests of the Soviet Russians, recognition as an "autonomous delegation and duly qualified representation of the Ukrainian People's Republic." [12] On January 24 the Ukrainian Rada proclaimed the full sovereignty of their republic,[13] and on February 9 the world was surprised by the announcement that a peace treaty had been concluded between the Central Powers and the Ukrainian People's Republic.[14] The authorities of the puppet "Kingdom of Poland" that had been created by the proclamations of November 5, 1916, were not even allowed to attend the Conference. When the provisions of the treaty were disclosed, the British Government made the following announcement:

His Majesty's Government have instructed their agent at Kiev to

---

If any nation whatsoever is detained by force within the boundaries of a certain State, and if, contrary to its expressed desire . . . is not given the right to determine the form of its State life by free voting and completely free from the presence of the troops of the annexing or stronger State and without the least pressure, then the adjoining of that nation by the stronger State is annexation, i.e. seizure by force and violence.

(Text in Wheeler-Bennett, *The Forgotten Peace,* 373, and in Korovin, "The USSR and Disarmament," *Int. Conc.* 292, 310)

[10] Taracouzio, *The Soviet Union and International Law,* 29

[11] 2 *Polish Doc.* 291; Buell, *Poland, Key to Europe,* 266 (The Proclamation is known as the "Third Universal.")

[12] 2 *Polish Doc.* 306

[13] *Ibid.* 307; Buell, *op. cit.* 267 ("The Fourth Universal")

[14] *For. Rel.* 1918, Russia, II 665; Wheeler-Bennett, *op. cit.* 392

make a declaration to the effect that they do not recognize the peace recently concluded between the Ukraine and the Central Powers.[15]

This declaration appears to be the first instance of an explicit application of non-recognition policies to territorial changes stipulated in a treaty signed by a European Great Power. A week later the Allied Governments issued a collective declaration to the effect that any peace treaty concluded outside the Entente and contrary to the principle of nationality would be considered null and void.[16] The climax in these two documents is interesting: the first spoke of "non-recognition," the second of "nullity." The Germans, of course, were not deterred by such declarations from the pursuit of their predatory plans. On March 3 they forced Soviet Russia to sign the Russian Treaty of Brest-Litovsk;[17] a few weeks later, on May 7, 1918, they imposed on Rumania the Treaty of Bucharest,[18] and on August 27, 1918, they implemented the former by a "Supplementary Convention" signed at Berlin.[19] Before signing the Brest-Litovsk Treaty, the Russian plenipotentiary, Sokolnikov, made a statement which clearly forecast that Russia would repudiate the treaty at the earliest opportunity. He said:

This peace is no peace of understanding and agreement, but a peace which Russia, grinding its teeth, is forced to accept. This is a peace which, whilst pretending to free Russian border provinces, really transforms them into German States and deprives them of their right of self-determination. Under the present conditions the Soviet Government is unable to withstand the armed offensive of German imperialism and is compelled, for the sake of saving revolutionary Russia, to accept the conditions put before it. . . . We declare . . . that we are going to sign immediately the treaty presented to us as an ultimatum, but at the same time we refuse to enter into any discussion of its terms.[20]

On November 11, 1918, Germany surrendered. One of the terms of the armistice, Article 15, was the renunciation of the Treaties of Bucharest and Brest-Litovsk and comple-

[15] 2 *Polish Doc.* 359
[16] *Ibid.* 400
[17] Text of the treaty in *For. Rel.* 1918, Russia, I 442; Wheeler-Bennett, *op. cit.* 403
[18] 3 Temperley 44
[19] Text of the treaty in Wheeler-Bennett, *op. cit.* 427
[20] *Ibid.* 268

mentary treaties.[21] Two days later the Soviet Government issued the following Decree:

The All-Russian Central Executive Committee of Soviets hereby solemnly declare that the conditions of peace with Germany signed at Brest on March 3, 1918, are null and void. The Brest-Litovsk Treaty, and equally the annexed agreement signed at Berlin on August 27, 1918, in their entirety and in all their articles, are herewith declared as annulled. All obligations assumed under the Brest-Litovsk Treaty and dealing with . . . the cession of territories and regions are declared void.[22]

[21] *Ibid.* 450
[22] *Ibid.* 447

CHAPTER IV

THE BIRTH OF THE BALTIC STATES

THE self-determination granted by the new rulers of Russia to the nationalities of the former Russian Empire led to the secession of many of them and the formation of new States such as Estonia, Latvia, and Lithuania. On the other hand, the establishment of a government that not only advocated but effectively carried out the abolition of the capitalistic system prompted a great number of Powers to withhold for a considerable length of time recognition from it. With the details of these developments this work is not concerned. What needs to be mentioned, however, is that the reluctance of certain Powers to recognize on the one hand the independence of the Baltic States, on the other hand the Soviet Government, favored the emergence of a new terminology in the field of recognition. While hitherto diplomatic language had sometimes used the terms "recognition of a government as government de jure" or "as government de facto," now diplomatic documents began also to speak of "de facto States" and "de jure States" and their recognition as such, and finally of "de facto recognition" and "de jure recognition" without clearly stating the meaning of these terms.[1]

The reluctance to recognize the independence of the new border States was predominantly due to the consideration that recognition should not be granted until the mother country, Russia, would herself recognize the secession, and would do it through a government itself recognized by the Powers. This position was clearly expressed in a declaration made by the British, French, and Italian members of

---

[1] The question of the meaning of the new terminology arose as early as 1920, at the First Assembly of the League of Nations, in connection with the issue of the admission of new Members. One of the delegates suggested that the exact meaning of the term "de jure recognition" should be defined by an Assembly resolution. The suggestion, however, was not acted upon. (*Records of the First Assembly of the League of Nations* (1920), *Plenary Meetings*, 578, 623, 636)

the Commission on Baltic Affairs of the Peace Conference on May 28, 1919.[2] In 1920 the Soviet Government concluded peace treaties with the Baltic States, thereby recognizing their independence.[3] Each of these treaties contained the following clause:

> By virtue of the right, proclaimed by the Russian Socialist Federated Soviet Republic, of all nations to free self-determination, even up to the point of complete separation from the State of which they form part, Russia recognizes without reservation the sovereign rights and independence of the . . . State, with all the juridical consequences arising from such recognition, and voluntarily and for all times abandons the sovereign rights of Russia over the . . . people and their territory.[4]

In spite of the conclusion of these treaties, the western Powers maintained at first their position regarding Baltic recognition on the ground that the Russian Government itself was not yet recognized. This point of view was emphasized in the American document of August 10, 1920, known as the Colby Note.[5] On January 26, 1921, however, the Supreme Council of the Allied Powers resolved to recognize Estonia and Latvia as "States de jure," while it reserved decision regarding Lithuania on account of her unsettled dispute with Poland over Vilna.[6] Yet the attitude of the United States remained unchanged. It is true that the Secretary of State of the Administration which took office on March 4, 1921, Mr. Hughes, ordered the American Commissioner at Riga, Mr. Young, to report on the Baltic situation with a view to recognition.[7] Mr. Young reported that there was no indication that the Bolsheviks intended to attempt through military measures the conquest and absorption of the Baltic States, and that he recommended the "immediate de jure recognition" of the latter.[8] But no action

[2] Graham, *The Diplomatic Recognition of the Border States*, 271

[3] Russian-Estonian Treaty, concluded Tartu, February 2, 1920 (11 *LNTS* 51). Russian-Lithuanian Treaty, concluded Moscow, July 12, 1920 (3 *LNTS* 106). Russian-Latvian Treaty, concluded Moscow, August 11, 1920 (2 *LNTS* 196)

[4] Art. 2 Estonian Treaty, Art. 1 Lithuanian Treaty, Art. 2 Latvian Treaty

[5] *For. Rel.* 1920, III 463

[6] Graham, *op. cit.* 290 and 444

[7] *For. Rel.* 1921, II 755

[8] *Ibid.*

was taken by the Department of State, and the issue was kept in abeyance for many months.[9]

On April 6, 1922, Commissioner Young, apparently acting on his own initiative, submitted a further, very thorough report on the Baltic situation in which he once again advocated recognition.[10] The most interesting part of the report read:

It is entirely possible, or even probable, that some time in the indefinite future these so-called States may once again become an integral part of Russia. It seems most probable, however, that until that time comes they will be able to maintain their political stability, and with that their independence. . . . Admitting that, from our viewpoint, a strong Russia is greatly to be desired, it is still difficult for an observer here to suggest any course of action other than the immediate recognition of these States. . . . Later it is not improbable that through the operation of fundamental economic laws these countries will become a part of a federated Russia or will retain autonomous powers, but will be linked with the Russian Government through close economic and political treaties and agreements.

The Department of State still hesitated. But on June 30, 1922, it was informed by the American Ambassador in France that at a meeting, held that morning, the Conference of Ambassadors had decided that the principal Allied Powers would recognize Lithuania de jure.[11] Thereupon the

[9] On July 1, 1921, the Russian Ambassador, Mr. Bakhmetiev, submitted to the Department of State a Memorandum in which he stated:
"The fundamental feature of the problem of the so-called Baltic States is the temporary character of their present orientation. Their actual tendency to sever relations with Russia and gain complete independence is not based on permanent economic factors or deep-rooted historical traditions. . . .
"The future will undoubtedly bring a reunion of the Baltic States with restored Russia. This reunion will probably materialize in the form of a broad federation. . . . Powerful economic factors will actuate such a reunion. . . .
"Should the status of the small States be established at this time on the basis of unreserved recognition, such a solution would possess only a semblance of permanency and would last only while Russia remained inarticulate.
"Unreserved recognition . . . is pregnant with complications of a formal character. In this case reunion with Russia would mean a fusion of sovereign States. . . . It would become a case of international concern requiring international sanction. . . . A Power desirous of perpetuating the dismemberment of Russia would have simply to oppose the change of the status quo. . . ." (*Ibid.*)
[10] *For. Rel.* 1922, II 869
[11] *Ibid.* 873. The Conference of Ambassadors was the successor of the Supreme Council. Its decision to extend de jure recognition to Lithuania was taken although the Vilna question was anything but settled.

issue was reconsidered, and on July 25, 1922, the Secretary of State instructed Mr. Young to notify on July 28 the Foreign Offices of Estonia, Latvia, and Lithuania that the United States extended to each of them full recognition.[12]

[12] *Ibid.*

CHAPTER V

THE SOVIET-POLISH AND
THE SOVIET-RUMANIAN BORDER DISPUTE
BETWEEN THE TWO WORLD WARS

W<small>HEN</small> the surrender of the
Central Powers made the rebirth of Poland a certainty, the
problem of her future borders became acute. There was little
dispute among the Poles about the western and southern
borders. Yet regarding the east, the situation was different.
An extremist party claimed the pre-1772 frontiers, others
were more moderate, but on one point all agreed: that in the
east the new State must not be limited to the ethnically
Polish areas, and that it must include all of Galicia as well
as the territory of Vilna. It is clear that even the program
of the moderates was bound to make conflict with Soviet
Russia, Lithuania, and the Ukraine inevitable. The details
of this multi-cornered struggle cannot be narrated here. By
July, 1919, the Poles had occupied the whole of Galicia and
destroyed the West Ukrainian People's Republic. The war
between the Soviets and the East Ukrainian People's Republic ended with the defeat of the Ukrainian leader, Petlura,
and the establishment of a Ukrainian Soviet Republic
(April, 1920). In the Polish-Soviet War the Red Army was
defeated at the gates of Warsaw (August, 1920), whereupon the Soviet Government decided to make peace with the
Poles. Vilna was taken by force from the Lithuanians by the
Polish General Żeligowski (October, 1920).

The Allied and Associated Powers were by no means sympathetic with exaggerated Polish claims. Yet they were unable to reach definite conclusions regarding the settlement
in the east. For this reason they inserted into the Treaty of
Versailles a clause regarding the Polish borders which left
the door open for future arrangements.[1] In December, 1919,

[1] Art. 87, par. 3: "The boundaries of Poland not laid down in the present
Treaty will be subsequently determined by the Principal Allied and Associated Powers."

the Supreme Council made a tentative suggestion to fix the eastern border at what became subsequently known as the Curzon line. Nothing came out of it. Regarding eastern Galicia, various projects were adopted and abandoned in turn.[2]

The issue was ultimately decided by the outcome of the Polish-Soviet War. On March 18, 1921, a peace treaty was concluded at Riga between Poland on the one hand and the Russian and Ukrainian Soviet Republics on the other, the Russian also acting with the authorization and on behalf of the Byelorussian Soviet Republic.[3] Article 2 fixed the eastern border of Poland roughly halfway between the pre-1772 border and the Curzon line. Under Article 3, Russia and the Ukraine abandoned all claims to the territories situated to the west of the frontier laid down in Article 2. Poland, on her part, abandoned in favor of the Ukraine and Byelorussia all rights and claims to the territory situated to the east of that frontier. The following part of Article 3 concerned the Vilna dispute:

> The two contracting parties agree that, in so far as the territory situated to the west of the frontier fixed in Art. 2 of the present treaty includes districts which form the subject of a dispute between Poland and Lithuania, the question of the attribution of these districts to one of those two States is a matter which exclusively concerns Poland and Lithuania.

In signing the treaty, the Soviet representatives refrained from making any statement similar to that made by the Russian plenipotentiary at Brest-Litovsk. Yet how they felt about the future of the Riga settlement may be gathered from the provisions of another treaty which the Soviet Government signed two days before the Riga Treaty, namely, the Russo-Turkish Treaty of March 16, 1921.[4] It contained the following interesting provision:

> Art. 1. Each of the Contracting Parties agrees not to recognize any peace treaty or other international agreement imposed upon the other against its will. The Government of the RSFSR agrees not to recognize any international agreement relating to Turkey which is not recognized by the National Government of Turkey, at present represented by the Grand National Assembly.

[2] Buell, *op. cit.* 270
[3] 6 *LNTS* 123
[4] 118 *BFSP* 991

As far as could be ascertained, this provision was the first instance that non-recognition of changes effected by force—and it is obvious that the article was primarily aimed at territorial changes—was made a legal duty under treaty law, even if such changes would be confirmed by a peace treaty or other agreement.

The Poles tried very hard to secure from third Powers recognition of the territorial changes stipulated in the Riga settlement, and to this effect they approached the former "Principal Allies" with a request for explicit recognition. They were kept waiting for two years. Possibly the Powers hesitated to give their formal approval to an arrangement against which they had repeatedly advised. Their decision may also have been delayed by the fact that most of the Powers had not yet fully recognized the Soviet Russian Government. Finally, however, they yielded to the Polish request. On March 15, 1923, the Conference of Ambassadors decided to accord recognition to the territorial status created by the Treaty of Riga, and also to the Polish seizure of Vilna.[5] The United States Government made no public statement of recognition, but it accepted the situation created by the Riga Treaty and the seizure of Vilna for the practical purposes of its domestic administration.[6]

Thus, in the cases of the Baltic States, eastern Poland, and Vilna, the Powers ultimately abandoned their initial position that no questions affecting the territorial integrity of the former Russian Empire could be decided until the Russian people were represented by a recognized government. But they could claim that the new status had been accepted by the non-recognized government of Soviet Russia.

Not even this could be asserted in the case of Bessarabia.[7] Soon after the Russian Revolution of March, 1917, an autonomist movement started to develop in that province of the former Tsarist Empire. In October a Bessarabian Congress proclaimed the election of a National Assembly (*Sfatul Tzearii*). The Assembly met on November 21, and resolved that Bessarabia should be an autonomous republic. On Janu-

5 *Ibid.* 961
6 Below, 33, n. 5
7 The following narrative is based on Milioukov, *La Politique Extérieure des Soviets,* and Boldur, *La Bessarabie et les Relations Russo-Roumaines.*

ary 5, 1918, the Bolsheviks captured the provisional capital, Kishinev. Thereupon the Sfatul invoked the aid of Rumania. On January 13 the Rumanian troops arrived; the Soviet Government at once severed relations with Rumania. On January 24 the Sfatul proclaimed the full independence of the Bessarabian Republic. On March 5 the Soviets concluded an agreement with the Rumanian commander under which the Rumanians had to evacuate Bessarabia; yet the pact failed of ratification, and on April 9 the Sfatul voted the reunion of Bessarabia with Rumania. When the Peace Conference met, the Bessarabian question presented itself together with the other Russian border problems; and as in the Baltic case, the Powers held at first the view that it was impossible to sever Bessarabia from Russia without the consent of the Russian people.[8] In 1920, however, they reversed their position. In April, 1920, the Commission on Yugoslav and Rumanian Affairs drew up a draft treaty providing for the recognition of the Rumanian annexation of Bessarabia by the Principal Allied Powers, and in May, 1920, the Secretariat General of the Peace Conference approached the Government of the United States with a request to participate in this step.[9] The United States flatly refused "to become a party to any treaty tending to Russia's dismemberment." After several months of fruitless efforts to change the minds of the Americans,[10] the Principal Allied Powers signed the treaty on October 28, 1920, without the participation of the United States.[11] The Soviet Governments answered at once with a declaration of non-recognition.[12] The

[8] Boldur, *op. cit.* 93

[9] *For. Rel.* 1920, III 420

[10] *Ibid.* 426-434

[11] Treaty between the British Empire, France, Italy and Japan (the Principal Allied Powers) and Roumania relative to Bessarabia (113 *BFSP* 647). The main provisions were:

"(Art. 1) Les Hautes Parties contractantes déclarent reconnaître la souveraineté de la Roumanie sur le territoire de la Bessarabie. . . .

"(Art. 9) Les Hautes Parties contractantes inviteront la Russie à adhérer au présent Traité, dès qu'il existera un Gouvernement russe reconnu par elles."

[12] *For. Rel.* 1920, III 434: "Having learned that a treaty has just been signed between the Allied Great Powers and Rumania dealing with the annexation of Bessarabia by latter, the Governments of Russia and the Ukraine declare herewith that they cannot recognize any transaction as to Bessarabia carried out without their participation as having any force or validity and that they do not consider themselves tied by a treaty concluded by other governments on the subject."

treaty was first only ratified by Rumania and Great Britain. France followed suit in 1924, but the efforts of Rumania to obtain the ratification of her second "Latin sister," Italy, failed; the Duce was obviously not willing to get embroiled with the Soviets on account of the descendants of Emperor Trajan's legionnaires. In 1926 an Italo-Rumanian treaty of friendship was concluded, yet Mussolini informed the Rumanian Government that the ratification of the Convention of 1920 would only take place "if and when it could be done without damaging effect to the general interests of Italy." [13]

Russia never acquiesced in the loss of Bessarabia. This attitude prompted the Rumanians to seek explicit recognition of their Bessarabian annexation from other Powers not directly concerned. They were successful with the Poles; Article 1 of the Treaty of Mutual Guarantee between Poland and Rumania, concluded at Bucharest on March 26, 1926,[14] committed both parties to maintain against external aggression their territorial integrity including Bessarabia.[15] The Soviet Government retorted by denouncing the Polish seizure of Vilna. On September 28, 1926, the Soviet Foreign Commissar Chicherin declared that

> The de facto violation of the frontiers of Lithuania did not affect the recognition of her territorial sovereignty as recognized in the Russo-Lithuanian Treaty of 1920.[16]

The Poles protested against this note as a violation of the Treaty of Riga,[17] and emphasized that the Vilna question had been finally solved by the Conference of Ambassadors. The Soviet Government replied on November 19, 1926, that

> The decisions of the so-called Conference of Ambassadors cannot entail any obligation on the part of the USSR and continue to be contested by Lithuania; as regards the agreement between Poland and Lithuania provided in the Treaty of Riga, it is unknown to Moscow.[18]

13 Boldur, *op. cit.* 98
14 125 *BFSP* 981
15 Milioukov, *op. cit.* 320
16 *Ibid.* 322
17 Art. 3, last sentence, of the treaty (above, 27)
18 Milioukov, *op. cit.* 323

The Bessarabian question again played an important role in 1932 when the Soviet Union and Rumania entered into negotiations aiming at the conclusion of a non-aggression pact. The Soviet Government demanded the insertion of a clause providing that the pact did not affect the question of Bessarabia; the Rumanians, in turn, insisted on the explicit recognition by the Soviets of Rumanian sovereignty over Bessarabia. The negotiations broke down.[19] The following year, however, both the Soviet Union and Rumania became parties to two multilateral conventions without returning to the Bessarabian issue.[20]

The foregoing justifies the conclusion that the territorial changes which followed in the wake of the Russian Revolution favored the development of the idea that territorial changes should receive the recognition of third Powers, even of such as had not participated in the establishment of the previous status. Evidence for this may be seen in the attempts of the Principal Allied Powers to secure the adherence of the United States to their Bessarabian recognition treaty, and in the efforts of the Poles to obtain from the western Powers recognition of their eastern borders, and from the Soviet Government recognition of the annexation of Vilna, or at least a declaration of non-interference. It would, of course, be unwarranted to claim that by that time the recognition of an annexation by all other Powers, or at least by the leading Powers, had become a legal requirement of its full effectiveness.

[19] *Ibid.* 399
[20] The two Conventions for the Definition of Aggression, signed London, July 3–4, 1933 (below, 73)

CHAPTER VI

THE ATTITUDE OF THE
UNITED STATES UNTIL 1932

THROUGHOUT the nineteenth century the United States had never sought from third Powers recognition of its territorial acquisitions. Conversely, the United States had normally abstained from making statements of recognition with respect to the various territorial changes effected in Europe and elsewhere in the era before the First World War. The treaties drafted at the Paris Peace Conference of 1919 represented the first attempt to sanction by the American signature territorial changes not directly affecting the American sphere. The attempt failed, and the state of war with the former enemies (or what was left of them) was terminated in July, 1921, by Joint Resolutions, not by regular peace treaties. Thereupon, treaties "restoring friendly relations" were concluded in August, 1921, with Germany, Austria, and Hungary.[1] Their text clearly showed the unwillingness of the United States Government to have anything to do with any territorial settlement in Europe. Thus Article 2, paragraph 3, of the Treaty with Germany explicitly provided "that the United States assumes no obligations under or with respect to the provisions of Part II, Part III . . . of the Treaty of Versailles."[2] Similar provisions were inserted into the Austrian and Hungarian treaties. As far, however, as the territorial changes consisted in the formation of new States, this position could not be strictly upheld due to the necessity of entering into diplomatic relations with them. It was for this reason that the Government of the United States granted explicit recognition to the Baltic States, but otherwise it persistently refused to participate in discussions regarding territorial

[1] *USTS* 658 (Germany), 659 (Austria), 660 (Hungary)
[2] Part II of the Treaty of Versailles fixed the boundaries of Germany; Part III contained "Political Clauses for Europe," among them also many territorial provisions.

problems of Europe.[3] These problems, however, had to be dealt with in the domestic sphere of the United States. Many urgent questions, such as the disposition of enemy property, the resumption of prewar trade relations and of consular activities, matters of extradition, immigration, and so forth, frequently depended for their solution on a decision regarding the acceptance of new boundaries by the Government of the United States, and consequently, at least by implication, on the recognition or non-recognition by the latter of certain territorial changes.[4-5]

[3] This is illustrated by a correspondence between the American Chargé in Paris and the Department of State, which took place soon after the recognition of the Baltic States. On August 24, 1922, the Chargé reported that the Conference of Ambassadors was about to take up the question of the disposition to be made of the Territory of Memel, and asked for instructions. The Department of State replied on September 25, 1922: "It is felt that the subjects in question are primarily matters of European concern, in the settlement of which this Government is not necessarily called upon to participate. You should refrain from any expression of views. . . ." (*For. Rel.* 1922, II 875)

[4] Sec. 2 (c) of the Act to Limit the Immigration of Aliens to the United States, approved May 19, 1921, (U. S. *Statutes at large,* V. 42/I, p. 5) provided with regard to the determination of the immigration quotas that "in case of changes in political boundaries in foreign countries occurring subsequent to 1910 and resulting (1) in the creation of new countries, the Governments of which are recognized by the United States, or (2) in the transfer of territory from one country to another, such transfer being recognized by the United States," the Secretary of State, the Secretary of Commerce, and the Secretary of Labor, "jointly, shall estimate the number of persons resident in the United States in 1910 who were born within the area included in such new countries or in such territories so transferred, and revise the population basis as to each country involved in such change of political boundary. . . ."

[5] According to information obtained from the U. S. Dept. of State, Division of Geography and Cartography, under date August 11, 1944, the line recognized by the Conference of Ambassadors as the frontier between Poland and the Soviet Union (above, 28) has served for the purpose of immigration quotas as the eastern limit of the quota area of Poland since late in March, 1923, when the Secretaries of State, Commerce and Labor, who were charged with the administration of the Restrictive Immigration Act, agreed that the immigration quotas theretofore maintained for the regions of Pinsk and Eastern Galicia (which lie to the west of that line) should be merged with that of Poland.

CHAPTER VII

THE NON-RECOGNITION IDEA
IN THE AMERICAS PRIOR TO 1932

Wʜɪʟᴇ in the Old World the idea developed rather slowly that territorial changes should not only politically, but also legally, be a matter of concern for third States, similar ideas occupied the minds of the Latin-American world since the early days of Latin-American independence, and led to endeavors to establish a doctrine, or even a law, of what was termed "the legal validity of conquest." During the century that preceded the outbreak of the First World War, provisions attempting to circumscribe the said "law of conquest" were repeatedly written into treaties concluded among Latin-American States; none of these treaties, however, was able to secure ratification.

At the first Inter-American Conference (Panama, 1826) a "Treaty of Union, League, and Perpetual Confederation" was concluded by several American States. Its Article 22 provided that as soon as the boundaries were delimited, they would be placed under the guarantee and protection of the Confederation; further articles (16 and 19) stated that no Signatory Power should declare war on another Treaty Power unless it had previously invoked the conciliatory decision of the General Assembly of the Confederation. The treaty was ratified only by Colombia.[1] Similar provisions were written into an equally abortive "Treaty of Confederation" concluded at the Inter-American Congress of Lima (1847–48).[2] At the Inter-American Conference held at Santiago de Chile in 1856 seven republics signed a "Treaty of Union of the American States" (commonly known as the "Continental Treaty") which was the first instrument that tried to establish a legal duty of non-recognition of territorial changes.[3] Its Article 13 provided that

[1] Alvarez, Le Droit International Américain 49-50
[2] Ibid. 52-54
[3] Ibid. 55-56

The High Contracting Parties undertake not to cede nor alienate, under any form, to another State or government any part of their territories, nor to permit, within said territories, the establishment of a foreign Power; the other Parties pledge themselves not to recognize such an establishment, on whatever grounds.

The "Treaty of Union and Defensive Alliance," signed at the Inter-American Congress of Lima in 1865, contained provisions of mutual territorial guarantees as well as pledges not to make territorial cessions, but no clauses regarding non-recognition of territorial changes.[4]

All the efforts of the Latin-American world to outlaw the right of conquest were engulfed in the Pacific War between Chile, Peru, and Bolivia (1879–1883), the outcome of which deprived Bolivia of her entire seacoast, Peru of valuable provinces. The annexationist tendencies which manifested themselves while the war was still in progress prompted the United States Government, which had hitherto kept aloof from the disputes between Latin-American States, to issue through Secretary of State Blaine the following statement:

This Government feels that the exercise of the right of absolute conquest is dangerous to the best interests of all the republics of this continent. . . .

This Government also holds that between two independent nations hostilities do not, from the mere existence of war, confer the right of conquest until the failure to furnish the indemnity and guarantee which can rightfully be demanded.

Nor can this Government admit that a cession of territory can be properly exacted far exceeding in value the amplest estimate of a reasonable indemnity.[5]

No action, however, was taken by the United States Government when victorious Chile imposed on her defeated opponents the treaties which mutilated their territories.[6] Yet the idea that the right of conquest should be outlawed within the orbit of the Latin-American world tried again to assert

[4] *Ibid.* 59
[5] *For. Rel.* 1881, 143 and 147
[6] Treaty of Peace between Chile and Peru, signed Lima, October 20, 1883 (Martens, *Nouv. Rec. Gén.*, S. 2, X 191); Armistice Convention between Bolivia and Chile, signed Valparaiso, April 4, 1884 (*Ibid.* 611); Treaty of Peace between Chile and Bolivia, signed Santiago de Chile, October 20, 1904 (*Ibid.* S. 3, II 174).

itself. In the very year that marked the end of the Pacific War—1883—representatives of several Latin-American republics, meeting at Caracas on the occasion of the Bolivar Centenary, issued a declaration, known as the Caracas Protocol, in which they stressed the duty to uphold the integrity of Latin-American territory and the obligation to ignore "the so-called right of conquest." [7]

Once more an attempt to curb that right was made in 1890. In that year an "International Conference of American States" was held at Washington, D. C., under Secretary Blaine's chairmanship. It adopted the following "recommendation":

(1) That the principle of conquest shall not, during the continuance of the treaty of arbitration, be recognized as admissible under American public law.

(2) That all cessions of territory made during the continuance of the treaty of arbitration shall be void if made under threats of war or in the presence of an armed force.

(3) Any nation from which such cessions shall be exacted may demand that the validity of the cessions so made shall be void if made under threats of war or in the presence of an armed force.

(4) Any renunciation of the right to arbitrate, made under conditions named in the second section, shall be null and void.[8]

This recommendation, however, was contingent on the coming into force of a treaty of arbitration, simultaneously adopted by the Conference. As the treaty failed of ratification, the recommendation lapsed.[9]

Since the turn of the century, the endeavors of the Latin-American world to develop a law of territorial change were encompassed in the plans—in which soon also the United States participated—to codify the American international public and private law. This period, covering the years 1901 to 1928, produced much valuable spade work in the form of projects of Law Institutes, Committees of Jurists, and so on. These projects formed the material out of which in subsequent years important treaty law was created.

At the Second Inter-American Conference, held at Mexico City in 1901–2, a convention was signed which aimed at the

[7] Alvarez, *op. cit.* 106
[8] 1 Moore, *Dig.* 292
[9] *Ibid.;* Alvarez, *op. cit.* 217

codification of the "public and private international law to govern the relations between the American nations." [10] In furtherance of this aim the Third Conference, held at Rio de Janeiro in 1906, decided to appoint an International Committee of American Jurists.[11] This committee met for the first time at Rio in 1912 and began its work on the basis of a project submitted by the Brazilian Pessoa and a memorial drawn up by the Chilean Alvarez, yet it made little headway.[12] In 1916 the American Institute of International Law adopted a draft Declaration of the Rights and Duties of Nations [13] of which Articles 4 and 5 touched on the problem of territorial change:

Art. 4. Every nation is entitled to a territory enclosed in delimited boundaries, and to exercise exclusive jurisdiction over this territory and over all persons, nationals as well as aliens, who find themselves on that territory.

Art. 5. Every nation possessed of a right under international law is entitled to demand that this right be respected and protected by the other nations, because right and duty are correlated, it being incumbent on all to respect the right of each.

This draft was incorporated in the so-called Havana Declarations of the Institute, adopted at Havana in 1917, which proposed to define the line of conduct that the international policy of the American nations should follow in their mutual relations as well as in those with the rest of the world.[14]

The official codificatory work was interrupted by the First World War. The Fifth Inter-American Conference, held at Santiago de Chile in 1923, resolved that the International Committee of American Jurists should resume the work on the basis of the project Alvarez.[15] In 1924 the Pan American Union requested the Board of Directors of the aforementioned Institute to draft proposals which were to be submitted to the Committee at its projected Rio meeting. The Board entrusted three members (Brown Scott, Alvarez, and Anderson) with the task. In 1924 the Committee of the In-

10 *Second Pan-American Conference, Minutes and Documents,* 525 and 715
11 *Third International American Conference, Minutes, Resolutions, Documents,* 625
12 Alvarez, *La Codification du Droit International Américain,* 5
13 10 *AJIL* 126
14 11 *AJIL,* Suppl., 47 A
15 Alvarez, *op. cit.* 6

stitute met at Havana and drew up a text known as the Thirty Projects. In 1925 Secretary Hughes submitted the draft to the Pan American Union, and in 1927 the Institute, meeting at Montevideo, decided to present it as a basis of discussion to the Jurists' Committee.[16]

Project No. 30 dealt with the problem of conquest. It read:

> The American Republics . . . solemnly declare as a fundamental concept of American international law that, without criticizing territorial acquisitions effected in the past, and without reference to existing controversies,
>
> In the future territorial acquisitions obtained by means of war or under the menace of war or in presence of an armed force, to the detriment of any American Republic, shall not be lawful; and that
>
> Consequently territorial acquisitions effected in the future by these means cannot be invoked as conferring title; and that
>
> Those obtained in the future by such means shall be considered null in fact and in law.[17]

The Jurists' Committee met at Rio in April, 1927. It based its discussion on the following material: (1) Pessoa's draft code of international public law; (2) Alvarez' project of 1923; (3) the Thirty Projects; (4) various suggestions from delegates to the Montevideo session of the Institute. Yet none of these projects met in its entirety with the Committee's approval. Instead, the Committee drew up a proposal of its own, known as the Twelve Projects.[18] In this draft some of the previous projects were combined, while others were completely suppressed, among them Project 30. The problem of territorial change by force was only indirectly and vaguely touched upon in the following provision (Project II, Art. 9):

> A State loses its international personality only when it separates into two or more States, when it voluntarily incorporates itself with another State, or when it unites with another to form a single State.

The Twelve Projects were submitted to the Sixth Inter-American Conference, held at Havana in 1928. Some of them found their way into various conventions which are

16 *Ibid.* 7; 19 *AJIL* 333
17 20 *AJIL*, Spec. Suppl., 384
18 22 *AJIL*, Spec. Suppl., 234

outside the scope of this analysis. The issue of aggression was referred to only in one sentence of a resolution, adopted at the suggestion of the Mexican delegation, to the effect that

(1) All aggression is considered illicit and as such is declared prohibited;

(2) The American States will employ all pacific means to settle conflicts which may arise between them.[19]

Still in another direction the theoretical work done in the Americas in the first quarter of the twentieth century was fruitful: it enabled Latin-American scholars and statesmen to make many valuable suggestions in their capacity as delegates to the League of Nations, to which the narrative has now to turn.

[19] *U. S. Dept. of State, Report of the Delegates to the Sixth International Conference of American States* (1928), 320

CHAPTER VIII

THE LEAGUE OF NATIONS:
ARTICLE X OF THE COVENANT

I<small>N</small> his address to Congress of January 8, 1918, President Wilson declared in the last of his Fourteen Points that

A general association of nations must be formed under specific covenants for the purpose of affording mutual guarantees of political independence and territorial integrity to great and small States alike.[1]

This statement contained already in an embryonic form what became Article 10 of the Covenant of the League.

The legislative history of this provision cannot be discussed here in detail. Its original version, however, drafted by Wilson himself, may be quoted in full:

The Contracting Parties unite in guaranteeing to each other political independence and territorial integrity; but it is understood between them that such territorial readjustments, if any, as may in the future become necessary by reason of changes in present racial conditions and aspirations or present social and political relationships, pursuant to the principle of self-determination, and also such territorial readjustments as may in the judgment of three-fourths of the Delegates be demanded by the welfare and manifest interest of the people concerned, may be effected, if agreeable to those peoples; and the territorial changes may in equity involve material compensation. The Contracting Parties accept without reservation the principle that the peace of the world is superior in importance to every question of political jurisdiction or boundary.[2]

This text combined a somewhat vague guarantee of the status quo with an equally vague blueprint for what was subsequently termed "machinery for peaceful changes." Opposition arose from many quarters. Ultimately the following text was adopted as Article 10:

[1] *For. Rel.* 1918, Suppl. 1, I 12
[2] 3 Temperley 56

The Members of the League undertake to respect and preserve as against external aggression the territorial integrity and existing political independence of all the Members of the League. In case of any threat or danger of such aggression the Council should advise upon the means by which this obligation shall be fulfilled.

Les Membres de la Société s'engagent à respecter et à maintenir contre toute agression extérieure l'integrité territoriale et l'indépendence politique présente de tous les membres de la Société. En cas d'agression, de menace ou de danger d'agression, le conseil avise aux moyens d'assurer l'exécution de cette obligation.

The problem of territorial readjustment was completely severed from the guarantee of political independence and territorial integrity and made the subject of a separate provision, Article 19, worded as follows:

The Assembly may from time to time advise the reconsideration by Members of the League of treaties which have become inapplicable and the consideration of international conditions whose continuance might endanger the peace of the world.

It has been frequently asserted that the language of Article 10 is so vague that it could not possibly be regarded as a source of legal obligations. This view is believed to be exaggerated. No doubt the text left many problems unsolved: the term "external aggression" was not defined; nothing was said about the relationship between aggression and self-defense; nothing, either, about the question whether and how far an aggressor who was a League Member was himself protected against successful counteraction of the attacked State. Yet in spite of these deficiencies, the text appears clear and precise enough to form the basis of a legal obligation. This assertion is supported by the history of the attempts to eliminate Article 10 from the Covenant, for they were made just because certain quarters felt the pinch of the legal duty embodied in its wording.

On December 6, 1920, the Canadian delegate, Doherty, submitted to the First League Assembly the proposal "that Article 10 of the Covenant of the League be and is hereby struck out." [3] The proposal went through various committees. Finally, the First Committee submitted to the Second Assembly (1921) a report [4] which proposed not to strike

[3] *Records of the First Assembly* (1920), *Plenary Meetings,* 279
[4] *Records of the Second Assembly* (1921), *Minutes of the First Committee,* 107 and 191

out Article 10, but to adopt instead an "interpretative resolution" with the following text:

> The purpose of Article 10 is not to perpetuate the territorial and
> political organisation as established and existing at the time of the
> conclusion of the recent peace treaties. Modifications may be in-
> troduced by various legitimate means, and even by war, provided
> that the peaceful means laid down in the Covenant have been ex-
> hausted. The Covenant admits of this possibility.
> The purpose of Article 10 is to affirm the principle that for the
> future the civilized world will not tolerate acts of aggression as a
> means of altering the territorial status and political independence
> of the States of the world.
> To this end the Members of the League have in the first place
> undertaken to respect the territorial integrity and existing political
> independence against any external aggression on the part of a State
> whether a Member of the League or not. The Council shall advise
> upon the means by which this obligation shall be fulfilled.

In the ensuing discussion Mr. Doherty motivated his proposal to eliminate Article 10 in the following words:

> Even if certain reasons appeared to justify the maintenance of
> the territorial integrity of various nations, it was impossible to
> justify an article which imposed such an obligation on all the na-
> tions of the world alike. It might possibly be conceded that strong
> and powerful nations would consider it necessary, in the general
> interest, to guarantee the possessions of the weaker nations, but it
> was impossible to understand how such an obligation could also be
> imposed on the weaker nations and on all nations alike.[5]

Thus, Mr. Doherty explicitly admitted that Article 10
contained a legal obligation, and that he wanted it deleted
just on that ground. In the end, the Second Assembly decided to leave the further discussion and decision to the
Third Assembly,[6] which, in turn, postponed it.[7] Final action
was taken by the Fourth Assembly in 1923. The matter occupied first the Committee.[8] There the Canadian delegate,
Sir Lomer Gouin, declared that the Canadian delegation
realized that it would be impossible to obtain the elimination
of Article 10; instead he proposed an amendment to Article
10 reading:

[5] *Ibid.* 109
[6] *Ibid., Plenary Meetings,* 833-5
[7] *Records of the Third Assembly* (1922), *Plenary Meetings,* 217
[8] *Records of the Fourth Assembly* (1923), *Minutes of the First Committee,* 11-18, 24-28

That the following words should be added (to the last sentence): "Taking into account the political and geographical circumstances of each State."

That the following paragraph should be added: "The opinion given by the Council in each case shall be regarded as a matter of the highest importance and shall be taken into consideration by all Members of the League, which shall use their utmost endeavor to conform to the conclusions of the Council, but no Member shall be under the obligation to engage in any act of war without the consent of its parliament, legislature or other representative body."

Mr. Rolin (Belgium) suggested the adoption of an "interpretative resolution" instead of an amendment to Article 10 in view of the fact that the amending procedure was not yet completely defined. Against this suggestion Mr. Scialoja (Italy) objected on the ground that

Any interpretation by the Assembly of an article of the Covenant could have no effective intrinsic value and could not bind the League for the future. Such an interpretation could only serve as a guide for the Council and the Assembly, because behind these bodies were the Members of the League which did not regard themselves bound by a vote of the Assembly. Thus the moral authority of the interpretation, although considerable, could not be regarded as binding on future Assemblies. If the Governments did not ratify any amendment which had been unanimously adopted by the Assembly, the amendment ceased to exist, because in the last resort the decision rested with the Governments and not with the Assemblies or the Delegates.

The Committee appointed a Subcommittee which proposed the following draft-resolution to be submitted to the Assembly:

The Assembly, desirous of defining the scope of Article 10 of the Covenant, adopts the following resolution:

It is in conformity with the spirit of Article 10 that, in the event of the Council considering it to be its duty to recommend the application of military measures in consequence of an aggression or danger or threat of aggression, the Council shall be bound to take account more particularly of the geographical situation and of the special conditions of each State.

The opinion expressed by the Council shall be regarded as an invitation of the utmost weight which all the Members of the League shall take into consideration in the sincere desire of executing in all good faith their engagements.

It is for the constitutional authorities of each Member to decide whether the circumstances do give rise to the obligation of preserving the independence and the integrity of the Members, and in what degree the Member is bound to assure the execution of this obligation by employment of its military forces.

Mr. Rolin, acting as rapporteur of the Subcommittee, declared that Article 10 implied international obligations, and that the draft emphasized their legal nature. But he continued:

It had been repeated many times that the League of Nations was not a Super-State, and that its Members had not surrendered their sovereignty. It followed, therefore, that the Members of the League who had, in virtue of the Covenant, contracted various engagements, were, in accordance with the traditions of international law, the proper judges of those engagements. Unless any special exception was made, they retained the right to estimate the extent of their obligations. . . . Each Member of the League was therefore pledged to fulfil its obligations, which existed independently of the deliberations of any parliament; but, just as the various parliaments were free to decide whether the casus foederis had arisen and whether the guarantee came into action, the Members of the League of Nations were free to determine the limits and conditions of their obligations and the manner in which these were to be carried out.

The draft-resolution was opposed by Barthélémy (France) and others on the ground that

To adopt the text of the Sub-Committee would be to destroy the authority of Article 10 by transforming an obligation into merely facultative action; it would be contrary to all principles of law to make the legality of an obligation depend upon the appreciation of the party on whom the obligation lay.

The Committee laid the draft-resolution before the Assembly;[9] there, too, Mr. Rolin acted as rapporteur. His views on the value of Assembly resolutions are of interest. After explaining why the Committee proposed an "interpretative resolution" instead of an amendment, he continued:

I admit that the interpretative resolution before you is not of very definite value from a legal point of view. Mr. Scialoja . . . pointed this out to the Committee. He said that the Covenant was an international convention which had been ratified by the various States, and that, without this ratification, we could not adopt any interpretation which was juridically and definitely binding upon States. From a legal standpoint this is incontestable. Any interpre-

[9] *Ibid., Plenary Meetings*, 75-86

tation, however, which you embody in a resolution will certainly possess very great authority from a moral point of view. . . .

The vote on the resolution was taken by roll call. Twenty-nine members voted for it; twenty-two abstained from voting; one vote, that of Persia, was cast against it. Thereupon the President announced that, as unanimity had not been obtained, the resolution was not adopted.[10]

[10] *Ibid.* 87

CHAPTER IX

THE LEAGUE OF NATIONS:
THE NON-RECOGNITION IDEA
BEFORE 1932

T HE Second Assembly of the League of Nations (1921) appointed a Committee for the purpose of suggesting measures to ensure the thorough execution of the provisions of the Covenant regarding blockade and disarmament. This Committee was the first League agency to discuss non-recognition of territorial changes as a sanction against aggression. One of its members, Dr. Braga (Brazil), proposed the following amendment to the Covenant:

All the Members of the League of Nations consider null and void, pleno jure, the provisions of any international treaty concluded in the future which grant to a State which has made war contrary to Articles 12, 13 and 15 of the Covenant, the following:

(a) Indemnity for war costs and reparations for damage caused by the war;

(b) Clauses relating to the economic pressure against the conquered country;

(c) The annexation of territory.

Consequently all the Members of the League of Nations agree to introduce at once into their legal systems provisions for the purpose of investing their Governments with the following Powers:

. . . .

(6) Not to recognize in any form in their diplomatic and consular services, the sovereignty of the aggressor over the territories of the State attacked.[1]

From the language used by Dr. Braga it is not quite clear whether he conceived of non-recognition as a duty implied in the Covenant. For he motivated his suggestion in the following words:

[1] *Records of the Second Assembly* (1921), *Minutes of the Third Committee,* 320 and 396

This amendment would consist in establishing a legal system in accordance with which no aggressor State could, even after the war, continue to enjoy a tranquil and prosperous existence.

Mr. Braga's proposal was shelved, and so was a suggestion made the following year to the League by the Danish Government to the effect that

In the future territorial acquisitions in Europe shall not be lawful if resulting from war, conquest or the conclusion of a peace treaty.

Any agreement or arrangement made to the contrary shall be null and void and will not be recognized by the High Contracting Parties.[2]

This suggestion expressed the idea embodied in the Soviet-Turkish Treaty of 1921 that the consent of the dispossessed State to a loss of territory, even though given in treaty form, should not relieve third States of their duty to withhold recognition of such transfer.[3]

The issue of non-recognition of territorial changes was, oddly enough, completely left out in the discussion which preceded the signature of the Protocol for the Pacific Settlement of International Disputes (Geneva, October 2, 1924).[4]

The first to assert explicitly that Article 10 of the Covenant implied a legal duty not to recognize territorial changes brought about by aggression was the Finnish statesman and scholar Erich, who wrote in 1926:

Even in case the League of Nations should not have succeeded in repelling an aggression or in preventing an occupation—perhaps a total one—of the territory of a Member, the other Members must not recognize that de facto change as final and valid de jure. If one of the direct consequences of that unlawful aggression has been the establishment of a new State, the Members of the League of Nations should, on that account, refuse to recognize that new State the existence of which is conflicting with the supreme values whose inviolability Art. 10 wants to safeguard.[5]

Mr. Erich's suggestion was taken up two years later by his countryman, Mr. Procope, at the Ninth League As-

2 Quoted from Prof. Jessup's Report on the Harvard Research Draft Convention on Rights and Duties of States in Case of Aggression (33 *AJIL*, Spec. Suppl., 892).

3 Above, 27

4 *LNOJ*, Spec. Suppl. 23, 501; Hudson, *International Legislation* II 1378

5 "La Naissance et la Reconnaissance des États" (13 *Hague Rec.* 430 at 456)

sembly (September, 1928). During a discussion of the previous work of the Security Committee of the League, the latter made the following statement:

Viewed as a means for the comprehensive settlement of international relations, an undertaking in regard to non-aggression is not sufficient in itself. Non-aggression is intimately bound up with the question of mutual assistance. It represents to a certain extent an obligation provided for under Art. 10 of the Covenant, namely, to respect the territorial status and political independence of a State.

Mutual assistance represents a second obligation under the same article, namely, that of causing the political and territorial integrity of a State to be respected. Mutual assistance represents the positive aspect of international interdependence and is an expression of international solidarity.

Art. 10, however, implies a further obligation which must be mentioned. We may, indeed, we must, infer from it that Members of the League cannot recognize as final or admissible a situation resulting from an act of aggression or from any other act incompatible with the provisions of the article itself.[6]

This statement went beyond Mr. Braga's suggestion of 1921, since it considered non-recognition to be implied in the League Covenant as a legal obligation, while Mr. Braga, judging by his language, was merely thinking in terms of future amendments. On the other hand, Mr. Procope's wording, "cannot recognize as final or admissible," was less clean-cut than Mr. Braga's: "not to recognize, in their diplomatic and consular services, the sovereignty of the aggressor over the territories of the State attacked." The latter language emphasized what constitutes the very essence of non-recognition.[7]

A few weeks before Mr. Procope made the foregoing statement, on August 27, 1928, the so-called Briand-Kellogg Pact of Paris was concluded.[8] The text[9] contained nothing

---

[6] *LNOJ*, Spec. Suppl. 64, 75
[7] Below, 96, 100
[8] 4 *U. S. Treaties* 5130
[9] The essential provisions were:

"(Art. I) The High Contracting Parties solemnly declare in the names of their respective peoples that they condemn recourse to war for the solution of international controversies, and renounce it as an instrument of national policy in their relations with one another.

"(Art. II) The High Contracting Parties agree that the settlement or solution of all disputes or conflicts of whatever nature or whatever origin they may be, which may arise among them, shall never be sought except by pacific means."

regarding a duty not to recognize changes effected in violation of its provisions, and it appears unwarranted to read such an obligation into it.

The following year (1929) the Tenth League Assembly resolved to undertake what was called the co-ordination of the Covenant with the Pact of Paris. During the protracted discussions which accompanied the attempts of Committees and Subcommittees to harmonize the text of the former with the Briand-Kellogg Pact, the issue of non-recognition was sporadically injected. Thus the Peruvian delegate, Mr. Cornejo, suggested that a formula be devised whereby a peace treaty imposed after an unjust war, waged in defiance of the Briand-Kellogg Pact and the Covenant, would not be recognized.[10] He also proposed the following amendment to Article 18:

The Secretariat of the League may not register any treaty of peace imposed by force as a consequence of a war undertaken in violation of the Pact of Paris. The League of Nations shall consider as null and void any stipulations which it may contain, and shall render every assistance in restoring the status quo destroyed by force.[11]

No action was taken on these suggestions, which followed the pattern of the Danish proposals of 1922. The problem of the relationship between Article 10 of the Covenant and non-recognition was shelved until the initiative of a non-member State—the United States of America—spurred the organs of the League to take it up again.

[10] *LNOJ*, Spec. Suppl. 75, 168
[11] *LNOJ* 1930, 78

CHAPTER X

THE MANCHURIAN INCIDENT. THE STIMSON NOTES AND THE LEAGUE ASSEMBLY RESOLUTION OF MARCH 11, 1932

For many decades the three northeastern provinces of China—Fengtien, Kirin, and Heilungkiang—commonly known as the Manchurian provinces or Manchuria, had formed a bone of contention between China, Japan, and Russia. Wedged in on the north between Transbaikalia and coastal Siberia, bordering in the southeast on Korea (Cho-sen), their southernmost portion, the Liaotung peninsula, jutting into the Gulf of Chili, they constitute an area of great strategic importance to each of those three countries. In 1894 Japan made war on China over the latter's claims to the suzerainty over Korea. China was defeated, and Japan imposed on her the Treaty of Shimonoseki, signed on April 17, 1895.[1] Under its terms China undertook to cede to Japan "in perpetuity and full sovereignty" not only Formosa and the Pescadores group, but also "the southern part of Fengtien province," that is, the Liaotung peninsula with its seaports of Liushunkoo (Russian: Port Arthur) and Talienwan (Russian: Dalny; Japanese: Dairen). The Liaotung cession, however, was opposed by Russia, Germany, and France on the ground "that the permanent possession of this district by Japan would be detrimental to the lasting peace of the Orient." Yielding to the diplomatic pressure of the three Great Powers, Japan gave up that part of her spoils.[2] Before long Russia's good services found their reward. In 1896 the Chinese Government granted for a term of eighty years to the Russo-Chinese Bank, a corporation sponsored and partly financed by the Russian Government,[3] the right to build and operate

[1] Martens, *Nouv. Rec. Gén.*, S. 2, XXI 642; Rockhill 14; MacMurray 18
[2] The renunciation was made in form of a retrocession treaty, signed Peking, November 8, 1895 (Rockhill 26).
[3] The Russo-Chinese Bank was subsequently merged with the Russo-Asiatic Bank.

on Manchurian territory a section of the Trans-Siberian trunk line connecting Chita (Transbaikalia) with Pogranichnaya (Ussuri region). The Bank was to organize a subsidiary, the Chinese Eastern Railway Company, which received from the Chinese Government, in addition to the rights originally granted to the Bank, a series of important industrial and commercial privileges.[4] In 1898 Russia took a further step in her pacific penetration of Manchuria. By an agreement signed at Peking on March 15 (o.s.) of that year she obtained from China for a period of twenty-five years the lease of the Liaotung peninsula for the purposes of establishing bases in Port Arthur and Talienwan, and moreover, the extension of the Chinese Eastern Railway concession so as to include the right to connect by rail these two ports with the Manchurian section of the Trans-Siberian.[5]

During the Boxer uprising (1899–1900) Russian troops occupied all of Manchuria. After peace had been restored, China as well as other Powers, in the first place Japan, was eager to see the Russian occupation terminated. The Russians promised evacuation by stages,[6] but the schedule was not observed, and Russia even seemed to have designs on Korea. The Japanese decided to make war on the Tsarist Empire, and they started it on February 10, 1904, by a sneak attack on the Russian fleet in Port Arthur harbor. There can be little doubt that Japan's action was encouraged by the attitude of the British Government, for on January 30, 1902, the latter had concluded with Japan a treaty, signed at London,[7] which explicitly mentioned Japan's "special interests" in Korea. The land war was fought in Manchuria, and consequently, since China did not enter the conflict, on neutral territory. For many months Japan was successful on land and at sea; in the long run, however, Russia might have recovered her breath. Yet in the summer of 1905 both parties

[4] Agreements of August 28, 1896 (MacMurray 78) and of September 8, 1896 (Ibid. 74)
[5] Convention, signed Peking, March 27, 1898 (Rockhill 50) and Additional Convention, signed St. Petersburg, May 7, 1898 (Ibid. 53)
[6] Russo-Chinese Convention, signed Peking, March 26/April 8, 1902 (Ibid. 99). Under Article I the Tsar agreed to the restoration of Chinese authority in Manchuria, "qui reste une partie intégrante de l'Empire de Chine."
[7] MacMurray 324; 95 BFSP 83

decided to accept the forthcoming offers of mediation, and
peace was finally concluded on September 5, 1905, at Portsmouth, N. H., U. S. A.[8] Again a friendly hand guided Japan's steps. For a few weeks earlier, on August 12, 1905,
the British Government had concluded with the Japanese
Government a new treaty, again signed at London.[9] By its
terms both contracting parties undertook to ensure the independence and integrity of China, while Great Britain,
emphasizing once more that Japan possessed "paramount
political, military, and economic interests" in Korea, recognized the former's right "to take measures of guidance, control, and protection" in that country.

Backed by these treaty provisions and not opposed by the
United States, Japan was able to secure from Russia the
pledge (Art. 2 of the Portsmouth Treaty) not to interfere
with her measures in Korea. Furthermore, Russia agreed to
transfer to Japan, subject to the consent of China, the
Liaotung lease (Art. 5) and the railway and railway rights
from Changchun to Port Arthur.[10] Under Article 3 both
parties mutually engaged to evacuate completely and simultaneously all of Manchuria except the area affected by the
Liaotung lease, and to restore to the exclusive administration of China all portions of Manchuria in occupation of
Japanese or Russian troops except the said peninsula. On
December 22, 1905, the Chinese Government gave its assent
to these transfers and even granted Japan additional rights
in South Manchuria.[11] In 1906 Japan organized the railway
system Changchun—Port Arthur and its branch lines under
the name of the South Manchuria Railway Company, Ltd.,
and established in the leased area, henceforth known as the
Kwantung peninsula, a Government General which ruled it
as though its sovereignty belonged to Japan.[12] As regards
Korea, Japan was not remiss in filling out the blank endorse-

[8] MacMurray 522; 98 *BFSP* 735
[9] MacMurray 516; 98 *BFSP* 136
[10] The line from Port Arthur makes connection with the Trans-Siberian
at Kharbin, some 120 miles north of Changchun. Consequently, the section
Changchun-Kharbin of the former remained after 1905 part of the Chinese
Eastern Railroad System.
[11] MacMurray 549
[12] Japanese Imperial Orders of June 7 and July 31, 1906 (MacMurray 555
and 565)

ments obtained at London and Portsmouth. On November 17, 1905, the Korean Government was made to sign a treaty [13] yielding to Japan the conduct of Korea's foreign affairs and providing for the installation of a Japanese resident general in the nation's capital, Seoul. Thus, Korea was officially transformed into a Japanese protectorate; the transaction, however was only the prelude to full absorption. After a treaty, concluded on July 12, 1909,[14] had handed over to Japan the administration of justice, the Emperor of Korea was finally induced to sign on August 22, 1910, at Seoul a convention [15] by which he ceded his whole empire to the Mikado.[16] The transfer was not opposed by any of the Great Powers, and internationally Korea was henceforth regarded and treated as an integral part of the Japanese Empire.

In Manchuria outside the Kwantung area Chinese administration was restored, subject to the rights of Japan and Russia in their respective zones. This regime led often to friction between the territorial sovereign and the grantees, but the incidents were always ironed out without leading to dangerous complications.[17] On July 4, 1910, Russia and Japan concluded at St. Petersburg a treaty by which they mutually pledged themselves to the maintenance of the status quo in Manchuria.[18] Yet in 1911 a revolution broke out in China, and the following year the rule of the Manchu dynasty was finally overthrown. China became a republic, but the new government was utterly weak and unable to prevent one of the "war lords," Marshal Chang Tso-lin, from establishing himself as dictator in Manchuria. The

[13] Martens, *Nouv. Rec. Gén.*, S. 2, XXXIV 727.
[14] *Ibid.* S. 3, II 669
[15] *Ibid.* S. 3, IV 24
[16] The main provisions of the treaty were: (Art. I) The Emperor of Korea makes complete and permanent cession of all rights of sovereignty over Korea; (Art. II) The Emperor of Japan accepts the cession and consents [sic!] to complete annexation of Korea to the Empire of Japan.
[17] See, e.g., Russo-Chinese Agreement of April 27, 1909 (*China Treaties*, Vol. 3, p. 13): "Des divergences d'opinion s'étant produites dans l'interprétation du Contrat pour la construction et l'exploitation du Chemin de Fer Chinois de l'Est du 27 août 1896, les Gouvernements de Chine et de Russie ont arrêté les dispositions générales suivantes: (I) Comme principe fondamental les droits souverains de la Chine sont reconnus sur les terrains du Chemin de Fer; aucun préjudice ne peut leur être porté. . . ."
[18] MacMurray 803

position of Russia and Japan, however, remained at first un-changed by the new state of affairs.

The prolonged weakness of the Chinese Government and the involvement of the European Great Powers in the First World War encouraged Japan to embark on an expansion-ist policy in China. In the spring of 1915 she presented the Chinese Government with the so-called "Twenty-One De-mands." [19] Their acceptance would have made China in fact, if not in name, a Japanese protectorate. But this time the Japanese action met with the opposition of the Government of the United States. On May 11, 1915, Secretary of State Bryan dispatched the following note to the Japanese Gov-ernment:

In view of the circumstances of the negotiations which have taken place and which are now pending between the Government of Japan and the Government of China, and of the agreements which have been reached as the result thereof, the Government has the honor to notify the Imperial Japanese Government that it cannot recognize any agreement or undertaking which has been entered into or which may be entered into between the Governments of Japan and China, impairing the treaty rights of the United States and its citizens in China, the political and territorial integrity of the Republic of China, or the international policy relative to China commonly known as the open door policy.[20]

It is interesting to note that the American diplomatic step assumed the form of a statement of non-recognition, and that, by contrast with the diplomatic correspondence relat-ing to the Balkan situation of 1908, the threat to resort to non-recognition was not limited to potential violations of treaty rights. For at that time the political independence and territorial integrity of China was not yet protected by a multilateral convention after the pattern of the great European compacts concluded in the course of the nine-teenth century. The intercession of the United States prompted Japan to desist for the time being from her most extreme demands, but it could not prevent her from wresting from China considerable concessions. Thus, China was made to sign on May 25, 1915, a convention which granted to Japan the extension to a period of 99 years of the Kwan-

[19] *For. Rel.* 1915, 178-206
[20] *Ibid.* 146

tung lease and the railway rights in South Manchuria, and numerous further privileges.[21]

The Russian Revolution of 1917 led to inter-Allied intervention in eastern Siberia in which Japan played a prominent part. Thus, not only the Russian railway zone in North Manchuria, but also parts of eastern Siberia were occupied by the Japanese. Again, as in 1915, it was the Government of the United States that opposed their expansionist aspirations, and yielding to American representations, Japan agreed at the International Conference on the Limitation of Armaments, held at Washington from 1921 to 1922, to evacuate Siberia.[22] The evacuation was carried out by October, 1922, and as a consequence the control of the Soviet Government was extended over eastern Siberia as well as over the Chinese Eastern Railway. A further achievement of the Washington Conference, which lent a new legal aspect to Far Eastern affairs, was the conclusion, on February 6, 1922, of the so-called Nine Power Treaty.[23] Under its Article 1 the Contracting Parties agreed

(1) To respect the sovereignty, the independence, and the territorial and administrative integrity of China;
(2) To provide the fullest and most unembarrassed opportunity to China to develop and maintain for herself an effective and stable government.

It will be remembered that previously the principle expressed in the first paragraph of this article had only found its way into certain bilateral treaties. Now the legal status of China was placed under the protection of a multilateral convention which enabled its signatories to oppose encroachments on the independence and integrity of China not only as affecting their interests, but also as violating their treaty rights. Subsequently, all the signatories of the Nine Power Treaty became also parties to the Briand-Kellogg Pact of Paris.[24] This added another legal basis for opposing acts of aggression against China as a violation of treaty law.

[21] MacMurray 1220
[22] *For. Rel.* 1922, II 842-865
[23] Treaty between the United States of America, Belgium, the British Empire, China, France, Italy, Japan, the Netherlands, and Portugal relating to the Principles and Policies to be Followed in Matters Concerning China (3 *U. S. Treaties* 3120).
[24] Above, 48

The following years witnessed a marked growth of Chinese national consciousness, and soon the wave of Chinese nationalism swept also to Manchuria.[25] There the ethnical structure had considerably changed since the end of the Russo-Japanese War. Previously rather sparsely settled, the Manchurian provinces had become since 1905 the goal of millions of Chinese who trekked from the over-populated interior to the northeastern border provinces.[26] The Manchurian dictator, Marshal Chang Tso-lin, had originally lived on good terms with the Japanese. The national upsurge prompted him to change his attitude. Before long he was dead, killed in 1928 in an explosion on his railway car. His son and successor, Chang Hsueh-liang, not deterred by his father's fate, openly joined the Chinese National Party (Kuomintang) and thereby lent new impetus to Chinese national feeling in Manchuria. In 1929 the Chinese clashed with the Soviet Government over the Chinese Eastern, but they achieved nothing.[27] In 1930 and 1931 the tension between Chinese and foreigners increased and led to a series of serious incidents.[28] On the night of September 18, 1931, a minor explosion occurred on the tracks of the South Manchurian near Mukden.[29] It was never ascertained who had planted the bomb, which, by the way, caused so little damage to the rails that the train which was due shortly thereafter passed the spot of the explosion without being derailed. The Japanese, however, used the incident as a pretext for sweeping measures. Their action must have been planned in advance since it extended within a few days over the whole Japanese railroad zone, and within a few weeks over all of Manchuria. A few hours after the explosion Japanese troops occupied Mukden and Changchun; a few days later Kirin fell to them; on January 3, 1932, Chinchow was occupied and thereby the last remaining authority of the Chinese Republic in South Manchuria destroyed. On February 5, 1932, the Japanese entered Kharbin on the Trans-Siberian.[30] The military operations were closely followed by administrative

[25] Stimson, *The Far Eastern Crisis* 23
[26] *Ibid.* 18
[27] *Ibid.* 25
[28] *Lytton Report* (below, 68, n. 4), Ch. III
[29] *Ibid.* Ch. IV
[30] *Ibid.*

measures.[31] As soon as the Japanese military had established effective control in any one of the Manchurian provinces, the Chinese civil authorities were replaced by Japanese puppet agencies purporting to be local self-governing administrations. On February 17, 1932, a "Supreme Administrative Council" was constituted at Mukden; it published the following day a Declaration of Independence, and thereafter resolved to ask the former Emperor of China, Huan-tung, who had been dethroned in 1912 when a boy and now called himself Mr. Pu-yi, to assume the headship of the new State, "Manchukuo." He accepted, and on March 9, 1932, an "Organic Law" was promulgated as the constitution of the new State.

At the time of the Mukden incident the Council of the League of Nations was in session. On September 21, 1931, the Chinese representative, Dr. Sze, invoked its attention under Article 11 of the League Covenant.[32] The Council instituted proceedings of a rather formal character, carefully avoiding any steps which might have hurt the feelings of the aggressor. One of the more positive measures of that League body was the decision to establish contact with the Government of the United States on the ground that the Manchurian situation involved not only obligations under the League Covenant, but also such under the Briand-Kellogg Pact of Paris to which the United States was a party.[33] After a number of adjournments and other procrastinations the Council decided on December 10, 1931, to appoint a commission of five members which was to study the situation on the spot.[34] The commission became subsequently known as the Lytton Commission. Its members were selected by the Council President and finally approved by the Council on January 14, 1932.[35]

In the meantime, however, the Japanese seizure of South Manchuria had been completed with the fall of Chinchow. The latter event convinced the Government of the United

---

[31] For the following see *Ibid.* Ch. VI; also *LNOJ* 1932, 925-6 (Chinese Statement of February 22, 1932, and letter from the Chinese Delegation, dated March 3, 1932).

[32] *LNOJ* 1931, 2453

[33] Stimson, *op. cit.* 41 and 62

[34] *LNOJ* 1931, 2374-8

[35] *LNOJ* 1932, 284

States that, as Mr. Stimson put it,[36] "all hope for a solution
of the Manchurian problem by conciliation and for a fair
settlement by even-handed negotiation with China was ended
for the present," and that harm to the interests of the
United States might result from the situation. It was decided
in Washington to give Japan a solemn notice of the rights
of the United States under the Nine Power Treaty and the
Pact of Paris. On January 7, 1932, the Secretary of State
of the United States, Mr. Stimson, dispatched the following
note to the Governments of China and Japan:

> In view of the present situation and of its own rights and obli-
> gations therein, the American Government deems it to be its duty
> to notify both the Imperial Japanese Government and the Govern-
> ment of the Chinese Republic that it cannot admit the legality of
> any situation de facto nor does it intend to recognize any treaty or
> agreement entered into between those Governments, or agents
> thereof, which may impair the treaty rights of the United States or
> its citizens in China, including those which relate to the sover-
> eignty, the independence, or the territorial or administrative in-
> tegrity of the Republic of China, or to the international policy
> relative to China, commonly known as the open-door policy; and
> that it does not intend to recognize any situation, treaty, or agree-
> ment which may be brought about by means contrary to the cove-
> nants and obligations of the Pact of Paris of August 27, 1928, to
> which Treaty both China and Japan, as well as the United States,
> are parties.[37]

Mr. Stimson's own narrative proves that it was the precedent of the Bryan note of May 11, 1915, that prompted him
to issue his warning to Japan in terms of a declaration of
non-recognition.[38] The comparison of the two notes, how-

[36] Stimson, *op. cit.* 88
[37] 6 *D. S. Press Rel.* 41
[38] Stimson, *op. cit.* 93: "As soon as the actual taking of Chinchow by the
Japanese army signalized the final flouting of all our efforts . . . , I set to
work upon the second step—the winding up of discussion by a final notice
of our rights. The idea of using a notice of non-recognition as a warning to
an aggressive power of course was not new. In 1915 Secretary Bryan had
sent such a notification to China and Japan at the time when Japan had
served the Twenty-One Demands upon China and was exercising pressure
upon China to make agreements with her which might violate the rights of
the United States under the Open Door policy or otherwise. The thought of
using such a method to emphasize our position in the present controversy
had been in our minds for many weeks. I find from my diary that as early
as November 9th I discussed it with my assistants as an ultimate possible
weapon to be used, and thereafter it was constantly cropping up in our discussions. Mr. Bryan had used it as an individual notification from the

ever, shows that each is partly wider, partly narrower in scope than the other. Bryan's note threatened to resort to non-recognition only with regard to changes effected by means of agreements; Stimson's declaration was not limited to this contingency since it used the terms "any situation de facto" besides the words "treaty or agreement." On the other hand, Bryan's note envisaged non-recognition of changes regardless of whether they constituted violations of treaty rights of the United States, whereas Stimson's non-recognition statement referred only to such violations, more specifically to violations of the rights accrued to the United States in its capacity as a party to the Nine Power Treaty and the Briand-Kellogg Pact.

The United States Government had anticipated that the British Government would view its action sympathetically even if it felt unable for any reason to follow the American lead.[39] What really occurred was disappointing. On January 11 His Majesty's Government published in the press a communiqué stating that it would stand by the Open Door policy, and that, since the Japanese had made statements to the same effect, "His Majesty's Government have not considered it necessary to address any formal note to the Japanese Government on the lines of the American Government's note. . . ." [40] Commenting on that communiqué, Mr. Stimson wrote:

Its omissions were the most important features of the communiqué. It was entirely silent as to the preservation of the sovereignty, independence and integrity of China, the Kellogg-Briand Pact, and the assertion of the principle of non-recognition of the fruits of unlawful aggression. . . .[41]

As could hardly be expected otherwise, the position of the British Government was backed by editorials of the British

---

United States based upon rights of our Government under treaties relating to China alone. But even on November 9th we were beginning to discuss the greater potentialities of the doctrine should the other nations of the world join us in establishing it. The force of a non-recognition of the fruits of aggression when concurred in by the entire world would manifestly have a more powerful deterring influence upon the aggressor than when used by a single nation."

[39] *Ibid.* 99
[40] *Ibid.* 101
[41] *Ibid.*

press. On the very day of the issuance of the communiqué the London *Times* contained an article which praised the "wisdom" which the British Government had shown "in declining to address a communication to the Chinese and Japanese Governments on the lines of Mr. Stimson's notes" and continued:

> Nor does it seem the immediate business of the Foreign Office to defend the "administrative integrity" of China until that integrity is something more than an ideal. It did not exist in 1922 and it does not exist today. On no occasion since the Nine Power Treaty was signed has the Central Government of China exercised any real administrative authority over large and varying areas of its huge territory. Today its writ does not run in Yunnan and in other important provinces, and, while its sovereignty over Manchuria is not disputed [sic!], there is no evidence that it has exercised any real administration there since Nanking became the Chinese capital.[42]

On January 16, 1932, the Japanese Government replied to the American note of January 7. The Japanese communication, which, by the way, used almost literally the same language as the foregoing article of the London *Times* claimed

> that the treaties which related to China must necessarily be applied with due regard to the state of affairs from time to time prevailing in that country, and that the present unsettled and distracted state of China is not what was in the contemplation of the high contracting parties at the time of the Treaty of Washington. . . .[43]

The attitude of the British did not discountenance Secretary Stimson, as witnessed by the following sentences which he wrote on February 23, 1932, to Senator Borah:

> If a similar decision should be reached and a similar position taken by the other governments of the world, a caveat will be placed upon any action which, we believe, will effectively bar the legality hereafter of any title or right sought to be obtained by pressure or treaty violation, and which . . . will eventually lead to the restoraton to China of rights and titles of which she may have been deprived.[44]

The assertion that non-recognition would "bar the le-

[42] *Ibid.* 102
[43] *Ibid.* 106; 6 *D. S. Press Rel.* 68
[44] *Ibid.* 201 at 205

gality of title" drew fire from international lawyers who asserted that under existing international law recognition by third Powers was no prerequisite for the validity of a title to territory.[45] Yet soon the events took a turn which led to a world-wide endorsement of Stimson's undertaking. By the middle of January Japan had apparently reached all her objectives—military as well as diplomatic—in Manchuria. Unable to secure assistance from the Great Powers, China resorted to the only weapon at her disposal—economic boycott. The Japanese answered by carrying their aggression from Manchuria to Shanghai. On January 28, 1932, they launched a large-scale attack on the city. The Chinese opposed stubborn resistance, and weeks of desperate fighting ensued.[46]

At this juncture, the Chinese Government took further action at Geneva. On January 29, 1932, the Chinese representative on the League Council, Mr. Yen, invoked the application of Articles 10 and 15 of the Covenant in addition to the measures taken, or which might be taken, by the League in the exercise of its functions under Article 11.[47] The League Council was then in session. It devoted much time to the discussion of the Manchurian situation, but nothing was achieved. Therefore, the Chinese took a further step. On February 12, 1932, Mr. Yen requested that the dispute be referred to the League Assembly under Article 15, paragraph 9, of the Covenant.[48] The request was complied with, and the Assembly convoked for March 3.[49] Prior to its meeting, however, the Members of the League Council other than Japan, possibly feeling that they owed some contribution, and obviously influenced by the American note of January 7, 1932, addressed on February 16, 1932, to the Government of Japan the following appeal:

The Twelve Members of the Council recall the terms of Article 10 of the Covenant of the League by which all Members of the League have undertaken to respect and preserve the territorial integrity and existing political independence of the other Members.

[45] See, e.g., Fischer Williams, "La Doctrine de la Reconnaissance en Droit International" (44 *Hague Rec.* 203)
[46] Stimson, *op. cit.* 109; *Lytton Report,* Ch. V
[47] *LNOJ* 1932, 373
[48] *Ibid.* 386
[49] *Ibid.* 387

It is their friendly right to direct attention to this provision, particularly as it appears to them to follow that no infringement of the territorial integrity and no change in the political independence of any Member of the League brought about in disregard of this article ought to be recognized as valid and effectual by the Members of the League.[50]

This appeal was the first League document that officially linked non-recognition to Article 10 of the Covenant. Japan replied on February 23, 1932, by a note which tried to place the whole blame for the events in Shanghai on Chinese "aggression." Regarding the threat of non-recognition the note said:

4. The appeal invokes Article 10 of the Covenant of the League of Nations. The measures of Japan, strictly defensive, do not infringe the provisions of that article. . . . It is a very proper provision; but it does not exclude self-defense, nor does it make China a "chartered libertine" free to attack other countries without their having any right to repel the attack.

5. As Japan does not . . . contemplate any attack on the territorial integrity or independence of a Member of the League of Nations, it is superfluous to say that the bearing of the observation that attacks of such a character made in defiance of Article 10 of the Covenant cannot be recognized as valid and effective is notably obscure to the Japanese Government. They take this occasion of once more firmly and emphatically declaring that Japan entertains no territorial or political ambitions whatsoever in China.[51]

The Mikado's Government was soon to get more light on the bearing of the non-recognition statement. For the exchange of the correspondence quoted above was merely the prelude to an action of the League Assembly which culminated in the adoption, on March 11, 1932, of the following resolution:

The Assembly
Considering that the provisions of the Covenant are entirely applicable to the present dispute, more particularly as regards:
(1) The principle of a scrupulous respect for treaties;
(2) The undertaking entered into by Members of the League of Nations to respect and preserve as against external aggression the territorial integrity and existing political independence of all the Members of the League;

[50] *Ibid.* 383
[51] *Ibid.* 384

(3) Their obligation to submit any dispute which may arise between them to procedure for peaceful settlement;

Adopting the principles laid down by the acting President of the
Council, M. Briand, in his declaration of December 10, 1931;

Recalling the fact that twelve Members of the Council again invoked those principles in their appeal to the Japanese Government
on February 16, 1932, when they declared that no infringement of
the territorial integrity and no change in the political independence
of any Member of the League brought about in disregard of Art. 10
of the Covenant ought to be recognized as valid and effectual by
Members of the League of Nations;

Considering that the principles governing international relations
and the peaceful settlement of disputes between Members of the
League above referred to are in full harmony with the Pact of
Paris, which is one of the cornerstones of the peace organization
of the world and under Art. 2 of which "the High Contracting
Parties agree that the settlement or solution of disputes or conflicts,
of whatever nature and whatever origin they may be, which might
arise among them shall never be sought except by pacific means";

Pending the steps which it may ultimately take for the settlement
of the dispute which has been referred to it;

Proclaims the binding nature of the principles and provisions
referred to above and declares that it is incumbent upon the Members of the League of Nations not to recognize any situation, treaty
or agreement which may be brought about by means contrary to the
Covenant of the League of Nations or to the Pact of Paris.[52]

The legal significance of this resolution will be discussed
at a later stage.[53] This chapter, however, would not be complete without reporting its legislative history.[54]

The Assembly met on March 3 in special session and appointed a General Commission, which discussed Article 10
and its relationship to the Pact of Paris. It was during that
discussion that the idea of the resolution was conceived.

On March 5 the Danish delegate, Mr. Munch, said:

The first thing to place on record is that a State will not be acting in conformity with the Covenant and the Pact of Paris merely
because it avoids declaring war. . . .

What the Covenant and the Pact forbid is not merely a declaration of war, but likewise any act of aggression, any recourse to
other than pacific methods as instruments of national policy.

The second need is a clear affirmation of the principle that, after
the establishment of the League as a great international organiza-

[52] *LNOJ,* Spec. Suppl. 101, 87
[53] Below, *96*
[54] The whole source material is contained in *LNOJ,* Spec. Suppl. 101.

tion based on law and the adoption of the Pact of Paris, no new right can be created by force. No agreement secured by force can be registered by the Secretariat under Art. 18 of the Covenant. That is a *sine qua non* for the validity of any agreement concluded between Members of the League.

In the view of many Members of the League, the guarantee contained in the Covenant against the creation of new rights by force is undoubtedly one of the most important achievements accomplished through the formation of the League.

To this Zulueta (Spain) added:

We hold that Art. 10 is the Magna Carta of the League. Consequently Spain reaffirms in this Assembly the axiom, enunciated by twelve Members of the Council, including Spain, in an appeal recently sent to the Government of Japan, to the effect that the Members of the League cannot recognize any political or administrative changes brought about by force or in disregard of the principles of the Covenant or the Pact of Paris. Spain believes that the Assembly would be acting wisely if all Members composing it were to express themselves explicitly on this point.

On March 7 Titulescu (Rumania) said with reference to Article 10:

This article, which is the keystone of the League, contains obligations, that of assisting any Member of the League against foreign aggression, and first and foremost that of respecting the existing territorial integrity of the Members of the League. . . .

May I point out that the Pact of Paris, which forbids war as an instrument of national policy and contains a pledge that resort will be had only to pacific means to settle international disputes, thereby entails, for those who have signed it, an obligation identical with that in Art. 10 concerning the respect for the existing territorial integrity of each state.

But the decisive speech was made by the delegate of the British Government, no lesser man than Sir John Simon:

I do not . . . mean that we can pronounce a judgment on matters which are in controversy. . . .

But none the less, there is a very important declaration which, without waiting for the full ascertainment of matters in controversy, the Assembly might, if it so willed—and, as it seems to me, properly should—make forthwith. . . .

Should we not take this opportunity now solemnly to reaffirm the fundamental principles on which the League is based, and by which every signatory in this room is bound? . . .

Should we not make reference therefore to Art. 10 of the Covenant, whereby all Members of the League have undertaken to respect and preserve as against external aggression the territorial integrity and existing political independence of all Members of the League? These propositions, therefore, are propositions which every Member of the League is bound to accept without regard to the merits of the controversy. . . . Changes brought about not as the result of methods of conciliation and peaceful adjustment, but by means contrary to the Covenant and the Pact of Paris manifestly could not receive the approval of Members of the Assembly of Nations which exists for the very purpose of observing these obligations and these principles.

Such are the general lines of the declaration which I would invite my colleagues here to join in formulating. It would not be the complete discharge of our duty, but it would be a step we can take now. . . .

What would such a declaration accomplish? It would reassert . . . the conditions under which every Member of the League is pledged to conduct relations with every other Member. . . .

It would be far better for the League to proclaim its principles, even though it failed to get them observed, than to forsake these principles by meaningless compromise.

On March 8 a Drafting Committee was appointed. The draft which it submitted to the General Commission was identical with the text as finally adopted; only the words, "or to the Pact of Paris," after "by means contrary to the Covenant of the League of Nations" were inserted at Sir John Simon's suggestion. The discussion of the draft in the Commission was rather summary; the question of the legal effect of the resolution, in case it should be adopted by the Assembly, was not ventilated except in the following question of the Chinese delegate, Mr. Yen:

I wish to point out that the French text of the last paragraph does not coincide accurately with the English. . . . The French text contains the words: *"les Membres de la Société des Nations sont tenus"* whereas the English text reads: "it is incumbent upon the Members of the League of Nations." I was wondering whether it is possible to make the two texts coincide a little bit more, because I do not know whether *"sont tenus"* means exactly "it is incumbent." The Members of the League are "bound," as someone said the other day, and it is better that the two texts should coincide as much as possible to prevent any misunderstanding.

Although this question offered an opportunity to consider the legal aspects and consequences of the planned action,

Mr. Yen's question was disposed of rather summarily by the President who referred it to the Secretary General as "a matter of language." The latter limited himself to the following statement:

> We have given this particular question very deep thought, and I think, if you consider it very carefully, you will see that probably the best translation of "it is incumbent" would be *"sont tenus."* I do not think you could find anything much better.

The draft resolution was adopted by the Plenary Assembly on March 11 without any further discussion. The vote took place by roll call. All the States represented at the meeting voted for it, except Japan and China; the latter declared its adherence the following day.[55]

The adoption of the resolution was immediately notified by the Secretary General of the League to the Government of the United States. Secretary Stimson commented on it on March 12 in the following words:

> This action will go far towards developing into terms of international law the principles of order and justice which underlie these treaties.[56]

[55] The following Member-States were not represented at the meeting: Abyssinia, Bolivia, Haiti, and Liberia. The following had not accredited at all delegates to the special session: the Argentine, the Dominican Republic, Honduras, Nicaragua, Paraguay. The League Members which voted for the resolution were: Albania, Australia, Austria, Belgium, Bulgaria, Canada, Chile, Colombia, Cuba, Czechoslovakia, Denmark, Estonia, Finland, France, Germany, Great Britain and Northern Ireland, Greece, Guatemala, Hungary, India, the Irish Free State, Italy, Latvia, Lithuania, Luxemburg, Mexico, Netherlands, New Zealand, Norway, Panama, Persia, Peru, Poland, Portugal, Rumania, El Salvador, Siam, Spain, Sweden, Switzerland, the Union of South Africa, Uruguay, Venezuela, Yugoslavia.

[56] Stimson, *op. cit.* 179

CHAPTER XI

THE CHACO DECLARATION AND THE LETICIA DISPUTE. THE LEAGUE RECOMMENDATIONS ON MANCHURIA. THE LITVINOV CONVENTIONS

THE adoption of the Assembly Resolution of March 11, 1932, marked the end of the first phase of the "Manchurian incident." For several months the League of Nations could take no further action since it had to wait for the results of the investigation which the League Council had entrusted in December, 1931, to the Lytton Commission. The interval was used by the Japanese for consolidating their position in Manchuria. To this effect, they decided to grant recognition to "Manchukuo" in open defiance of the Assembly Resolution. On September 16, 1932, the Japanese representative on the League Council informed the President of the Council

that the Japanese Government has concluded with the Manchukuo Government a Protocol, dated September 15th. . . . The Japanese Government has thus granted to that State its formal recognition. . . .[1]

The preamble of the Protocol stated that "Japan has recognized the fact that Manchukuo, in accordance with the free will of its inhabitants, has organized and established itself as an independent State. . . ." The Protocol provided that Manchukuo confirmed all rights and interests possessed by Japan and her subjects within the territory of Manchukuo by virtue of Sino-Japanese treaties and agreements, and that Japan and Manchukuo agreed to co-operate in the maintenance of their national security, and that such Japanese forces as might be necessary for this purpose would be stationed in Manchuria.

In the meantime, another dispute, dragging on in the

[1] *LNOJ*, Spec. Suppl. 111, 79

Western Hemisphere, also produced a solemn declaration of non-recognition. In the course of the Chaco war between Bolivia and Paraguay the representatives of the other nineteen American republics issued on August 3, 1932, the following statement:

The American nations . . . declare that they will not recognize any territorial arrangement of this controversy which has not been obtained by peaceful means nor the validity of territorial acquisitions which may be obtained through occupation or conquest by force of arms.[2]

It should be noted, however, that in the subsequent settlement of the Chaco conflict, although it was hardly in keeping with the standards of this declaration, non-recognition was never mentioned again.[3]

The Lytton Commission published its report on October 1, 1932,[4] and on December 6, 1932, the League Assembly met again in special session to deliberate on further steps. The Assembly referred the Lytton Report to a special committee called the Committee of Nineteen. The latter submitted its own report to the Assembly on February 15, 1933,[5] and the

[2] 7 *D. S. Press Rel.* 100. The diplomatic antecedents of the Chaco Declaration were the following: During a meeting at Washington of an International Conference of American States on Conciliation and Arbitration a protocol of conciliation was signed (January 3, 1929), providing for a Conference of Neutrals. The latter extended after a conference with the diplomatic representatives of the Argentine, Brazil, Chile, and Peru an invitation to all the American States to unite in applying the non-recognition doctrine to the Chaco conflict (see *Proceedings of the International Conference of American States on Conciliation and Arbitration,* Washington 1929, pp. 161-170). The outcome of this action was the Declaration of August 3, 1932.

[3] After the issuance of the Chaco Declaration a diplomatic stalemate ensued. Bolivia appealed to the League, the action of which was unsuccessful. The non-recognition issue was not raised again. Early in 1935 the Argentine and Chile approached the belligerents with proposals for a settlement of the conflict. On June 12, 1935, the latter signed a protocol providing for the meeting of a peace conference. The Chaco Peace Conference met in Buenos Aires in the summer of 1935. On July 21, 1938, a peace treaty was finally signed. Its Article 2 provided that the dividing line in the Chaco between Bolivia and Paraguay would be determined by the Presidents of the Republics of the Argentine, Chile, the United States of America, the United States of Brazil, Peru and Uruguay in their capacity as arbitrators in equity, who acting "ex aequo et bono" were to give their arbitral award within certain narrow zones defined in the treaty. The arbitral award was handed down on October 10, 1938 (text, 33 *AJIL* 180), assigning to Paraguay about three-fourths of the disputed area. According to Woolsey (33 *AJIL* 128), the award gave Paraguay more than her actual military possession at that time, but less than her farthest demands.

[4] *Report of the Commission of Enquiry* (known as the "Lytton Report"), League of Nations Document C. 663.M.320-1932.VII

[5] *LNOJ*, Spec. Suppl. 112, 56

Assembly adopted it on February 24 with all votes against that of Japan, while one of the Member States represented —Siam—abstained from voting.[6] Thereupon, Japan gave notice of her withdrawal from the League.[7]

The report as adopted contained a Statement of Recommendations which upheld the principle of non-recognition in the following language:

> The Assembly recommends as follows:
> Whereas the sovereignty over Manchuria belongs to China,
> . . . .
>
> In view of the special circumstances of the case, the recommendations made do not provide for a mere return to the status quo existing before September, 1931. They likewise exclude the maintenance and recognition of the existing regime in Manchuria, such maintenance and recognition being incompatible with the fundamental principles of existing international obligations and with the good understanding between the two countries on which peace in the Far East depends.
>
> It follows that, in adopting the present report, the Members of the League intend to abstain, particularly as regards the existing regime in Manchuria, from any act which may prejudice or delay the carrying out of the recommendations of the said report. They will continue not to recognize this regime either de jure or de facto.[8]

After adopting the report, the Assembly appointed an "Advisory Committee" which was "to follow the situation, to assist the Assembly in performing its duties under Article 3, paragraph 3, and, with the same object, to aid the Members of the League in concerting their action and their attitude among themselves and with the non-member States." [9]

During the following weeks the League Council had an opportunity to emphasize that the applicability of the Assembly Resolution of March 11, 1932, was by no means limited to the Sino-Japanese conflict. In the so-called Leticia dispute between Peru and Colombia, the League Council adopted on March 18, 1933, a report which recommended the evacuation of the Leticia district by the Peruvians, and recalled that "at its meeting of March 11, 1932, the Assembly of the League of Nations declared that it is incum-

[6] Ibid. 22
[7] LNOJ 1933, 657
[8] LNOJ, Spec. Suppl. 112, 75
[9] Ibid. 24-28

bent upon the Members of the League of Nations not to recognize any situation, treaty or agreement which may be brought about by means contrary to the Covenant of the League or the Pact of Paris.[10]

On June 14, 1933, the League Secretariat sent to the League Members and to certain non-member States a circular letter containing recommendations of the aforementioned Advisory Committee regarding measures proposed in connection with the non-recognition of "Manchukuo." [11] These recommendations represented the first attempt to translate the principle of non-recognition into the legal and administrative practice of everyday life. The recommendations covered the following subjects: participation of the "Manchukuo" Government in international conventions; postal services and stamps; currency of "Manchukuo"; acceptance by foreigners of concessions or appointments in "Manchukuo"; passports; position of consuls; application of the import and export certificate system under the Geneva Opium Convention of 1925 and the Limitation Convention of 1931.

Regarding multilateral conventions the Committee recommended the barring of the admission or accession of "Manchukuo" by means of proceeding in accordance with the peculiarities of the respective type of convention; this was also to apply should the question of accession of "Manchukuo" to the Universal Postal Union arise. Regarding the currency question the Advisory Committee held that "a domestic currency is created by domestic law, and is actually utilized in the same way as any other object of value that is bought or sold in the international market." Therefore, the Committee deemed it inexpedient to propose that governments should pass legislation prohibiting transactions in "Manchukuo" currency, but it desired "to call the attention of countries which have an official foreign exchange market to the desirability of taking any useful measures in order not to admit official quotations in 'Manchukuo' currency." Regarding concessions and appointments the Committee held that the report adopted on February 24, 1933, did not

10 *LNOJ* 1933, 526
11 *LNOJ*, Spec. Suppl. 113, 10

prohibit nationals of League Members from entering into contractual relations with anyone in Manchuria, nor from accepting concessions or appointments from the authorities established there, but the Committee felt

that it rests with each of the Members of the League to decide for itself whether it is desirable to call the attention of its nationals to the special risks attending upon the acceptance of concessions or appointments in Manchuria. In this sense, a Government might urge the difficulty it might experience in protecting such nationals, in view of the position created by the Assembly's report, and also the probable attitude of the Chinese authorities with regard to the validity of such concessions or appointments obtained in the present circumstances from the authorities established in Manchuria.

Regarding passports the Committee held that a government which did not recognize the existing regime in Manchuria either de jure or de facto could not regard as such documents issued by authorities dependent on the "Manchukuo Government" and could not, therefore, allow any of its own agents to visa such documents. The recommendation continued:

On the other hand, there is no reason why an inhabitant of a territory subject to the "Manchukuo" authorities who is desirous of proceeding abroad should not receive an identity document or a *laisser-passer* from the consul of the country which he wishes to visit. The same procedure might be adopted as regards countries of transit. . . .

The recommendation concerning consuls deserves quotation in full:

The Committee considers that States Members of the League of Nations can, without infringing the report adopted by the Assembly, make provision, if necessary, for replacing their consuls in Manchuria. The despatch of consuls under the circumstances does not imply recognition of "Manchukuo," as those agents are appointed for the purpose of keeping their Governments informed and protecting their nationals. Moreover, it is in conformity with the Assembly's recommendations that Governments should remind their consuls that, so far as possible, particularly in such contacts as their duties may lead them to make for that purpose, they should do nothing which could be interpreted expressly or by implication as a declaration that they regard the authorities established in Manchuria as the proper Government of the country.

Every Government may, when appointing its consuls in Manchuria, be guided by its special juridical situation as regards China, and, if necessary, by the precedents followed in certain parts of China such as Canton, the authorities of which have not, at certain times, recognized the authority of the Central Governments.

With reference to the Geneva Opium Convention of 1925 the Committee recommended that applications for export of opium to "Manchukuo" should not be granted unless the applicant produced an import certificate in accordance with the Convention of such a nature "as to satisfy the Government to which application is made that the goods in question are not to be imported into 'Manchukuo' territory for a purpose which is contrary to the Convention." The recommendation concluded:

A copy of the export authorisation should accompany the consignment, but Governments should refrain from forwarding a second copy of the export authorisation to "Manchukuo," since such action might be interpreted as de facto recognition of "Manchukuo."

From the foregoing it would appear that the Advisory Committee was reluctant to recommend measures which might have impaired the commercial interests of the nationals of the non-recognizing States, and that it resorted therefore to expedients and half-way solutions, such as the barring of official quotations of the Manchukuo currency while not prohibiting transactions in it, or the granting of opium export licenses for Manchukuo without forwarding the second copy thereof. The statement of the recommendations to the effect that the appointment of consuls did not involve recognition was obviously based on the fact that in China consular activities could be carried out without the grant of an exequatur from the local sovereign, for the application for such an exequatur undoubtedly implies recognition of that sovereign.[12] The recommendations of the Advisory Committee met with the approval of practically all of the States approached.[13]

*   *   *

During the first half of 1933 the League of Nations had also to deal with another issue related to the non-recognition

[12] Below, 102
[13] *LNOJ* 1934, 17

problem, namely, with the "definition of aggression." The subject came up in February of that year in the form of suggestions made by the Soviet delegation at the Conference for the Limitation and Reduction of Armaments. A special "Committee on Security Questions" was appointed which, working under the chairmanship of the Greek statesman and scholar, Mr. Politis, drew up a text known as the Politis Report.[14] Influential circles of the Conference, however, opposed its adoption. Therefore, the Soviet representative, Mr. Litvinov, dropped the issue at Geneva, but, seizing the opportunity offered by the presence of delegates from many countries at the International Monetary and Economic Conference held at London in July, 1933, he took it up again and succeeded in concluding on behalf of the Soviet Union two "Conventions for the Definition of Aggression." One was signed on July 3, with Afghanistan, Estonia, Latvia, Poland, Persia, Rumania, and Turkey;[15] the other was signed the following day, with Czechoslovakia, Yugoslavia, and again Rumania and Turkey.[16] The texts of these conventions are essentially identical. Their main provisions read:

Art. I. Each of the High Contracting Parties undertakes to accept in its relations with each of the other Parties, from the date of the entry into force of the present Convention, the definition of aggression as explained in the report, dated May 24, 1933, of the Committee on Security Questions (Politis Report) to the Conference for the Reduction and Limitation of Armaments, which report was made in consequence of the Soviet delegation's proposal.

Art. II. Accordingly, the aggressor in an international conflict shall, subject to the agreements in force between the parties to the dispute, be considered to be that State which is the first to commit any of the following actions:

1. Declaration of war upon another State;
2. Invasion by its armed forces, with or without a declaration of war, of the territory of another State;
3. Attacks by its land, naval or air forces, with or without a declaration of war, on the territory, vessels or aircraft of another State;
4. Naval blockade of the coasts or ports of another State;

[14] *League of Nations, Conference for the Reduction and Limitation of Armaments, Minutes of the General Commission*, 510, 547, 559; *Conference Documents*, I 679

[15] 136 *BFSP* 545 (above, 31, n. 20); 147 *LNTS* 69

[16] 136 *BFSP* 632; 148 *LNTS* 211

5. Provision of support to armed bands formed in its territory which have invaded the territory of another State, or refusal, notwithstanding the request of the invaded State, to take, in its own territory, all the measures in its power to deprive those bands of all assistance or protection.

Art. III. No political, military, economic or other consideration may serve as an excuse or justification for the aggression referred to in Article II. (For examples, see Annex.)

The Annex to Article III of the Conventions had the following wording:

The High Contracting Parties . . .

Desiring, subject to the express reservation that the absolute validity of the rule laid down in Article III of that Convention shall be in no way restricted, to furnish certain indications for determining the aggressor,

Declare that no act of aggression within the meaning of Article II of that Convention can be justified on either of the following grounds, among others:

A. The internal condition of a State:

E.g., its political, economic or social structure; alleged defects in its administration; disturbances due to strikes, revolutions, counter-revolutions or civil war.

B. The international conduct of a State:

E.g., the violation or threatened violation of the material or moral rights or interests of a foreign State or its nationals; the rupture of diplomatic or economic relations; economic or financial boycotts; disputes relating to economic, financial or other obligations towards foreign States; frontier incidents not forming any of the cases of aggression specified in Article II.

The High Contracting Parties further agree to recognize that the present Convention can never legitimate any violation of international law that may be implied in the circumstances comprised in the above list.

The Litvinov Conventions ended a period of attempts of European diplomacy to develop the law of territorial change. In the following months the scene shifted again to the Western Hemisphere.

CHAPTER XII

INTER-AMERICAN CONFERENCES AND TREATIES, 1933–1938

THE adoption of the Chaco Declaration of 1932 inspired the Foreign Minister of the Argentine, Sr. Dr. Saavedra Lamas, to suggest to the Latin-American world the conclusion of a formal treaty that was to be based partly on the principles of the older Latin-American drafts, partly on the recent trends reflected in the Stimson Doctrine, the League Resolution of March 11, 1932, and the Chaco Declaration. The draft was published in the fall of 1932 [1] and submitted to the Foreign Offices of various American republics. On October 10, 1933, the treaty was solemnly signed at Rio de Janeiro by the Argentine, Brazil, Chile, Mexico, Paraguay, and Uruguay.[2] The instrument of seventeen articles, officially called "Anti-War Treaty of Non-Aggression and Conciliation" and commonly known as the Saavedra Lamas Anti-War Treaty, proclaimed in its first articles the principle of non-recognition of certain territorial changes and contained furthermore detailed provisions regarding conciliation proceedings and instrumentalities. The preamble stated the object of the treaty as follows:

The States designated below . . .
To the end of condemning wars of aggression and territorial acquisitions that may be obtained by means of armed conquest and of making them impossible, of sanctioning their invalidity through the positive provisions of this treaty, . . . have agreed on the following:

The basic ideas of the treaty concerning the law of territorial change and, in particular, non-recognition, were formulated in the first two articles. It is important to note

[1] *Draft of an Anti-War Treaty,* translated and published by the Argentine Embassy, Washington, 1932
[2] 4 *U. S. Treaties* 4793

that the final text of these articles deviates in part from the original draft, as shown in the following juxtaposition:

DRAFT	FINAL TEXT
Art. I. The High Contracting Parties solemnly declare that they condemn wars of aggression in their mutual relations, and that the settlement of disputes and controversies shall be effected only through the pacific means established by international law.	Art. I. The High Contracting Parties solemnly declare that they condemn wars of aggression in their mutual relations or those with other States, and that the settlement of disputes or controversies of any kind that may arise among them shall be effected only through the pacific means established by international law.
Art. II. They declare that territorial questions must not be settled by violence, and that they will not recognize any territorial arrangement which is not obtained by pacific means nor the validity of an occupation or acquisition of territory that may be brought about by force.	Art. II. They declare that as between the High Contracting Parties territorial questions must not be settled by violence, and that they will not recognize any territorial arrangement which is not obtained by pacific means, nor the validity of an occupation or acquisition of territory that may be brought about by force.

The treaty was to remain open to the adherence of all States (Art. 16).

Annexed to the draft was a Statement of Reasons. The following portions of it deserve quotation:

This draft Anti-War Treaty . . . aims at the consolidation of world peace inasmuch as it begins by creating a peaceful system to insure it in a continent, recording the obligation not to resort to a war of aggression or to settle territorial controversies by armed force. To that end it creates a permanent system of conciliation . . . open to universal accession.

Art. I condemns wars of aggression in the relations between the Contracting States. . . . The Argentine draft retains the right of self-defense of States, which must be inalienable.

Art. II includes two principles which supplement each other. The first declares that territorial disputes shall not be settled by violent means. . . . The second principle, which flows from the first, provides that no territorial arrangement secured by other than pacific means, nor the validity of any occupation or acquisition of territory by force of arms, shall be recognized. These doctrines which exclude resort to arms, were originated at the very dawn of American emancipation. . . . The need for respecting territorial integrity was acknowledged by successive Congresses of American nations.

Numerous States, American as well as European, adhered

to the treaty. By July 1, 1945, the status of adhesion and ratification was the following: *

AMERICAN STATES:

Argentina, *Rd;* Bolivia, *AR;* Brazil, *Rd;* Colombia, *ARdr;* Costa Rica, *A;* Cuba, *ARd;* Chile *Rdr;* Dominican Republic, *ARd;* Ecuador, *ARdr;* Guatemala, Haiti, *ARd;* Honduras, *ARdr;* Mexico, *Rd;* Nicaragua, Panama, *ARd;* Paraguay, *Rd;* Peru, Salvador, *ARdr;* Uruguay, *Rd;* U. S. A., Venezuela, *ARdr.*

NON-AMERICAN STATES:

Bulgaria, Czechoslovakia, Finland, *ARdr;* Greece, Italy, Norway, *Ar;* Portugal, *AR;* Rumania, *ARdr;* Spain, *ARd;* Turkey, *ARr;* Yugoslavia, *ARdr.*

Consequently, the treaty is in force regarding the following European States: (a) Czechoslovakia and Yugoslavia; (b) Bulgaria, Finland, Rumania; (c) Spain.[3] Numerous reservations were affixed to the Treaty, among them the following by the United States:

In adhering to this treaty the United States does not hereby waive any rights it may have under other treaties or conventions or under international law.

A few weeks after the signature of the Anti-War Treaty the Seventh Inter-American Conference met at Montevideo (December, 1933), and resumed the work of codification. Among the projects that secured adoption was a "Convention on the Rights and Duties of States."[4] Its Article 11 deals with non-recognition of territorial changes as follows:

The Contracting States definitely establish as the norm of their conduct the precise obligation not to recognize territorial acquisitions or special advantages which have been obtained by force whether this consists in the employment of arms, in threatening diplomatic representations, or in any other effective coercive measure. The territory of a State is inviolable and may not be the object of military occupation nor of other measures of force imposed by other States directly or indirectly or for any motive whatever even temporarily.

* Abbreviations: A—Adhesion; R—Ratification; d—instruments of ratification deposited; r—reservations.

[3] *Status of the Pan American Treaties and Conventions,* revised to July 1, 1945, by the Juridical Division of the Pan American Union, Washington, 1945

[4] 4 *U. S. Treaties* 4807

The Convention was signed by all American States except Bolivia; by July 1, 1945, instruments of ratification had been deposited by all the signatories except the Argentine, Peru, and Uruguay.[5]

A non-recognition provision after the pattern of Article 2 of the Argentine Anti-War Treaty and Article 11 of the Montevideo Convention was also contained in Article 4 of the so-called "Peace Code," which was submitted to the Montevideo Conference by the Mexican delegation,[6] but it was shelved without detailed discussion. The Article read:

> The High Contracting Parties declare that territorial questions must not be solved by violence, and that they will not recognize any territorial settlement that is not obtained by pacific means and without coercion of any sort, nor will they recognize the validity of the occupation or acquisition of territories accomplished by force of arms.

In December, 1936, an extraordinary "Inter-American Conference for the Maintenance of Peace" met at the invitation of the President of the United States at Buenos Aires in order to discuss the international situation. Among the projects submitted to the Conference was a "Convention for the Maintenance of Peace," drafted by Dr. Saavedra Lamas. Its Article 6 undertook to set up a formal procedure of non-recognition,[7] yet it did not find its way into the "Convention for the Maintenance, Preservation and Re-establishment of Peace" as finally adopted.[8] On the other hand the Buenos Aires Conference reaffirmed the principle of non-recognition in two instruments: The "Declaration of Principles of Inter-American Solidarity and Cooperation," adopted on December 21, 1936,[9] stated among the principles "accepted by the American Community of Nations" the "proscription of territorial conquest, and that, in consequence, no acquisition made through violence shall be recognized." The "Convention to Coordinate, Extend and Assure the Fulfillment

[5] See n. 3

[6] *Minutes and Antecedents of the Seventh International Conference of American States*, Montevideo, 1933, *Meetings of the First Committee*, 76; *Plenary Sessions*, 83

[7] *Draft of a Convention for the Maintenance of Peace*, Washington 1938, 8

[8] 4 *U. S. Treaties* 4817

[9] *Report of the Delegation of the United States of America to the Inter-American Conference for the Maintenance of Peace*, 227

of the Existing Treaties between the American States," signed on December 23, 1936,[10] provided in Article 6 that the Contracting Parties reaffirmed their loyalty to the principles enunciated in the following five agreements: the Gondra Treaty of May 3, 1923; the Briand-Kellogg Pact of Paris of August 27, 1928; the Conventions of January 5, 1929, on Inter-American Conciliation and Arbitration; and the Argentine Anti-War Pact.

At the Eighth Inter-American Conference, held at Lima in 1938, no treaties or conventions were concluded; the principle of non-recognition, however, was again reaffirmed in the following resolution, adopted on December 22, 1938:

The . . . Conference . . . declares that it reiterates as a fundamental principle of the Public Law of America, that the occupation or acquisition of territory or any other modification of territorial or boundary arrangement obtained through conquest by force or by non-pacific means shall not be valid or have legal effect.[11]

[10] 4 *U. S. Treaties* 4831
[11] Resolution No. 26, Final Act p. 45 (*Int. Conc.* 349, 187)

CHAPTER XIII

JURISTS' DRAFTS, 1934–1939.
THE ACTS OF HAVANA AND CHAPULTEPEC.
THE ATLANTIC CHARTER
AND THE CAIRO DECLARATION

THE period between the adoption of the Montevideo Convention and the outbreak of the Second World War witnessed several efforts of jurists to close the gaps and solve the various moot points discernible in the body of rules created during the preceding five years by the Briand-Kellogg Pact, the Litvinov Treaties, the Anti-War Pact, and the Montevideo Convention.

At a meeting held in Budapest, 1934, the International Law Association endeavored to define the effect of the Briand-Kellogg Pact on international law. The results of the deliberations were embodied in a resolution known as the "Budapest Articles of Interpretation." [1] Article 5 dealt with non-recognition in the following words:

> The signatory States are not entitled to recognize as acquired de jure any territorial or other advantages acquired de facto by means of a violation of the Pact.

The language of this article was obviously influenced by the distinction, by that time already familiar to the legal world, between de jure and de facto recognition.[2]

The topic of recognition was predominant at the Brussels

---

[1] Text 29 *AJIL* 93. The meaning of the Articles was the subject of a debate in the English House of Lords. On February 20, 1935, Lord Askwith asked whether the Articles correctly represented the effect of the Briand-Kellogg Pact on international law. Answering for the Government, the Lord Chancellor, Viscount Sankey, said: ". . . It is necessary to emphasize . . . that the Conference, whatever the weight of its authority, and whatever consideration is due to its conclusions, was a purely private and unofficial conference." He added: ". . . It is not desirable . . . for H. M. Gvt. to attempt to give their imprimatur to any particular article of interpretation adopted by the Budapest Conference. . . ." Regarding Art. 5 he remarked that it was "apparently based upon the resolution passed by the Assembly of the League of Nations on March 11, 1932." (95 *H. L. Deb.* 1042)

[2] Above, 22; below, 112

Conference of the Institute of International Law (1936). The discussion, however, was limited to problems connected with the recognition of new States and new governments. Within this scope, attempts were made to clarify the distinction between de jure and de facto recognition, and also such aspects of recognition as revocability and retroactivity. The results of the Conference were embodied in a Final Resolution.[3] Its Article 17 undertook to define the effects which should be attributed to the acts of a non-recognized government before the courts and other authorities of the non-recognizing Power. Since the same problem has to be dealt with in the field of non-recognition of territorial changes,[4] the article deserves quotation:

Recognition "de jure" of a government implies the recognition of the judicial, administrative, or other organs, and the attribution of extraterritorial effect to their acts, in conformity with the rules of international law and particularly under the customary reservation of respect for public order, even if these acts had been consummated before any previous de facto recognition.

These extraterritorial effects, however, do not depend on the formal act of recognition of the new government. Even in the absence of recognition, they should be acknowledged by the competent jurisdiction and administrations when, considering especially the actual character of the power exercised by the new government, these effects are in conformity with the interest of good justice and the interest of individuals.

The last jurists' project in which the problem of non-recognition of territorial changes played a definite role was the "Draft Convention on the Rights and Duties of States in Case of Aggression," [5] a work of the Harvard Research in International Law. The draft did not explicitly mention non-recognition as a legal consequence of aggression; instead, its Article 4 (paragraph 2) provided that

Situations created by an aggressor's use of armed force do not change sovereignty or other legal rights over territory.

This provision, however, was apparently not designed to apply in case the victim of aggression had been forced to sign

[3] Text 30 *AJIL*, Suppl., 185
[4] Below, 103 ff.
[5] Text 33 *AJIL*, Suppl., 823. See also the exhaustive comment on the project, written by the rapporteur on the draft, Professor Jessup. (*Ibid.*)

an instrument conveying territorial rights or other advantages to the aggressor. For the third paragraph of Article 4 provided that a treaty brought about by an aggressor's use of force should merely be voidable, not absolutely void.

During the Second World War the main concern of the American States was the prevention of territorial changes in the Western Hemisphere effected by acts of aggression on the part of a non-American Power. On October 3, 1939, a meeting of the Foreign Ministers of the American States, held at Panama, adopted a resolution providing for consultation "in case any geographic region of America subject to the jurisdiction of any non-American State should be obliged to change its sovereignty and there should result therefrom a danger to the security of the American continent." [6]

After the invasion of western Europe by the Germans the Congress of the United States passed, on June 17–18, 1940, a Joint Resolution to the effect

(1) That the United States would not recognize any transfer, and would not acquiesce in any attempt to transfer any geographic region of this hemisphere from one non-American Power to another non-American Power, and

(2) That if such transfer or attempt to transfer should appear likely, the United States shall . . . immediately consult with the other American republics.[7]

In July, 1940, a second meeting of the Foreign Ministers of the Americas was held at Havana. It adopted a series of Declarations, among them one (No. XV) to the effect that

Any attempt on the part of a non-American State against the integrity or inviolability of the territory, the sovereignty or the political independence of an American State shall be considered as an act of aggression against the States which sign this Declaration.[8]

In February–March, 1945, an Inter-American Conference on Problems of War and Peace was held at Mexico, D. F. On March 6, 1945, it adopted a "Declaration on Reciprocal Assistance and American Solidarity," [9] which became known as the "Act of Chapultepec" since it was signed

[6] Doc. Am. For. Rel., II 86
[7] H. J. Res. 556, S. J. Res. 271, 76th Congress, 3d Session
[8] 3 D. S. Bull. 136
[9] 12 D. S. Bull. 339

at Chapultepec Castle. Its preamble emphasized the principle of non-recognition in the following language:

Whereas:

. . . .

5. The American States have been incorporating in their international law, since 1890, by means of conventions, resolutions and declarations, the following principles:

(a) The proscription of territorial conquest and the non-recognition of all acquisitions made by force (First International Conference of American States, 1890). . . .

The Declaration also attempted to define aggression as follows:

The Governments Represented at the Inter-American Conference on War and Peace Declare:

. . . .

Third: That every attack of a State against the integrity or the inviolability of territory, or against the sovereignty or political independence of an American State, shall . . . be considered as an act of aggression against the other States which sign this Declaration. In any case invasion by armed forces of a State into the territory of another, trespassing boundaries established by treaty and demarcated in accordance therewith, shall constitute an act of aggression.

While the foregoing statements, resolutions, and declarations referred merely to the Western Hemisphere, the war against the Axis produced also a series of declarations of global scope. In August, 1941, President Roosevelt and Prime Minister Churchill met at sea off the shore of New England. At the close of their meeting, on August 14, 1941, a Joint Declaration was issued, known ever since as the Atlantic Charter.[10] This document contained the following provisions bearing on the problem of territorial change:

[They] deem it right to make known certain common principles in the national policies of their respective countries on which they base their hopes for a better future for the world.

First, their countries seek no aggrandizement, territorial or other;

Second, they desire to see no territorial changes that do not accord with the freely expressed wishes of the peoples concerned. . . .

In a message, sent to Congress on August 21, 1941, President Roosevelt commented on the Charter in the words:

[10] 5 D. S. Bull. 125

"The declaration of principles at this time presents a goal which is worth while for our type of civilization to seek." [11]

Adherence to the principles of the Atlantic Charter by the governments allied with Great Britain was formally declared at a meeting of the Inter-Allied Council, held in London on September 24, 1941.[12] The position of the Soviet Government was given by the Soviet Ambassador in London, Mr. Maisky, in the following terms:

The Soviet Union defends the right of every nation to the independence and territorial integrity of its country. . . .

Thereupon the following resolution was unanimously adopted:

The Governments of . . . having taken note of the declaration recently drawn up by the President of the United States and by the Prime Minister (Mr. Churchill) on behalf of His Majesty's Government in the United Kingdom, now make known their adherence to the common principles of policy set forth in that declaration and their intention to cooperate to the best of their ability in giving effect to them.

On similar lines as the Atlantic Charter, the Treaty of Alliance concluded on May 26, 1942, between the United Kingdom and the Soviet Union proclaimed the determination of both parties to act in future in accordance with the principle "of not seeking territorial aggrandizement for themselves." [13]

On December 1, 1943, at the end of a meeting, held at Cairo between President Roosevelt, Generalissimo Chiang Kai-shek, and Prime Minister Churchill, a Declaration was released which contained the following statement:

The Three Great Allies are fighting this war to restrain and punish the aggression of Japan. They covet no gain for themselves and have no thought of territorial expansion. . . .[14]

All these documents—the Atlantic Charter, the Anglo-Soviet Treaty, and the Cairo Declaration—although not es-

11 *Ibid.* 147
12 *Ibid.* 234
13 Below, 269
14 9 *D. S. Bull.* 393

tablishing a legal obligation not to take territory, form joint declarations of policy implying at least a moral undertaking in that direction. The principle of non-recognition, it is true, is not mentioned in any of those texts, yet it would not seem unwarranted to see it involved in their implications.

CHAPTER XIV

THE UNITED NATIONS CHARTER

ALREADY during the early stages of the Second World War it had become obvious that the League of Nations would not survive its failure to prevent the outbreak of the universal conflagration. The pitiful attitude adopted by the League as a whole, as well as by most of its Members, in all cases of aggression ever since the Manchurian "incident" [1] forecast its collapse. The exclusion of the Soviet Union, proclaimed by the League Council in December, 1939,[2] shattered all hopes that at the end of the war new life could be instilled into the Geneva institution. Yet the ideas and ideals which had led to the establishment of a world organization in 1919 were not dead, in spite of the disillusionment over the failure of the first attempt. To put in the place of the old League a new, better system of international organization became before long the object of a vast sector of public opinion. It was adopted by the leading statesmen of the nations united in the fight against Axis aggression. At the close of the Inter-Allied Conference held at Moscow in October, 1943, the following "Four Nations Declaration on General Security" was released:

The Governments of the United States of America, the United Kingdom, the Soviet Union, and China: . . .
Jointly declare:
1. That their united action, pledged for the prosecution of the war against their respective enemies, will be continued for the organization and maintenance of peace and security. . . .

. . . .

4. That they recognize the necessity of establishing at the earliest practicable date a general international organization, based on the principle of the sovereign equality of all peace-loving States, and open to membership by all such States, large and small, for the maintenance of international peace and security.
5. That for the purpose of maintaining international peace and security pending the re-establishment of law and order and the

[1] See Part III.
[2] Below, 261

inauguration of a system of general security, they will consult with one another and as occasion requires with other members of the United Nations with a view to joint action on behalf of the community of nations.

6. That after the termination of hostilities they will not employ their military forces within the territories of other States except for the purposes envisaged in this Declaration and after joint consultation.[3]

In August, 1944, delegates of the signatory Powers of the above Declaration met at Dumbarton Oaks, Washington, D. C. The results of their deliberations were embodied in a document called the Dumbarton Oaks Proposals for the Establishment of a General International Organization.[4] The proposals envisaged the formation of an organization for the maintenance of peace and security, open to all peace-loving States, and consisting of the following principal organs: a General Assembly, a Security Council, an International Court of Justice, and a Secretariat. To the Security Council was assigned the main task of determining the existence of any threat to the peace, breach of the peace or act of aggression, and of making recommendations or of deciding upon the measures which should be taken to maintain or restore peace and security.

The draft, however, did not contain any provision analogous to Article 10 of the League Covenant. The reason for this omission has not yet been disclosed. The United States documents on the proposals [5] were completely silent in this respect. The British commentary on the draft undertook to motivate the omission as follows:

15. By the Principles the members would enter into undertakings as regards their own individual conduct as well as regards their conduct in the Organisation itself. The first Principle gives effect to the provision in the Moscow Declaration that the Organisation should be based on the principle of the "sovereign equality" of all peace-loving States. The first criterion for action is thus not power but the equal rights of all States to the maintenance of their political independence. In the League of Nations the political independence and territorial integrity of all members was guaranteed against external aggression, but no definite obligation was laid

---

[3] 9 *D. S. Bull.* 308
[4] 11 *D. S. Bull.* 368
[5] *Dumbarton Oaks Documents on International Organization* (U. S. Dept. of State, Publication 2223, Conference Series 60), 5

upon other members to give effect to this provision. Many of them indicated their dislike of this obligation from time to time. The greatest threat to the political independence and territorial integrity of States comes from war, and the Covenant machinery for the prevention of war was incomplete.

16. Now that the undertaking to prevent war is absolute and much more definite responsibilities to secure that end are laid on all States, such a guarantee, if literally interpreted, would prevent any change in frontiers being carried out, even if all the other members of the Organisation thought such a change was just and desirable. It is considered that the recognition of this general principle of "sovereign equality" gives protection to States against arbitrary action by other States, or by the Organisation itself, while at the same time it does not involve the maintenance of the status quo for all time.[6]

This attempt to motivate the elimination from the future international charter of what President Wilson had called the "backbone" of the old world organization is anything but convincing. It is true that the principle expressed in Article 10 of the League Covenant, and consequently the duty of non-recognition inherent in that principle, must be properly delimited in order to be consonant with the problem of changes in the status quo. A later chapter of this work will undertake to outline this delimitation.[7] But to abandon the principle altogether would seem to be warranted only in case a fully adequate equivalent were inserted in the law of the new organization. The mention of the "general principle of sovereign equality" is entirely out of place in this respect and appears to indicate the inability—or unwillingness—to state the true reasons for the abandonment of the principle embodied in Article 10 of the League Covenant.

At the invitation and under the sponsorship of the signatory Powers of the Moscow Four Power Declaration the delegates of fifty States met on April 25, 1945, at San Francisco, California, U. S. A., for the final consideration of the Dumbarton Oaks Proposals as made public on October 9, 1944, and of the hundreds of amendments and modifications which were offered following their governmental and public study. The delegation of New Zealand—one of the few

6 *A Commentary on the Dumbarton Oaks Proposals for the Establishment of a General International Organization* (Cmd. 6571)
7 Below, Ch. XIX

countries which, in their capacity as League Members, had to a certain extent endeavored to live up to their obligations under Article 10—submitted a number of amendments apparently intended to offer an adequate equivalent for the omission of this article.[8]

To Chapter I of the Dumbarton Oaks Proposals ("Purposes") the amendment was proposed to specify as one of the intentions of the new organization "to preserve as against external aggression the territorial integrity and political independence of every member of the organization" by inserting this clause after the following words of paragraph 1:

The purposes of the Organization should be:
1. To maintain international peace and security;

To Chapter II ("Principles") the New Zealand delegation proposed to insert after the text of paragraph 4 which read

All members of the Organization shall refrain from the threat or use of force in any manner inconsistent with the purpose of the Organization

the following paragraph 4a:

All members of the Organization undertake collectively to resist every act of aggression against any member.

The amendment to Chapter I was ultimately dropped in favor of an Australian amendment which called upon the members, not to *preserve* the territorial integrity and political independence of every member, but merely to *refrain* from the threat or use of force against these rights. The withdrawn amendment, however, had primarily been intended to introduce the above amendment to Chapter II.[9] The latter amendment was defeated in the Subcommittee but brought up again in the Committee. There the New Zealand delegate stated [10] that the proposal was regarded by the New Zealand delegation as covering one of the most serious inadequacies of the Dumbarton Oaks Proposals, and that it appeared to

8 *United Nations Conference on International Organization, Documents,* III 486
9 *United Nations Conference on International Organization, Report on the Conference held at San Francisco 25 April–26 June 1945 by the Right Honorable Peter Fraser, Chairman of the New Zealand Delegation,* 22
10 *Ibid.* 24

the New Zealand delegation to go to the very core and kernel of any system of collective security. He continued:

If no such system of mutual insurance was included in the Charter the organization being set up in San Francisco might, when tested, prove to be a container without content. The cause of the failure of the last great and noble experiment, the League of Nations, was just on this point, that in essence the League failed because its members were not prepared mutually to support each other against aggression. With such an undertaking as the New Zealand delegation proposed, and with a firm determination to carry it out, it was, and is, our belief that war would in fact be prevented, that if this determination were fully understood by potential aggressors there would be no aggression. The omission of this provision in fact left the door open to—and indeed invited—evasion, appeasement, and perhaps the sacrifice of smaller and less influential peoples.

In the Committee, the New Zealand amendment was opposed by the delegates of the United States and Great Britain on the ground that aggression could not be defined; that it was unnecessary as it merely expressed the intention of the Charter; and, by the United States delegate, on the ground that the word "collective" in the New Zealand proposal might involve the South American republics in war in Europe, in Asia, and throughout the world. The amendment was strongly supported by the Belgian representative, Mr. Rolin. When it finally was put to vote, it received 26 votes against 18. This majority fell short by four votes of the two-thirds necessary to make a substantive alteration. Subsequently, the same proposal was moved again by the Panamanian delegate with the addition of the words "and to preserve the territorial integrity and political independence of each member of the Organization." But this amendment, too, which would have restored the essence of Article 10 of the League Covenant, failed to obtain the necessary two-thirds majority, since it received only 21 votes against 18, with three abstentions.[11]

On June 26, 1945, the final text of the constitution of the new international organization was adopted under the title "United Nations Charter." [12] In it Chapters I and II of the Dumbarton Oaks Proposals became Articles I and II; the

11 *Ibid.* 26
12 12 *D. S. Bull.* 1119

aforementioned Australian amendment was inserted in paragraph 4 of the latter which now reads:

All Members shall refrain in their international relations from the threat or use of force against the territorial integrity or political independence of any State, or in any other manner inconsistent with the purposes of the United Nations.

The protection of these rights of the Members, which the Covenant of the League had intended to achieve by establishing the legal obligation of its Article 10, is now sought by empowering one of the organs of the new organization, the Security Council, to take action in case they should be endangered. The essential provisions are embodied in the following articles of Chapter VII of the Charter ("Action with Respect to Threats to the Peace, Breaches of the Peace, and Acts of Aggression"):

Art. 39. The Security Council shall determine the existence of any threat to the peace, breach of the peace, or act of aggression and shall make recommendations, or decide what measures shall be taken in accordance with Articles 41 and 42, to maintain or restore international peace and security.

. . . .

Art. 41. The Security Council may decide what measures not involving the use of armed force are to be employed to give effect to its decisions, and it may call upon the Members of the United Nations to apply such measures. These may include complete or partial interruption of economic relations and of rail, sea, air, postal, telegraphic, radio, and other means of communication, and the severance of diplomatic relations.

Art. 42. Should the Security Council consider that the measures provided for in Article 41 would be inadequate or have proved to be inadequate, it may take such action by air, sea, or land forces as may be necessary to maintain or restore international peace and security. Such action may include demonstrations, blockade, and other operations by air, sea, or land forces of Members of the United Nations.

The composition and voting of the Security Council is fixed in Chapter V as follows: The Council shall consist (Art. 23) of eleven Members of the United Nations; the Republic of China, France, the Union of Soviet Socialist Republics, the United Kingdom of Great Britain and Northern Ireland, and the United States of America shall be permanent members of the Council; the General Assembly shall elect six other Members of the United Nations to be non-permanent members of the Security Council, these non-permanent members to be elected for a term of two years. Each member of the Security Council shall have one representative and one vote. Decisions of the Council on other than procedural matters shall be made (Art. 27) by an affirmative vote of seven members including the concurring votes of the permanent members.

Consequently, any action of the Security Council in case of an act of aggression against the political independence or territorial integrity of a member State of the new organization may be blocked by the veto of one of the permanent members or by the impossibility of obtaining a seven to four majority.

On October 24, 1945, the Charter of the United Nations came into force as adopted at San Francisco.[13] Gone by the board was the right which the International Organization of 1919 had granted to its members under Article 10 of the League Covenant, the right, though weak, yet still an absolute right, to have their political independence and territorial integrity respected and preserved by their fellow-members.[14]

---

[13] 18 *D. S. Bull.* 679

[14] The British Government's Report to Parliament (*"A Commentary on the Charter of the United Nations, signed at San Francisco on the 26th June, 1945,"* Cmd. 6666) mentioned this fact, without, however, trying to motivate it otherwise than by referring to the explanation attempted in the Dumbarton Oaks Commentary (above, n. 6). This was done in the following language (p. 6): "19. The obligation of Members to refrain from the threat or use of force against 'the territorial integrity or political independence of any state' has been laid down in the fourth principle (Art. 2 (4)). This obligation was inherent in the original text but has been made explicit. It should be noted that the United Nations do not guarantee the territorial integrity or political independence of all the Members, for the reasons given in Cmd. Paper 6571, Paras. 15 and 16."

PART II

Legal Aspects

CHAPTER XV

NON-RECOGNITION AS A LEGAL DUTY

Extensive research, backed by a great amount of case law, has tried to disentangle the legal problems involved in the recognition and non-recognition of new States and new governments.[1] Scant attention, however, has been given hitherto to the legal aspects of the non-recognition of territorial transfers.

As shown in the preceding chapters of this work, general enunciations of the principle of non-recognition of territorial changes effected by force are to be found in the following public acts:

(a) The Stimson notes of January 7, 1932, and the subsequent reaffirmations of the principles contained therein;

(b) The Resolution of the League of Nations Assembly of March 11, 1932;

(c) The Chaco Declaration of August 3, 1932

(d) The Saavedra Lamas Anti-War Treaty of October 10, 1933;[2]

(e) The Montevideo Convention on the Rights and Duties of States of December 21, 1933.

Certain of these acts, namely, the Stimson notes and the Chaco Resolution, were unilateral declarations; others, namely, the Anti-War Treaty and the Montevideo Convention, international compacts. It is clear that the former constituted merely statements of policy, not entailing any legal duty, while the latter created for the contracting parties legal obligations not to recognize certain territorial transfers. The question, however, whether such an obligation

---

[1] Below, 105, n. 10

[2] Regarding the Anti-War Treaty, doubts were raised as to whether the non-recognition provisions of its Article 2 (above, 76) refer only to changes affecting the territories of the signatories. According to Professor Jessup ("The Argentine War Pact," 28 *AJIL* 538), the question should be answered in the affirmative.

was created within the framework of the League, is utterly controversial. Those who hold that it should be answered in the affirmative rely on Article 10 of the Covenant, some also on the Assembly Resolution of March 11, 1932.

The text of Article 10 did not mention non-recognition explicitly. This, however, would not exclude that it implied such a duty. The preparatory work gives no clue whether the idea of non-recognition ever occupied the minds of the draftsmen of the Covenant. The first to claim that Article 10 really implied such a duty was Mr. Procope at the Ninth League Assembly (1928).[3] His view, which won the support of a number of scholars,[4] would appear to be warranted. Article 10 created for the League Members an obligation to respect and preserve as against external aggression the political independence and territorial integrity of the other Member States. The essence of non-recognition of a territorial transfer is the refusal, on the part of the non-recognizing Power, to regard the sovereignty of the dispossessed Power superseded by that of the dispossessing Power and to give to the acts of the latter the effects attaching to the acts of a rightful sovereign. It is hard to see how without such a refusal the obligation to respect the political independence and territorial integrity of a sovereign dispossessed by external aggression could be complied with. Therefore the view that Article 10 implied a duty of non-recognition is believed to be sound.

Even more controversial than the foregoing issue is the question whether, and if so, to what extent such a duty was created by the Assembly Resolution of March 11, 1932.[5] Those who deny its binding force argue that the Covenant, being an international compact, established certain definite obligations and no others, and that additional duties could only be imposed by amending it as provided in its Article 26.[6] Others defend the position that an Assembly Resolution

[3] Above, 47

[4] See, e.g., Garner, "Non-Recognition of Illegal Territorial Annexations" (30 *AJIL* 679) (quoted below, n. 7)

[5] Above, 62

[6] Among the writers who doubted or denied the binding force of an Assembly resolution the following deserve quotation: Brierly (in "The Meaning and Legal Effect of the Resolution of the League of Nations of March 11, 1932," 16 *Br. Y. Bk.* 159) holds that the Covenant did not confer general

created a legal obligation at least for those League Members whose delegates voted for it.[7] Thus, in spite of a great

---

authority on the League or any of its organs to take action which would have the effect of creating obligations legally binding on its members. "Sometimes the League of Nations drew up pacts for signature and ratification, but never suggested that a resolution of the Assembly should replace any of the accepted formalities of treaty making." Further: "The juristic analysis of an ordinary League resolution is a simple matter. It is not a legal act, not a treaty between Members, but a concordant declaration of will, a formal declaration of intention, not immutable." But he adds that it should not be lightly departed from, and that the ordinary decency required that it should not be departed from without notice to, and consultation with, the other concurring Members.

Hill (in "Recent Policies of Non-Recognition," *Int. Conc.* 293) finds it doubtful whether the resolution of March 11, 1932, was binding on the Members.

Fischer Williams wrote (in "Some Thoughts on Recognition," 47 *Harv. L. Rev.* 776): "It cannot be said how far that resolution of the Assembly constitutes an engagement binding even those Members of the League whose representatives concurred in voting for it."

[7] Schindler (*Die Verbindlichkeit der Beschlüsse des Völkerbundes*) reaches the conclusion (p. 14) ". . . dass ein einstimmig gefasster Beschluss für die zustimmenden Staaten eine Bindung erzeugen kann." He quotes a. o. a report submitted by Viviani and Rowell to the First League Assembly stating that ". . . il faut qu'il reste bien entendu qu'au moment où il vote, le représentant engage le membre qui l'a délégué. . . ." (*Ibid.* 35-36); furthermore a report of the First Commission of the Fifth League Assembly: "L'unanimité n'est, en effet, requise aux séances plénières de l'Assemblée que pour l'adoption des résolutions constituant des décisions proprement dites, liant les États, et non relatives à la procédure. . . ." (*Ibid.* 37); and finally the opinion of the Permanent Court of International Justice in the Mossul case (Publ. Ser. B, no. 12), which, speaking of the Council, states: "Il s'agit donc de représentants des membres, c'est à dire de personnes mandatées par leurs gouvernements respectifs, dont elles reçoivent les instructions et dont elles engagent la responsabilité." Schindler holds his view also to be applicable to the so-called "interpretative resolutions" of which the object is to define, by way of interpretation, rights and duties implied in the provisions of the Covenant.

Among the other writers who assumed that an Assembly resolution might be able to create legal obligations for the League Members whose delegates voted for it, the following should be quoted:

Schücking (in Le Développement du Pacte de la Société des Nations," 20 *Hague Rec.* 353): "Ce sont les résolutions du Conseil et de l'Assemblée qui dans leur contenu représentent un développement du droit constitutionnel, sans que le texte du pacte ait été complété. . . ."

Middlebush (in "Non-Recognition as Sanction in International Law," 27 *ASIL* 40): ". . . Presumably the action of the Assembly [in adopting the resolution of March 11, 1932] is binding upon them [the League Members]."

Sharp (in *Non-Recognition as a Legal Obligation,* at 191): ". . . It appears that all States members present and voting [for the resolution] were bound. Its legal content may . . . be said to have consisted in the affirmation of a preexisting obligation which, although only implied, was binding."

The same author (in *Duties of Non-Recognition in Practice, 1775–1934,* 13): "The question remains to be analyzed whether these resolutions and reports impose additional duties on League Members. A clear case can be argued in support of the reasoning that the primary obligation not to recognize situations brought about in violation of the Covenant, especially Art. 10,

amount of learning, the issue remains somewhat doubtful.

Controversy arose also over the question whether the said
League Resolution referred only to the Manchurian case or
was intended to be of general applicability. The latter is believed to be true for the following reasons: First of all, nothing in the wording of the resolution points to any intent of
limiting its applicability to the Manchurian case. Furthermore, its fourth paragraph explicitly referred to the Council's Appeal of February 16, 1932; [8] the latter, however,
undoubtedly stated a general principle ("of any Member of
the League"). Finally, the League itself re-emphasized on
the occasion of the Leticia dispute that the validity of the
Resolution was by no means limited to the Sino-Japanese
dispute.[9] Exactly the same conclusions may be derived from
the legislative history of the Resolution.[10] In particular the

---

is and has been imposed by the Covenant itself as long as it has been in
force. To be sure, this obligation was only implied prior to 1932. The resolution of March 11, 1932, is the basic instrument among the secondary actions.
It is held by some authorities that resolutions adopted by the Council or the
Assembly are binding, to the limited extent of the competence entrusted to
these organs, upon State-Members without the necessity of subsequent ratification by their governments. A distinction is sometimes made between
Members present and voting, and those absent. The former are admitted to
be bound, and many authorities contend that the latter are also. All of these
points are disputed. It remains indisputable that a Member which has officially sanctioned an interpretation of its Covenant obligation as including
the duty to refuse recognition to situations resulting from violations of that
instrument, can hardly deny that it is so bound."

Garner (in "Non-Recognition of Illegal Territorial Annexations," 30 *AJIL*
679): "The duty of non-recognition may logically be deduced from its [that
is Art. 10] spirit and purpose. It would be a strange interpretation of the
article to hold that while it forbids Members of the League from despoiling
one another of its territory, it nevertheless leaves them free to recognize the
results of spoliations made by one of them in violation of the prohibition. In
practice the interpretation here defended is that which was adopted by the
Assembly of the League in its resolution of March 11, 1932. Adopted by a
unanimous vote excluding that of Japan, it would seem that the duty of
non-recognition here declared was binding upon all the League Members
whose delegates voted for it."

Lauterpacht (in "Règles Générales du Droit de Paix," 62 *Hague Rec.* 99
at 293): "Outre qu'elle [that is the resolution of March 11, 1932] est une
déclaration d'obligations existentes, elle est par elle-même une source d'obligations. La nature juridique de cette obligation formulée dans la résolution
est sujette à controverse. D'une part il semble qu'il n'y ait aucune raison
pour qu'une décision de l'Assemblée ou du Conseil ne soit pas obligatoire
pour les États qui l'acceptent. Un traité ratifié n'est pas le seul moyen
d'assumer des obligations internationales. . . ."

[8] Above, 61

[9] Above, 69

[10] Above, 63

language used by Sir John Simon [11] would appear to reveal the intention to suggest the adoption of an act of general significance and applicability.

[11] Above, 65 ("What should such a declaration accomplish? It would re-assert . . . the conditions under which every Member of the League is pledged to conduct relations with every other Member.")

CHAPTER XVI

THE LEGAL IMPLICATIONS
OF NON-RECOGNITION

THE essential content of non-recognition of a territorial transfer is, as was stated in the preceding chapter, the refusal, on the part of a non-recognizing Power, to regard the sovereignty of the dispossessed Power over the area in question as ended and the sovereignty of the dispossessing Power as established. This was clearly expressed in the recommendations of the League Assembly of February 24, 1933,[1] and is supported by recent decisions of common law courts.[2] Similarly, the Harvard Draft Convention on the Rights and Duties of States in Case of Aggression [3] provided that "situations created by an aggressor's use of force do not change sovereignty or other legal status over territory."

The practical application of the principle will have to differentiate according to the various possible patterns of aggression: the seizure of foreign territory may take place by means of international war (belligerent seizure) or by the use or threat of force against a Power unable to oppose warlike resistance (non-belligerent seizure, as in the cases of Austria 1938, Czechoslovakia 1938 and 1939) or by crushing the resistance of the victim in its initial stage (Albania 1939); the seizure may affect only part of a foreign State (Manchuria 1932, Czechoslovakia 1938), or absorb its whole territory (Austria, Albania, Czechoslovakia 1939); it may assume the form of outright annexation (Austria, Sudeten-area), or it may be veiled by the establishment of a puppet state (Manchukuo, Slovakia), of a protectorate (Bohemia-Moravia), or of a personal or real union (Albania). In case the whole territory of a State is seized, the practice of non-

---

[1] "Whereas the sovereignty of Manchuria belongs to China. . . ." (*LNOJ*, Spec. Suppl. 112, 75) (above, 69)
[2] Below, 266 ff.
[3] Above, 81

recognition may partly differ according to whether all governmental authority of the dispossessed sovereign has been destroyed, or whether it survives in some form or other (government-in-exile, ministers who continue to be accredited as official representatives of their countries, etc.) Different problems are also bound to rise (a) during the occupation, (b) after the ejection of the occupant and the return of the dispossessed sovereign.

A Power that adopts a policy of non-recognition is bound to take certain measures in two main spheres: in the field of its external relations, and in that of its domestic—judicial as well as administrative—activities. In the former, problems of diplomatic and consular representation and of international agreements have to be solved; in the latter questions of personal status, of property, and of the validity of acts effected by, or under the authority of, the dispossessing sovereign.

From the principle that the sovereignty of the dispossessed sovereign over the seized area legally continues to exist, it follows that the diplomatic relations between the non-recognizing Power and the former regarding that area have to continue if this is possible at all, that is if a governmental body of the dispossessed sovereign survives either in a non-occupied part of his territory or in exile. Conversely, it would be incompatible with non-recognition if a non-recognizing Power established such relations regarding the seized area with the dispossessing sovereign. The practical application of these principles, of course, will differ in case the seizure led to the erection of an allegedly independent State establishing its own diplomatic service, or in case the conduct of the foreign affairs of the seized area is openly taken over by the dispossessing Power. In the first case no diplomatic relations could be established between the non-recognizing State and the puppet of the dispossessing State without stultifying the non-recognition policies of the former. In the second case difficulties may arise, since between the dispossessing sovereign and the non-recognizing Power diplomatic relations may already have been in existence regarding the former's original territory, and it may at times not be easy for the latter to limit the diplomatic intercourse to the agenda concerning this territory, while declining it with reference to the seized area. But in no case should a non-recognizing State admit diplomatic interposition on the part of the occupant on behalf of inhabitants of the occupied territory. On the other hand, it would not appear incompatible with non-recognition if a non-recognizing Power asserted the responsibility of the dispossessing Power (but not of its puppet) for wrong done to the former's nationals. For in such cases interposition is not based on the sovereignty of the dispossessing Power, but on the mere fact of its control—exercised directly or through its puppet—over the seized area.[4]

In the field of consular representation earlier theory has developed the maxim that the granting of an exequatur implies recognition.[5] The same would appear to be true of the application for an exequatur by a non-recognizing State.[6] Consequently such a State, if it wanted to remain true to its policy (or, as the case may be, to its duty) of non-recognition, would have to renounce consular representation in the seized area. This, however, involves a serious problem. For, in spite of non-recognition, personal and commercial intercourse between the nationals of the non-recognizing State and the inhabitants of the seized area normally continue. Consequently, in many respects the former might suffer from the lack of consular representation. Furthermore, such representation may, as recent instances demonstrated, even be urgently needed in the interest of those whom non-recognition is intended to protect, namely, the inhabitants of the seized area, who are at the mercy of the invader and for whom the visa of the non-recognizing sovereign may be the only way of salvation. Thus, a State may find itself in a serious dilemma between its practice—or even duty—of non-recognition on the one hand, and urgent administrative needs on the other. In certain cases the appointment of special agents without consular status, or the resort

---

[4] The American note of April 6, 1938 to the German Government, appears to imply similar views (below, 162 [2]).

[5] Hyde, *International Law as Chiefly Interpreted and Applied by the United States*, 2d ed., I 150, n. 2

[6] This position was taken by the British Government regarding Slovakia and the German Protectorate in Bohemia-Moravia (below, 224, 229).

to the good offices of third Powers may offer a way out; yet an overbearing conqueror may ask explicit and unreserved recognition as the price for allowing third Powers any official activities in the occupied territory.[7]

In the sphere of international agreements non-recognition of a territorial transfer would apear to entail the consequence that the non-recognizing Power is bound to regard its treaties with the dispossessed sovereign as legally still being in force, although their operation is rendered impossible for the duration of the occupation.[8] Conversely, it would seem inconsistent with non-recognition, should a non-recognizing Power conclude with the dispossessing Power agreements regarding the occupied area, at least if this is done without explicitly adding that the transaction does not imply recognition.

The second main sphere of official activities in which problems of non-recognition of a territorial transfer have to be dealt with, is that of the domestic judicial and administrative practice of the non-recognizing State. The basic issue in this sphere is whether and how far acts which have been consummated by, or under the authority of, a non-recognized occupant should be considered effective by the authorities of the non-recognizing State; the issue arises normally in connection with questions of personal status and of property rights of persons linked in some way to the occupied area.

In view of the scantiness of the theory and practice developed in this field it might appear proper to look to other fields for precedents which seem to offer certain analogies.

Thus, analogies may be seen between a non-recognized forcible transfer of territory and the situation prevailing in the case of a so-called de facto government. The latter term denotes a group which was able to establish by means of unconstitutional acts, such as a coup d'État or a revolution, effective control within its own country, and which acts as its government without, however, being recognized as such by

[7] This happened in fact in 1939 between Great Britain and Germany regarding the Bohemian-Moravian Protectorate (below, 230).

[8] This position was repeatedly taken by the United States Government; thus in the case of Czechoslovakia (below, 232), the Baltic republics (below, 264, n. 32), and Albania (below, 253).

other Powers.[9] Both cases have in common a state of affairs brought about by illegal means and resulting in the establishment of effective control over a given territory. The essential difference, however, consists in that a group which established control within its own country may still be considered as representing, in some way, the will of the people of the country, while it would be absurd to assume this of a

[9] Regarding de facto governments originating in domestic tours de force, one theory, reflected in the recognition policies of President Wilson and underlying the so-called Tobar Doctrine, advocates withholding of recognition until certain tests of "legality" are met. Thus, Art. 1 of a convention concluded 1907 between the five Central-American republics (text, 2 *AJIL*, Suppl., 229) provided that the governments of the signatory Parties "shall not recognize any other government which may come into power in any of the five Republics as a consequence of a coup d'État, or of a revolution against the recognized government, so long as the freely elected representatives of the people thereof have not constitutionally reorganized the country." This theory was strongly opposed by another school of thought whose most prominent representatives in the United States are John B. Moore and E. Borchard. Their basic tenet is that "facts are facts" and that to refuse recognition to a government which has firmly established itself within its country and is willing and able to fulfil the international obligations of the latter, would encroach upon the principle of the sovereign equality of the members of the international community. In this sense Moore wrote (in "Fifty Years of International Law," 50 *Harv. L. Rev.* 395 at 427 ff.): "Wilson's recognition policy . . . struck at the very roots of the legal equality of independent States. . . . Erroneous supposition that if de facto authorities were not 'recognized,' their acts would be invalid externally if not internally. . . . Recognition validates nothing. . . ." Similarly Sir John Fischer Williams (in "Some Thoughts on Recognition," 47 *Harv. L. Rev.* 776 at 785) wrote: "If an existing State disapproves of a new government in an old State, it may wholly or partially break off diplomatic intercourse; but to refuse to recognize the new government is both to pass upon the legality of a municipal event and to invite the courts of the non-recognizing State to enter the world of unreality and to pretend that events which have happened have not in fact come to pass." The same author in "La Doctrine de la Reconnaissance en Droit International et ses Développements Récents" (44 *Hague Rec.* 203 at 307): "Un événement peut être illégal; mais le qualifier ainsi ne suffit pas à l'abolir. Dire que ce qui résulte de moyens illégaux n'existe dans ou pour le droit international, c'est de la fantaisie pure." Along similar lines is the so-called Estrada Doctrine, laid down in a Declaration of the Mexican Foreign Secretary, Sr. Estrada, issued on September 27, 1930 (text, 25 *AJIL*, Suppl., 203). The Declaration denounced "the so-called theory of recognition" on the ground that it "allows foreign governments to pass upon the legitimacy or illegitimacy of the regime existing in another country. . . ." and announced that "the Government of Mexico has transmitted instructions to its Ministers or Chargés d'Affaires in the countries affected by the recent political crises, informing them that the Mexican Government is issuing no declarations in the sense of recognition, since that nation considers that such a course is an insulting practice and one which, in addition to the fact that it offends the sovereignty of other nations, implies that judgment of some sort may be passed upon the internal affairs of these nations by other governments." The Declaration concluded: "Therefore, the Government of Mexico confines itself to the maintenance or withdrawal, as it may deem advisable, of its diplomatic agents, and to the continued acceptance, also when it may deem advisable, of such similarly accredited diplomatic agents as the respective nations may have in Mexico."

foreign Power seizing control by force or by the threat of force. Therefore, the extensive body of theory and practice which has been developed around the problem of the non-recognized de facto government and the validity of its acts in foreign courts seems hardly applicable to the case of a non-recognized territorial transfer.[10]

[10] Already at an early stage the courts had to deal with the problem of the non-recognized government and the effectiveness of its acts; many decisions originated in the sphere of the American civil war, others arose out of situations prevailing at different times in various Latin-American republics. The problem assumed new proportions when the principle of non-recognition was applied to the Soviet Government.

A great number of authors as well as of judicial decisions of civil law and common law courts took the position that in the absence of recognition the acts of a Power that wielded effective control over an area were, in the eyes of the authorities of a non-recognizing State, devoid of the effects attending the acts of a sovereign. In this sense e.g. Gemma 1924 (in 4 *Hague Rec.* 97 at 377): "Le gouvernement, pour les États qui ne l'ont point reconnu, est sans existence juridique; les diverses mesures prises par lui tant en matière législative qu'en matière administrative sont reputées nulles et non avenues." Similarly Noël-Henry (in *Le Gouvernement de Fait devant le Juge* àt 90, 109, 135, 139, 142, 144); Lagarde (*La Reconnaissance du Gouvernement des Soviets,* 115); Raestad (in "La Reconnaissance Internationale de Nouveaux États," *Rev. Dr. Int.,* S. 3, XVII 257 at 292). The leading cases in British and American law courts are: the *Annette* and the *Dora* (Pro 105, 1919), Luther v. Sagor, 1 K. B. 456 (1921); Pelzer v. United Dredging Co., 193 N. Y. Suppl. 676 (1922); among civil law cases may be cited: Héritiers Bounatian v. Société Optorg, Tribunal de la Seine, December 12, 1923 (51 *Journ. Dr. Int.* 133); Jelenkova v. Serbulov, Cour de Bruxelles, June 5, 1923, *Ann. Dig.* 1925/6, No. 20; Bekker v. Willcox, do. November 10, 1923, *Ann. Dig.* 1923/4, No. 22; Digmelov, do. June 16, 1928, *Ann. Dig.* 1927/8, No. 45. Yet as the years went by and recognition was refused to governments for political reasons and not because it was thought they were not in control of their countries, difficulties arose in applying the foregoing theory. Textbook writers as well as judicial decisions now advanced the doctrine that non-recognition of a foreign government did not prevent courts of a non-recognizing State from according validity to certain of its acts unless they conflicted with the public policy of their government. It was particularly in the writings of the Americans Dickinson and Borchard that this view was strongly defended; thus by Dickinson in 22 *Mich. L. Rev.* 39 (1924); by Borchard in 26 *AJIL* 261 (1932). But also the British scholar Sir John Fischer Williams supported this doctrine, e.g. in "Recognition" (15 *Transactions of the Grotius Society* 5), and in "La Doctrine de la Reconnaissance" (44 *Hague Rec.* 203 at 252 ff.). Many American judicial decisions followed suit, above all Sokoloff v. National City Bank, 239 NY 158 (1924) at 164 ff., Russian Reinsurance Company v. Stoddard, 240 NY 149 (1925), at a later stage also some European decisions, e.g. the Brussels Civil Court in the d'Aivasoff case (February 28, 1927, *Ann. Dig.* 1927/8, No. 46), the Swiss Federal Court in the case Banque Internationale de Commerce de Petrograd (December 10, 1924, 52 *Journ. Dr. Int.* 488) and in the Schinz case (June 4, 1926, *Ann. Dig.* 1925/6, No. 23).

Along similar lines was the following statement, made by the Belgian Foreign Minister in 1933: "Si les tribunaux belges, dans la plénitude de leur indépendance, décidaient que la législation de la Russie d'aujourd'hui peut produire certains effets en Belgique, le gouvernement n'y verrait pas une opposition à la politique suivie par lui, de non-reconnaissance du gouvernement de l'URSS." (reported by Fischer Williams in 44 *Hague Rec.* 203 at 255). Dickinson's and Borchard's views were rejected by a recent American decision ("The *Maret*," below, 268, n. 43).

Analogies may also be seen between such a transfer and belligerent occupation. Regarding the latter, international law developed a body of principles which were partly codified at the Hague Conferences of 1899 and 1907.[11] The substance of the doctrine is that the belligerent occupant has no sovereignty over the occupied territory and is not allowed to proceed to its annexation while the war is still in progress,[12] but that he is entitled to measures necessary for the conduct of the war and for proper administration, the latter as a corollary of the obligation, incumbent on him, to provide for the maintenance of the normal life of the inhabitants.[13]

The analogy between belligerent occupation and non-recognized territorial transfer, however, can hardly be carried beyond the point that in either case the dispossessing Power is not regarded as the sovereign of the occupied territory, but that the authority of the dispossessed Power has in fact passed into his hands. From this it may merely be argued that also in the case of a non-recognized transfer the occupant has to provide for the continuance of life in the seized area and that the application of this principle entitles him to take certain measures.

Thus, very little can be derived from the doctrine and practice built up in other fields, and the problems which confront the non-recognizing State in its domestic sphere, judicial as well as administrative, must be solved by drawing the logical conclusions from the essence of the principle of non-recognition.

A distinction, however, has to be made between instances in which non-recognition is merely based on an established policy such as the Stimson Doctrine, and cases when it is a legal duty under international treaties. In the former the non-recognizing State may or may not take all the steps logically implied in that policy, while in the latter case a

[11] *Annex to the Hague Convention on the Laws and Customs of War on Land* (Fourth Convention of the Second Hague Conference 1907).

[12] Above, 17. The rule is also reflected in Art. 45: "It is forbidden to compel the inhabitants of occupied territory to swear allegiance to the hostile Power."

[13] (Art. 43) "The authority of the legitimate Power having in fact passed into the hands of the occupant, the latter shall take all the measures in his power to restore, and ensure, as far as possible, public order and safety, while respecting, unless absolutely prevented, the laws in force in the country."

failure in this respect may amount to the breach of an international obligation.

Since the essence of non-recognition of a territorial transfer consists in the survival, in the eyes of the non-recognizing Power, of the sovereignty of the dispossessed Power, it is incumbent on the former not to accord effect, within its jurisdiction, to decrees by which the dispossessing Power (or its puppet) undertook to change the nationality of the inhabitants of the area in question; instead he has to continue to treat them as nationals of the dispossessed sovereign.[14] This point is of particular importance in case war breaks out between the non-recognizing and the dispossessing sovereign. It would be inconsistent with the former's practice —or obligation—of non-recognition to treat such persons as nationals of the latter and consequently as enemy aliens. This, however, does not mean that the non-recognizing State would not be justified in taking proper measures against attempts of the enemy to "plant" his agents under the disguise of nationals of the seized territory.

Furthermore, it must be held inconsistent with the policy of a non-recognizing State to give effect to decrees of the dispossessing Power transferring to the latter the public property of the dispossessed sovereign. As far as such property is located within the jurisdiction of the non-recognizing Power, the latter would either have to leave it in the custody of such representatives of the dispossessed Power as may still be accredited, or in the absence of such, entrust its care to appropriate agencies. Nor could, in case war breaks out between the non-recognizing and the non-recognized Power, the former, without violating the principle—or obligation— of non-recognition, treat such property as property of the latter and consequently as enemy property. The same holds true of private property of nationals of the seized area. Only such measures of the non-recognizing Power would seem justified as might be required to prevent the enemy from camouflaging his own property as that of nationals of

[14] This applies to the nationals of the transferred area regardless of whether or not they were residing in it at the time of the transfer, while international law had already at an earlier stage established the maxim that a territorial transfer does not affect such nationals of the transferred area who found themselves abroad at the time when it took place. (Cf. Westlake "The Nature and Extent of Title by Conquest," 17 *L. Q. Rev.* 892)

the occupied territory, or from using the property of the
latter to his own advantage.

In all these respects the conduct implied in non-recognition would seem to be sufficiently clear. Doubts, however, may
arise regarding the effect which should be given in the courts
of a non-recognizing Power to other acts consummated in
the seized area by or under the authority of the non-recognized occupant, in particular to orders and decrees affecting
the personal status and to transfers—judicial or otherwise
—of property rights. Since the occupant is under the obligation to provide for the continuity of life in the seized
area, the non-recognizing Power would seem justified in
treating such acts as valid if they appear to serve that
purpose. Yet many of them are in reality nothing but more
or less cleverly concealed measures of spoliation, frequently
aiming at the total ruin of the inhabitants of the occupied
area. A certain safeguard against the danger of giving effect, on the part of the non-recognizing State, to such measures of spoliation and depredation may consist in the application of the principle, incorporated in the legal system
of many countries, that acts of a foreign Power that are
irreconcilable with the public policy of the State from which
enforcement is sought, are disregarded in the courts of the
latter. Yet beyond this, uttermost caution on the part of the
non-recognizing Power is imperative lest its non-recognition
policies—or obligations—be thwarted by its administrative
and judicial practice.

The problem of the validity of transfers effected by, or
under the authority of, an occupant assumed unprecedented
proportions during the Second World War, due to the German system of wholesale spoliation and looting, concealed
in many cases behind the screen of apparently strictly legal
transactions.[15] This system prompted the governments of
the nations at war with Germany to issue on January 5,

---

[15] A pamphlet, *The Postwar Settlement of Property Rights*, published by
the Council on Foreign Relations, New York, in 1945, contains a survey of
the policies and practices of the Axis and the United Nations regarding the
treatment of enemy property, and a series of recommendations regarding
the postwar settlement of property rights. These recommendations were
drafted by a Study Group of the said Council under the chairmanship of
John W. Davis and with the participation of Professors Edwin Borchard,
Philip C. Jessup, and Quincy Wright.

1943, the following Inter-Allied Declaration against acts of dispossession committed in territories under enemy occupation or control:

The Governments of the Union of South Africa; the United States of America; Australia; Belgium; Canada; China; the Czechoslovak Republic; the United Kingdom of Great Britain and Northern Ireland; Greece; India; Luxembourg; the Netherlands; New Zealand; Norway; Poland; the Union of Soviet Socialist Republics; Yugoslavia; and the French National Committee

Hereby issue a formal warning to all concerned, and in particular to persons in neutral countries, that they intend to do their utmost to defeat the methods of dispossession practised by the governments with which they are at war, against the countries and peoples who have been so wantonly assaulted and despoiled.

Accordingly, the Governments making this Declaration and the French National Committee reserve all their rights to declare invalid any transfers of or dealings with property, rights, and interests of any description whatsoever which are, or have been, situated in the territories which have come under the occupation or control, direct or indirect, of the governments with which they are at war, or which belong, or have belonged, to persons, including juridical persons, resident in such territories. This warning applies whether such transfers or dealings have taken the form of open looting or plunder, or of transactions apparently legal in form, even when they purport to be voluntarily effected.

The Governments making this Declaration and the French National Committee solemnly record their solidarity in this matter.[16]

This Declaration was subsequently also approved by the Inter-American Conference on War and Peace, held at Mexico City in February–March, 1945.[17] Its text did not explicitly state whether it was intended to apply to cases of belligerent occupation only, or also to other non-recognized seizures of territory.[18] This failure led especially in the

---

[16] 8 *D. S. Bull.* 21

[17] Resolution XIX, paragraph 1, lt. a, of the Final Act

[18] Recommendation VI of the Study Group (above, n. 15) read:

"The United Nations have the right to declare invalid in behalf of themselves or their nationals all transfers involving their own property or that of their nationals:

a) located in the territory of an Axis nation if made during hostilities and induced by duress exercised by or on behalf of an Axis nation or national;

b) located in Axis-occupied territory if made subsequent to the date of occupation under duress or pursuant to exceptional war measures adopted by the administration of an army of occupation or a puppet regime.

"The person in possession of such transferred property would have the burden of proving that his title, since the commencement of hostilities, has been based upon voluntary transfers.

Austrian case to complications in the question of the so-called "German assets." [19]

An important step, however, in the direction of the principles set forth in this chapter was taken by the Allied Control Council for Germany. The latter adopted late in 1945 a "Law on Vesting and Marshaling of German External Assets" which contained the following provisions:

Article I   A German External Property Commission (hereinafter referred to as "the Commission") composed of representatives of the four occupying powers in Germany is hereby constituted. . . .

Article II   All rights, titles and interests in respect of any property outside Germany which is owned or controlled by any person of German nationality inside Germany are hereby vested in the Commission.

Article III   All rights, titles and interests in respect of any property outside Germany which is owned or controlled by any person of German nationality outside of Germany or by any branch or corporation or other legal entity organized under the laws of Germany or having its principal place of business in Germany are hereby vested in the Commission.

For the purpose of this article the term "any person of German nationality outside Germany" shall apply only to a person who has enjoyed full rights of German citizenship under Reich law at any time since 1 September 1939 and who has at any time since 1 September 1939 been within any territory then under the control of the Reich, but shall not apply to any citizen of any country annexed or claimed to have been annexed by Germany since 31 December 1937.[20]

"If the invalidity of any such transfers involves only the rights in Axis-occupied countries of the nationals of such country and of Axis nationals, final determination should be left to the local courts. If the rights of nationals of other United Nations or of neutral nations are involved, provision should be made for resort to an international tribunal."

To this Recommendation the following observations were made by members of the Study Group: Professor Jessup was dubious about the practicability of the proposals in (a) and (b) and declared an objection "to any scheme which would create the anarchy of a wholesale cancellation of property rights." Messrs. Redmond, Micou, and Wright concurred in the recommendation, but expressed the belief that the settlement of property rights should be based not on the mere exercise of the superior power of the victor, but on established principles of international law "to be found, though inadequately developed, in the Briand-Kellogg Pact and, by extension to the economic as well as the political sphere, in the early Pan-American doctrine and the subsequent Stimson doctrine, refusing recognition to rights acquired through aggression or threat of aggression and denying to the aggressor the rights normally accorded to a lawful belligerent."

[19] Below, 198 ff.
[20] 14 *D. S. Bull.* 283

The last part of the preceding paragraph is highly significant. It proclaims, in a very important field, the invalidity of the nationality decrees of the occupant indiscriminately for belligerent as well as for non-belligerent occupation and annexation, and is consequently in line with a consistent application of the non-recognition principle.

CHAPTER XVII

DE JURE AND DE FACTO RECOGNITION. WITHDRAWAL OF RECOGNITION

Much speculation has been devoted to the meaning of the terms de jure recognition and de facto recognition, which were introduced into diplomatic practice after the First World War and also applied to the field of territorial change.[1] No official document offers adequate explanation regarding the criteria of the distinction between the two terms, and the comprehensive disquisitions of numerous textbook writers on the subject produced only meager results. Little more could be ascertained than that the term de facto recognition has the connotation of the qualified and provisional, that consequently a Power in granting de facto recognition makes it clear from the outset that the recognition may subsequently be withdrawn.[2] Even this, however, is not beyond doubt.[3] At any rate, as far as

[1] Above, 22.

[2] Erich, writing in 1926, ("La Naissance et la Reconnaissance des États," 13 *Hague Rec.* 430 at 458) called the terms de jure recognition and de facto recognition "actes extrêmement vagues quant à leur signification." He added: "Il paraît que l'État qui se borne à prononcer la reconnaissance de facto peut être guidé par les considérations suivantes; ou doutes juridiques ou raisons de pure opportunité. . . . On pourrait qualifier un pareil acte de reconnaissance par embarras ou par excuse."

Noël-Henry wrote in 1927 (*op. cit.* 62): "Les motifs qui, au cours des douze dernières années, ont conduit les gouvernements à introduire dans la pratique internationale les notions de reconnaissance de fait et de reconnaissance de droit, sont de nature très diverses; ce sont tantôt des considérations de légalité, tantôt des considérations de stabilité. . . . Le seul point commun, c'est que la reconnaissance de facto est, en théorie tout au moins, provisoire et revoçable, tandis que la reconnaissance de jure est définitive. . . ."

Fischer Williams ("Recognition," in 15 *Transactions of the Grotius Society* 53 at 66) reached regarding de facto recognition the following conclusion: "It is provisional and without prejudice to a withdrawal if circumstances change. . . . A de jure recognition, on the other hand, is express and as irrevocable as the nature of human affairs will allow." Revocability is also considered to be the essential feature of de facto recognition by Raestad (in "La Reconnaissance Internationale de Nouveaux États," *Rev. Dr. Int.*, S. 3, XVII 257).

[3] Professor Hyde (*op. cit.* I 193 ff.) offers the following analysis: "A state may see fit formally to acknowledge that a regime functioning within the territory of another is merely in fact governing it, without going the

the validity of the acts of a recognized Power before the courts or other agencies of the recognizing Power is concerned, the effects of a de jure and a de facto recognition are held to be identical.[4] This would appear to warrant the conclusion that a legal duty not to recognize a territorial transfer bars not only de jure, but also de facto recognition.[5]

Recognition may be, and in fact frequently is, withdrawn. The latter is also true of de jure recognition, in spite of views to the contrary advanced by some textbook writers.[6] In the field of territorial change the withdrawal of recognition implies that the withdrawing Power no longer regards the formerly recognized Power as the sovereign of the seized territory. Normally the withdrawal will be devoid of retro-

whole length and acknowledging that that regime is to be deemed for all purposes the government thereof, of whose pretensions as such the soundness is no longer open to question. Inasmuch as it is always possible to have informal intercourse for essential purposes with an unrecognized government, it is rarely necessary or expedient to make formal acknowledgment of the bare fact of its achievement, if for any reason there be reluctance to accord it full and complete recognition. If, however, a foreign State is disposed to make such an acknowledgment and yields what is oftentimes described as de facto recognition, it takes a step of which the consequences are not altogether clear. Such act may not in fact be followed by a renewal of diplomatic intercourse previously suspended. . . . Nevertheless, it is not apparent why an opposite course may not be pursued under appropriate declarations disavowing a design of broadening the character of what has been accorded. Again, the courts of the recognizing State may experience difficulty in distinguishing the effects of de facto recognition from those where full and normal recognition has been yielded; and they may derive from the former what they regard as a sufficient foundation for the conclusion that the regime so recognized is entitled for purposes of adjudication to the privileges and immunities commonly enjoyed by a foreign government fully recognized as such."

[4] This view is expressed by textbook writers as well as in judicial decisions. McNair ("Judicial Recognition of States and Governments," 2 *Br. Y. Bk.* 57) wrote: "So far as this country is concerned, either form of recognition is equally binding upon its courts." Briggs (in "De Facto and De Jure Recognition. The Arantzazu Mendi," 33 *AJIL* 689) held that ". . . it appears that the legal consequences of de facto and de jure recognition are essentially the same." The leading cases are (1) Republic of Peru v. Peruvian Guano, 36 *Ch. D.* 485 (1887) at 497: "So soon as it has been shown that a de facto government of a foreign State has been recognized by the government of this country, no further inquiry is permitted in a court of justice here. . . ." (2) Luther v. Sagor, 3 *K. B.* 532 (1921) at 551: "In my opinion there is no difference for the present purpose between a government recognized as such de jure and one recognized de facto. In the latter case as well as in the former, the government in question acquires the right to be treated by the recognizing state as an independent sovereign state. . . ."

[5] In this sense the Statement of Recommendations adopted by the League Assembly on February 24, 1933 (above, 69), declared: "They will continue not to recognize this regime either de jure or de facto."

[6] Below, 153, n. 66

active force, regardless of whether it refers to de jure or de facto recognition. The view that withdrawal of the latter is bound to be retroactive on account of the provisional character of that type of recognition is not borne out by diplomatic practice.

If, however, a Power declares that it regards a territorial change, previously recognized by it, as "null and void,"— as occurred in recent instances [7]—the conclusion would appear cogent that the withdrawal of recognition, implied in such a declaration, is bound to have retroactive force. For, what is "null and void" (in French: *"nul et non avenu"*) must be held invalid from its inception; this means that by virtue of the declaration the effects of the previously granted recognition are deleted "nunc pro tunc."

[7] See Gen. de Gaulle's and the Franco-Czechoslovak Declarations on the Munich Agreement (below, 238, 240) and the Moscow Declaration on Austria (below, 181). All these statements use the language: "... regard ... as null and void."

CHAPTER XVIII

THE RETURNING SOVEREIGN

$\mathbf{B}$ELLIGERENT as well as non-belligerent seizure of territory may come to an end by the ejection of the occupant and the restoration of the dispossessed sovereign. In either case the latter, known in legal terminology as the "restored" or "returning" sovereign, may claim the invalidity of acts consummated by, or under the authority of, the occupant, and may resort to their rescission. This process may affect rights and interests of nationals of third States, and lead to reclamations from the governments of the latter. In all such disputes the question of the powers of the occupant is bound to be of decisive influence. The solution of this question, in turn, depends to a great extent on the recognition issue. For, in the eyes of a non-recognizing Power, the sovereignty of the dispossessed Power cannot be regarded as extinguished, nor that of the dispossessing Power as established. Consequently the powers of the latter are to be considered limited to such measures as are required by the obligation, incumbent on the occupant, to provide for the continuity of life in the seized territory. Whether, however, a given act performed during the occupation is apt to meet that test, the returning sovereign would appear best qualified to decide. Therefore, the conclusion may be warranted that a non-recognizing Power should go a long way in acquiescing in measures of rescission taken by the former, even in case they are detrimental to rights and interests which nationals of the latter may have acquired during the control of the non-recognized occupant.[1] This, of course, does not mean that in resorting

[1] In the field of belligerent occupation similar views were expressed in the following resolutions of the London International Law Conference 1943 (38 *AJIL* 292):

"7. A person who acquires, even in good faith, any property, rights or interests which are or have been situated in occupied territory or are the property of nationals of that country will if his acquisition of them is derived directly or indirectly from acts of the occupant or his associates or agents not acquire an internationally valid title thereto as against the true

to such measures the returning sovereign should be free to disregard the rules which international law has developed regarding the treatment of foreign nationals. Yet the very possibility that measures of a non-recognized occupant may be invalidated by the returning sovereign and that this invalidation may be accepted by the judicial and other authorities of the non-recognizing State, even as against the latter's nationals, is apt to surround the position of the occupant with an atmosphere of uncertainty which, it is believed, adds a great deal to the moral value of non-recognition.[2]

owner unless such a title is valid by the law of the occupied country as applied by the reconstituted authorities after the liberation of the country.

"8. It will be for the lawful government to take steps, whether legislative or administrative in character, in order to restore any property or status wrongfully disposed of or altered by the occupant or his associates or agents; if taken within a reasonable time after the cessation of the occupation such measures are not to be deemed penal or confiscatory."

The foregoing Resolutions dealt only with questions of property; but the scope of rescinding measures of the returning sovereign is not limited to that field; such measures may e.g. affect the validity of marriages, divorces and other changes of personal status which took place during the control of the occupant.

[2] It is interesting to note that Fischer Williams—who, as far as non-recognition of governments is concerned, shares the views advanced by Borchard and Dickinson (above, 105, n. 10)—sees in this uncertainty a decided merit of the non-recognition of a territorial transfer. Although he asserts (44 *Hague Rec.* 203 at 302) that "le cours ordinaire de la vie internationale et des rapports en temps de paix ne sera pas serieusement troublé au détriment d'un État annexant par suite de l'absence de la reconnaissance," he admits that due to the withholding of recognition "l'annexion restera marquée d'une certaine insécurité capable en temps de crise de produire de graves effets."

CHAPTER XIX

THE TERMINATION OF NON-RECOGNITION

INTERNATIONAL law developed the principle that belligerent occupation could not lawfully be converted into sovereignty over the occupied territory as long as the war was still in progress.[1] Once the war was ended, either by the conclusion of a peace treaty, or by subjugation, the occupant was not deemed to be prevented from proclaiming the annexation of the occupied territory, and the other members of the international community normally accepted such an annexation as a fact.

This conception is bound to be affected by the modern idea of non-recognition as expressed in the Stimson notes, so far as it is acted upon, since its essential feature is just the refusal to accept a fait accompli. Accordingly, a State practicing non-recognition of forcible territorial changes as its settled policy would be justified in withholding recognition even after the victim was subjugated or forced to sign a treaty of cession.[2] In cases in which non-recognition is a legal duty under some treaty obligation, a State would not only be entitled but even required to withhold recognition without regard to the aforementioned contingencies.

Yet it was just this aspect of non-recognition that prompted many Internationalists to denounce the Stimson Doctrine on the ground that if consistently applied, it would "freeze" the status quo and make "peaceful change" impossible. This charge, it is believed, originated in a miscon-

[1] Above, 17, 106. In recent years, the principle was once again summarized in a note of the Minister of Yugoslavia to the U. S. Dept. of State, dated May 12, 1941, (4 *D. S. Bull.* 682) as follows: "It is . . . a cardinal principle of International Law that military occupation of territory in the course of hostilities does not change the juridical status of the territory thus occupied and that occupation by enemy armies provides no legal basis for the establishment of a new juridical status within such territory. . . ."

[2] This is expressed in the provisions of the Soviet-Turkish Treaty of 1921 (above, 22), the Saavedra Lamas Anti-War Treaty (above, 75 ff.), and the Montevideo Convention (above, 77).

ception. It is true that neither the League Covenant as interpreted in the Assembly Resolution of March 11, 1932, nor any of the international compacts which established a legal duty of non-recognition contained any provision regarding the termination of that duty. But does this mean that the status quo prevailing at the time the obligation of non-recognition was undertaken should thereby be considered frozen per omnia saecula saeculorum?

Such a conception would be so irreconcilable with the realities and exigencies of international life that it could not possibly claim validity. How long, then, should an obligation of non-recognition be considered to be binding?

In answer to this question, some assert that the lapse of time, of a considerably long time, is apt to consolidate any situation regardless of the means by which it was brought about.[3] The unqualified acceptance of this principle, however, would in the last resort again be tantamount to acquiescence in the fait accompli, to the acknowledgment of the right of conquest, of the maxim that "Might makes Right." Sounder, it is believed, would appear the theory that non-recognition, regardless of whether it is based on a mere policy or on a legal duty, cannot be held to outlast a change of the previous territorial status effected by means of a general arrangement in the wake of one of the major international crises which are bound to recur from time to time as long as the international system is based on the principle of the sovereign equality of a number of independent States.

It is true that in such general arrangements normally the will of the leading Powers prevails, and that consequently the aspirations of the smaller Powers are frequently bound to remain unfulfilled. Unsatisfactory as this result may be, it is still preferable to a system which accepts unilateral acts of aggression as faits accomplis. At any rate it seems to be the only way to establish from time to time a new legality in the territorial status. In fact, the experiences of the past seem to prove that the application of principles analogous to those underlying the "Concert of Europe" may prevent the outbreak of a general war for decades. On

[3] Below, 227 ff. (Speech of Mr. Alexander in the British House of Commons)

the other hand the new idea of non-recognition may, in spite of its shortcomings, contribute to curb individual acts of aggression. To demand more would hardly be reasonable, for in the field of political life there are no best, only second-best solutions.[4]

[4] It may be proper to recall at this juncture the following address, delivered by President Wilson at the Paris Peace Conference on May 31, 1919 (5 Temperley 130):

"We are trying to make a peaceful settlement. . . . And back of this lies this fundamentally important fact that when the decisions are made, the Allied and Associated Powers guarantee to maintain them. It is perfectly evident that the chief burden of their maintenance will fall on the Great Powers. . . . And therefore, we must not close our eyes to the fact that in the last analysis the military and naval strength of the Great Powers will be the final guarantee of the peace of the world."

PART III

Diplomatic Practice
1934–1946

CHAPTER XX

THE FAR EAST

For a year the Assembly Resolution of February 24, 1933, which had proclaimed that the League Members "will continue not to recognize the Manchurian State either de jure or de facto" [1] was strictly respected. The first inroad was made by El Salvador, which granted recognition to the Manchurian puppet state in March, 1934. [2] But the other Powers continued to respect the resolution; nor did the United States budge from the position enunciated in the Stimson notes. The Soviet Union was not bound by the resolution since it had not been a League Member when the latter was adopted; it was, however, bound by the duties under Article 10 of the Covenant. As stated before, [3] the Soviet Government exercised since 1922 the Russian rights concerning the Chinese Eastern Railway, and this state of affairs continued during the first years of the Manchurian puppet state. But at a given moment, the Soviet Government decided to end it, obviously in order to avoid frictions which it was not willing to face at that time; it entered into negotiations with the puppet government, and on March 23, 1935, an agreement was signed at Tokyo "between Manchukuo and the Union of Soviet Socialist Republics" [4] providing for the cession by the latter to the former of all rights concerning the Chinese Eastern Railway —henceforth called North Manchurian Railway—for a consideration of 140 million yen. In an additional note of the same date, the Japanese Government, "in accordance with the desire" expressed by the Soviet Ambassador, undertook "in view of the close and special relations existing between Japan and Manchukuo" to guarantee the exact fulfillments

[1] Above, 69

[2] *LNOJ* 1934, 965-7. Shortly before, on March 1, 1934, Mr. Pu-yi had proclaimed himself "Emperor" of the puppet state whose name was changed to "Manchutiku" (Manchu Empire).

[3] Above, 55

[4] Martens, *Nouv. Rec. Gén.*, S. 3, XXX 649

of the obligations of the Manchukuo Government under the agreement. By explicitly asking for the latter undertaking, the Soviet Government made it sufficiently clear that it regarded the Government of Manchukuo as a mere Japanese puppet. The conclusion, however, of an agreement, be it in a purely commercial matter, may be construed as implied recognition, although the Soviet Government was hardly able to dispose in another way of the unwanted asset.

Recognitions of a deliberately political character were granted to the Japanese puppet when a world-wide block of aggressors sprang up during the Italo-Ethiopian war. On November 25, 1936, Germany and Japan signed the Anti-Comintern Pact,[5] while already since the fall of 1935 close relations had been established between Germany and Italy. The power constellation was propitious for another installment of Japanese aggression against China. On July 7, 1937, a new "incident" occurred, this time at the Marco Polo Bridge near Peiping. Unlike 1931, the Chinese decided to defend the integrity of their country even if it meant war; and real warfare ensued, although it was not formally declared until December, 1941. On November 6, 1937, the Italian Government adhered to the Anti-Comintern Pact,[6] and on November 29 it granted formal recognition to the Manchurian puppet state. The Chinese Government sent at once a protest to the Italian Embassy in China and a copy of it to the Secretary General of the League of Nations.[7] The protest stressed that Italy's action was

in contravention of the Washington Nine Power Treaty of February 6, 1922, to which Italy is a party, and inconsistent with the provisions of the Covenant of the League of Nations and the resolutions repeatedly adopted by the League of Nations in regard to the Sino-Japanese controversy.

Subsequently, the following States recognized Manchukuo: Spain on December 2, 1937; [8] Germany in January, 1938; [9] Poland in October, 1938, soon after she had joined Germany in the dismemberment of the Czechoslovak Republic; [10]

5 *Ibid.* XXXIII 376
6 *Ibid.* XXXV 3
7 *LNOJ* 1938, 11
8 32 *AJIL* 359
9 15 *Bull. Int. News* 192
10 *Ibid.* 1037

Hungary in January, 1939;[11] Rumania on December 4, 1939 (the day on which the German-Rumanian trade agreement was signed) ;[12] and Finland on July 19, 1941,[13] after she had entered the German-Soviet war on Germany's side. The other Members of the League of Nations withheld recognition, including Great Britain in spite of her divergent attitude in other cases of aggression.

From the Soviet Government the Manchurian puppet state never secured a direct statement of recognition. On April 13, 1941, however, the Soviet Union concluded with Japan a Non-Aggression Treaty [14] to which the following "Frontier Declaration" was annexed:

The contracting Parties solemnly declare that the U.S.S.R. pledges itself to respect the territorial integrity and inviolability of Manchutikuo, and Japan pledges itself to respect the territorial integrity and inviolability of the Mongolian People's Republic.

It is hard not to see in this declaration a recognition of Manchukuo; yet the roundabout way the Soviet Government took demonstrated once more that it regarded the new State as a mere Japanese puppet.

On December 7, 1941, Japan attacked the United States in exactly the same way as she had attacked Russia in 1904. War was declared not only by the United States and Great Britain, but also by China. On December 9, 1941, the Chinese Government issued the following statement:

The Chinese Government hereby formally declares war on Japan. . . . The Chinese Government further declares that all treaties, conventions and contracts concerning the relations between China and Japan are and remain null and void.[15]

Thus, the anomalous status of undeclared warfare, which had prevailed in wide areas of the Chinese Republic ever since 1937, had come to an end. China became a member of the Grand Alliance and joined the United Nations. This opened the way to a resettlement of old territorial scores. In anticipation, as it were, of future decisions the United

[11] 33 *AJIL* 366
[12] 35 *AJIL* 373
[13] *Ibid.* 680
[14] 12 *D. S. Bull.* 812
[15] 5 *D. S. Bull.* 506

States Attorney General issued on February 9, 1942, an order to the effect that Koreans who had registered as such and not as Japanese during the alien registration of 1940 were exempted from the restrictions in force for enemy aliens, and that those who had involuntarily or mistakenly stated their nationality as Japanese were to be given an opportunity for reclassification.[16] The territorial war aims of the Allies regarding Japan, however, were not defined until the following year when at the end of the Cairo Conference [17] the following statement was issued:

. . . .

The three great Allies are fighting this war to restrain and punish the aggression of Japan.

They covet no gains for themselves and have no thought of territorial expansion.

It is their purpose that Japan shall be stripped of all the islands in the Pacific which she has seized or occupied since the beginning of the first World War in 1914, and that all the territories Japan has stolen from the Chinese, such as Manchuria, Formosa and the Pescadores, shall be restored to the Republic of China.

Japan will also be expelled from all other territories which she has taken by violence and greed.

The aforesaid three Great Powers, mindful of the enslavement of the people of Korea, are determined that in due course Korea shall become free and independent.

With these objects in view, the three Allies, in harmony with those of the United Nations at war with Japan, will continue to persevere in the serious and prolonged operations necessary to procure the unconditional surrender of Japan.[18]

The strategic councils of the Allies decided to press the war in Europe first, and not hurl their full might against Japan until Germany had been crushed. As the slow but steady advance of the Allied armies from the west, south, and east against the core of the German-held territory left no doubt of the impending doom of the Teuton, speculation arose whether at a later stage the Soviet Union would join in the war against Japan. The communiqué released at the close of the Crimea Conference, held at Yalta in February, 1945,[19] made no mention of the Far Eastern issue. The

16 Below, 170, n. 44
17 Above, 84
18 9 D. S. Bull. 393
19 Below, 187

Soviet-Japanese Non-Aggression Treaty of April 13, 1941, was then still in force since it had been concluded for a period of five years. Under its Article Three, in case neither of the Contracting Parties denounced the pact one year before the lapse of that term, it was to be considered prolonged for the next five years. On April 5, 1945, however, the Soviet Government denounced the pact,[20] thus barring its automatic renewal. But the treaty had still to run until April 13, 1946. Yet within little more than a month, on May 8, 1945, Germany surrendered unconditionally.[21] Had now the time come for the Soviet Union to enter the war in the Far East? While columnists and radio commentators outside the Soviet Union indulged in the usual comments and predictions, no official statement was forthcoming. Public opinion was largely focussed on the Far Eastern situation. This state of affairs prompted the United States Government to the following announcement, released on June 8, 1945:

In view of increased public interest in Korean affairs, . . . this is a proper occasion to review certain aspects of this Government's policy with respect to Korea and the Koreans.

There have been persistent rumors that an agreement concerning Korea was made at Yalta committing this Government to a policy contrary to the Cairo Declaration. These reports have already been denied by officers of the Department in reply to inquiries received. Various Korean leaders in China as well as in the United States have recognized that these rumors are baseless. The Cairo Declaration of December 1, 1943, included the statement that the three signatory powers, China, the United States, and Great Britain, "mindful of the enslavement of the people of Korea, are determined that in due course Korea shall become free and independent." There has been no change in this Government's intention to fulfill its commitments under the Cairo Declaration. . . .[22]

On July 17, 1945, the President of the United States of America, Harry S. Truman, the Chairman of the Council of People's Commissars of the Union of Soviet Socialist Republics, Generalissimo Stalin, and the Prime Minister of the United Kingdom, Winston S. Churchill, met in conference at Potsdam, Germany. The conference was interrupted

[20] 12 *D. S. Bull.* 811
[21] *Ibid.* 885
[22] *Ibid.* 1058

on July 25 for two days while the results of the British general elections were declared. On July 26 a Proclamation Defining Terms for Japanese Surrender was released, signed by the President of the United States and Prime Minister Churchill and concurred in by the President of the National Government of China, Generalissimo Chiang Kai-shek, who communicated with President Truman by dispatch.[23] The Proclamation fixed the military terms the acceptance of which was demanded of Japan, and provided further that

(8) The terms of the Cairo Declaration shall be carried out and Japanese sovereignty shall be limited to the islands of Honshu, Hokkaido, Kyushu, Shikoku and such minor islands as we determine.

The Soviet Government had not participated in the Proclamation. The conference was resumed on July 28; in the meantime Mr. Churchill, having lost his majority at the elections, had resigned and the leader of the opposition, Mr. Clement Attlee, returned to Potsdam as Great Britain's new Prime Minister. The conference ended on August 2, 1945. On the same day a report on its results was released, known as the Declaration of Potsdam.[24] Signed by the representatives of the Soviet Union, the United States, and Great Britain, it was silent on the Far Eastern war. Yet a few days later, on August 8, 1945, the Soviet Government announced that it had transmitted the following Declaration to the Japanese Government:

After the defeat and surrender of Hitlerite Germany, Japan is the only Great Power which still stands for the continuation of the war. The demand of the three Powers—the United States of America, Great Britain and China—of July 26 this year for the unconditional surrender of the Japanese Armed Forces, has been declined by Japan. Thus the proposal of the Japanese Government addressed to the Soviet Union on mediation in the Far Eastern war becomes groundless.

Taking into consideration Japan's refusal to surrender, the Allies proposed to the Soviet Government that it join the war against Japanese aggression and thus shorten the duration of the war, reduce the number of victims and facilitate the earliest restoration of general peace.

The Soviet Government, true to its duty to its Allies, has ac-

23 13 *D. S. Bull.* 137
24 *Ibid.* 153

cepted the Allies' proposal and has joined the declaration of the Allied Powers of July 26 this year. The Soviet Government considers that this policy is the only means capable of bringing peace nearer, relieving the peoples of further sacrifices and sufferings and enabling the Japanese people to avoid those dangers and destruction which Germany suffered after her refusal to surrender unconditionally.

In view of the above, the Soviet Government declares that from tomorrow, i.e., from August 9, the Soviet Union will consider itself in a state of war with Japan.[25]

By accepting the Allied Declaration of July 26, 1945, the Soviet Union had become a party to the Cairo Declaration and in particular to its pledges regarding Korea. The rapid advance of the Far Eastern Soviet forces and the use of the newly invented atomic bomb by the Americans brought Japan within a few days to her knees. The official surrender document, however, was not signed until September 1, 1945.[26]

Meanwhile, on August 14, 1945, a Treaty of Friendship and Alliance had been concluded at Moscow between the Soviet Government and the National Government of the Chinese Republic.[27] It remains in force (Art. VIII) for a period of thirty years and thereafter, unless terminated by giving one year's notice, for an unlimited period.

The Treaty was implemented by an exchange of notes between the Soviet People's Commissar for Foreign Affairs, Mr. Molotov, and the Chinese Minister for Foreign Affairs, Mr. Wang Shih-tse.[28] Mr. Molotov wrote:

Your Excellency,   August 14, 1945
With reference to the Treaty of Friendship and Alliance signed today between the Republic of China and the U.S.S.R., I have the honor to put on record the understanding between the High Contracting Parties as follows:

1. In accordance with the spirit of the aforementioned Treaty, and in order to put into effect its aims and purposes, the Government of the U.S.S.R. agrees to render to China moral support and aid in military supplies and other material resources, such support and aid to be entirely given to the National Government as the central government of China.

[25] 5 *Un. Nat. Rev.* 228
[26] 13 *D. S. Bull.* 299
[27] 14 *D. S. Bull.* 201
[28] *Ibid.* 204

2. In the course of conversations regarding Dairen and Port Arthur and regarding the joint operation of the Changchun Railway, the Government of the U.S.S.R. regarded the Three Eastern Provinces as part of China and reaffirmed its respect for China's full sovereignty over the Three Eastern Provinces and recognize their territorial and administrative integrity.

3. As for the recent developments in Sinkiang the Soviet Government confirms that, as stated in Article V of the Treaty of Friendship and Alliance, it has no intention of interfering in the internal affairs of China.

If your Excellency will be so good as to confirm that the understanding is correct as set forth in the preceding paragraphs, the present note and your Excellency's reply thereto will constitute a part of the aforementioned Treaty of Friendship and Alliance. . . .

In his reply note the Chinese Foreign Minister declared his full agreement with Mr. Molotov's letter. This exchange of notes canceled whatever recognition had been granted to the Manchurian puppet state by the Soviet Government.

Annexed to the Treaty were the following four Agreements:

(1) An "Agreement concerning Dairen" [29] declaring that city a free port for the trading and shipping of all countries.

(2) An "Agreement on Port Arthur" [30] under which the latter is to be jointly utilized for a period of thirty years as a naval base solely by the Soviet Union and the Republic of China, the defense being provided by the former, the civil administration by the latter.

(3) An "Agreement regarding relations between the Chinese administration and the Commander-in-Chief of the Soviet Forces after the entry of Soviet troops into the Three Eastern Provinces of China during the present joint military operations against Japan." [31] It provided that (Article 5)

As soon as any part of the liberated territory ceases to be a zone of immediate military operations, the Chinese National Government will assume full authority in the direction of public affairs and will render the Commander-in-Chief of the Soviet forces every assistance and support through its civil and military bodies.

29 *Ibid.* 205
30 *Ibid.*
31 *Ibid.* 206

(4) An "Agreement concerning the Chinese Changchun Railway." [32] It provided that the main trunk line of the Chinese Eastern Railway from Manchouli to Suifenho and the South Manchuria Railway from Kharbin to Dairen and Port Arthur should be united into one railway system under the name of "Chinese Changchun Railway," to be jointly owned and jointly operated by the Republic of China and the Soviet Union for a term of thirty years. After the expiration of this term the railway with all its properties shall be transferred without compensation to the ownership of the Republic of China.

At this writing Chinese sovereignty over Manchuria is fully restored, subject to the contest between the rivaling Chinese factions. As to Korea, the realization of the promises of the Cairo Conference seems still far away. At a conference, held by the Foreign Ministers of the United States, the Soviet Union, and Great Britain at Moscow in December, 1945, it was agreed to set up for a period not to exceed five years a joint trusteeship of these three Powers and China with the object of preparing Korea for her ultimate independence.[33] Little headway, if any, however, has been made so far toward this goal, and Korea is still governed by Soviet military occupation in the north, by American military occupation in the south, without prospect for an early unification of the two zones.

[32] *Ibid.* 207
[33] 13 *D. S. Bull.* 1030

CHAPTER XXI

ETHIOPIA

I_N the Manchurian case the aggressor had attacked with limited aims, namely, in order to wrest from the victim three provinces, and had refrained from open annexation, establishing instead a puppet state in the occupied territory. No such restraint was used by the Italian Government in its action against Ethiopia where outright annexation of the whole territory was the avowed goal.

On October 3, 1935, the Italian Government informed the League Council "that the warlike and aggressive spirit in Ethiopia had succeeded in imposing war against Italy." [1] On the same day the Ethiopian Government notified the Council that Italian airplanes had bombarded Ethiopian towns, that a battle was in progress on Ethiopian territory, and that these facts involved a violation of the frontiers of the Empire and a breach of the Covenant by Italian aggression.[2]

Both parties to the conflict being League Members, the bodies of the League had to take action. On October 9, 1935, the League Assembly adopted the following resolution:

> The Assembly . . .
> Taking into consideration the obligations which rest upon the Members of the League in virtue of Article 16 of the Covenant and the desirability of co-ordination of the measures which they may severally contemplate;
> Recommends to the Members of the League (other than the Parties) to set up a committee . . . to consider and facilitate the co-ordination of such measures. . . .[3]

The work of "co-ordinating the sanctions" led within a few months to the conquest of most of Ethiopia. On May 2, 1936, the Emperor left his country.[4] On May 5, Italian

---

[1] *LNOJ* 1935, 1613
[2] *Ibid.*
[3] *LNOJ*, Spec. Suppl. 138, 109, 114
[4] 12 *Bull. Int. News* 838

troops entered Addis Ababa, the Ethiopian capital. On
May 9 the King of Italy signed a decree-law of which
Article 1 read:

The territories and peoples which belonged to the Empire of
Ethiopia are placed under the full and entire sovereignty of the
Kingdom of Italy. The title of Emperor of Ethiopia is assumed by
the King of Italy for himself and his successors.[5]

These developments brought the issue of non-recognition
to the fore. On May 10, 1936, the Emperor of Ethiopia
sent to the Secretary General of the League a telegram
asking the League of Nations

to pursue its efforts to ensure the respect of the Covenant and to
decide not to recognize territorial extensions or the exercise of an
alleged sovereignty resulting from illegal recourse to armed force
and many other violations of international obligations.[6]

The following day, the League Council met at Geneva.
Since the Italian representative had announced that he
would make a statement as to the placing of the Italo-Ethiopian dispute on the agenda the Ethiopian representative
was invited to attend. The former stated that the Italian
delegation could not agree to the "self-styled" Ethiopian
representative's presence. He added:

Nothing resembling an organized Ethiopian State exists. The
only sovereignty in Ethiopia is Italian sovereignty. Any discussion
on a dispute between Ethiopia and Italy would accordingly be
pointless. I am bound, therefore, not to take part in it.[7]

Thereupon he left the Council room. On the following
morning the Italian delegation was recalled to Rome; it
never returned to Geneva. The same day—May 12—the
League Council adopted a resolution reading as follows:

The Council . . .
Recalls the conclusions reached and the decisions taken in the
matter in the League of Nations since October 3d, 1935,
Is of opinion that further time is necessary to permit its members
to consider the situation created by the grave new steps taken by the
Italian Government;
Decides to resume its deliberations on this subject on June 15th,

[5] *LNOJ*, Spec. Suppl. 151, 82
[6] *LNOJ* 1936, 660
[7] *Ibid.* 535

And considers that, in the meantime, there is no cause for modi-
fying the measures previously adopted in collaboration by the
Members of the League.[8]

On June 2, 1936, the Argentine Government asked that
the Assembly be convened, and expressed the view that the
latter should examine "the situation brought about by the
annexation of Ethiopia and also the position in regard to
the sanctions enacted by the League." The Assembly was
convened for June 30, and the session of the Council postponed until June 26.[9] On that day the Ethiopian delegation
sent to the Secretary General of the League, Mr. Avenol, a
letter stating that about half of the Ethiopian territory was
still unoccupied and under the control of a government appointed by the Emperor, and that the latter "affirms the
will of the Ethiopian Empire, a Member of the League of
Nations, to protest yet once more against the aggression
of which it has been the victim, and to claim at all times and
all places . . . respect for its territorial integrity and political
independence." [10]

The Assembly met on June 30; the Italian delegation
kept away, and nobody denied the Ethiopian delegation the
right to participate; in particular no doubts were raised
regarding the validity of its credentials.[11] The only real
purpose of the session, however, was to bring the sanctions
to an end. On July 4, 1936, the League Assembly adopted
with 44 votes against the vote of Ethiopia, 24 Members
abstaining, a resolution [12] recommending "that the Co-ordination Committee should make all necessary proposals to
the Governments in order to bring to an end the measures
taken by them in execution of Article 16 of the Covenant."

The preamble of the resolution contained the following
paragraphs:

(3) Noting that various circumstances have prevented the full
application of the Covenant of the League of Nations;
(4) Remaining firmly attached to the principles of the Covenant,

[8] *Ibid.* 540
[9] *LNOJ*, Spec. Suppl. 151, 82, n. 4
[10] *LNOJ* 1936. 782
[11] *LNOJ*, Spec. Suppl. 151, 18 (Report of the Committee on Credentials)
[12] *Ibid.* 65

which are also expressed in other diplomatic instruments such as the declaration of the American states, dated August 3, 1932, excluding the settlement of territorial questions by force; . . .

The day before the vote on this resolution was taken, the Ethiopian delegation had submitted two draft resolutions,[13] the first to the effect that

The Assembly recalls the terms of Articles 10 and 16, to which it declares its faithful adherence. Accordingly, it proclaims that it will recognize no annexation obtained by force.

The second recommended that the governments of the Member States give their guarantee to an Ethiopian loan.

The first resolution was not even brought to a vote. The President of the Assembly, Mr. van Zeland (Belgium), stressed a passage in the report of the General Committee to the effect that the resolution adopted by the Assembly "in one of its parts . . . relates, taking into account the views expressed in the debate, to the question which forms the subject of the first draft resolution of the Ethiopian delegation." [14] The second resolution was voted down by 23 against the Ethiopian vote, 25 Members abstaining.

The question whether Italy's conquest had ended Ethiopia's League Membership was raised by the Committee on Credentials at the next Assembly meeting, held in September, 1936. On September 23, the rapporteur of the Committee, Mr. Politis (Greece), reported that in view of the conditions prevailing in Ethiopia the Committee was confronted with the question whether the Head of the State from which the credentials of the Ethiopian delegation emanated "was exercising his legal title effectively enough to make those credentials perfectly in order." He proposed that the Assembly should consider the credentials submitted by the Ethiopian delegation, "despite the doubt as to their regularity," as sufficient to permit that delegation to sit at the present session. This, he said, would have the advantage that nothing would be done "to prejudice the future." His proposal was adopted with 39 votes against the votes of Italy's satellites (Austria, Hungary, and Albania) and Ecuador.[15] Thus, the

[13] *Ibid.* 60
[14] *Ibid.* 68
[15] *LNOJ*, Spec. Suppl. 155, 40-1

question whether conquest ended League Membership was dodged once more.

The issue of non-recognition, however, was taken up by Members of the British Parliament. On December 16, 1936, Mr. Noel-Baker asked the Secretary of State for Foreign Affairs

whether His Majesty's Government still adhere to the declaration made by the Committee of Twelve of the League Council on 16th February, 1932,[16] to the effect that no infringement of the territorial integrity and no change in the political independence of any Member of the League brought about in disregard of the Covenant ought to be recognized as valid and effectual by the Members of the League, and whether the principle thus expressed will guide their action with regard to Abyssinia.[17]

Mr. Eden replied that the Government adhered to the principle enunciated in the declaration, but must in Manchuria and elsewhere enter into such negotiations with the authorities on the spot "as are necessary to protect British interests." During the same session Mr. Leach asked the Foreign Secretary whether the Government had the intention to resist efforts at Geneva to recognize the Italian conquest of Abyssinia or to exclude Abyssinia from the League. To this Mr. Eden replied:

The question of the position of Abyssinia in relation to the League is not likely to arise before the next meeting of the Assembly, and when it does it will be for the Assembly to deal with it in the light of the circumstances as they then exist.[18]

Further asked by Miss Rathbone whether it was proposed to replace the Legation in Addis Ababa by a Consulate General, and whether this would imply the recognition of any change in the status of Abyssinia, consequent upon Italy's successful aggression, the Foreign Secretary replied:

The question of British representation in occupied Abyssinia has been for some time under consideration with special reference to the problems arising from the retention of a diplomatic mission accredited to a Government which no longer exercises any local authority. In any case it is not the intention of His Majesty's

16 Above, 61
17 318 *H. C. Deb.* 2432
18 *Ibid.* 2438

Government to accord de jure recognition of the annexation of Abyssinia.[19]

The Members who received these answers would probably have been somewhat surprised had they also been informed that at the very time when these discussions took place at Westminster, Downing Street had already made up its mind to accord to the Italian conquest "de facto recognition."

This was revealed a few months later in a law suit before the Chancery Division of the Supreme Court of Judicature. The issue underlying the case of *Bank of Ethiopia v. National Bank of Egypt and Liguori* [20] was the validity of an Italian decree dated June 20, 1936, by which the Bank of Ethiopia was dissolved and a liquidator appointed. The court, in accordance with British practice, inquired about the British Government's position regarding Italian sovereignty in Ethiopia. Thereupon a certificate from the Foreign Office was put before the judge stating that "in December, 1936, the British Government recognized the Italian Government as being in fact (de facto) the government of the area of Abyssinia then under Italian control." [21] It needs little acumen to see from this very statement that the British Government itself considered at that time the conquest of Abyssinia as not completed (". . . the area . . . then under Italian control"). Consequently, the correct answer would have been that the Italian army was in belligerent occupation of portions of Abyssinia. Instead, the British Government used a language which could quite well be construed as implying the de facto recognition of Italian sovereignty over the occupied portions of the victim of Italian aggression. That this was really the intention of His Majesty's Government may be inferred not only from its subsequent behavior, but also from the following statement, made by the Under-Secretary of State for Foreign Affairs, Mr. Butler, in the House of Commons on March 17, 1938:

His Majesty's Government have, since December, 1936, recognized the Italian Government as the Government de facto of the parts of Abyssinia which they control. From time to time the Sec-

[19] *Ibid.* 2439
[20] *Law Reports, Chancery Division* (1937), 513
[21] *Ibid.* 519

retary of State for Foreign Affairs has, in the course of the past
year, been asked for statements to produce in His Majesty's Courts
of Justice in connection with certain law suits in which the status
of Abyssinia has been involved. The first of such statements was
made on the 28th April, 1937, to the effect that, while detailed
information was hard to obtain, such information as His Majesty's
Government possessed tended to show that the Italian Government
controlled the whole of Abyssinia with the exception of certain
areas in the south and southwest of the country; that His Majesty's
Government regarded the Italian Government as the Government
de facto of the parts of Abyssinia which they controlled; and that
while it was difficult to fix a specific date on which His Majesty's
Government first accorded this measure of recognition to the Italian
position in Abyssinia, it might be said that that position had been
reached in the second half of December, 1936.

The last of these statements was made on the 29th December,
1937, when the Secretary of State for Foreign Affairs repeated
that His Majesty's Government recognized the Italian Government as the Government de facto of the parts of Abyssinia which
they controlled; that according to information in the possession of
His Majesty's Government the Italian Government were then in
control of virtually the whole of Abyssinia; and that therefore
His Majesty's Government recognized the Italian Government as
the Government de facto of virtually the whole of the country. No
later statement by His Majesty's Government on the particular
point at issue has been made.[22]

The verbiage in which Mr. Butler's statement was
couched, especially the words, "accorded this measure of
recognition to the Italian position in Abyssinia," would
appear to reveal with sufficient clearness the intention to
grant de facto recognition of Italian sovereignty over the
occupied parts of the country; for in order merely to inform the courts that the belligerent occupant had established
effective control over parts of the enemy country, no such
language was needed. Therefore, the circumlocution resorted to by the British Foreign Office is hardly apt to con-
ceal the fact that His Majesty's Government was not willing
to live up to its duties under Article 10 of the Covenant,
which would have required an unequivocal statement of non-
recognition, and not even to the duties under customary
international law which bars the annexation—and consequently also the recognition of the annexation—of enemy
territory before the enemy is completely subjugated. The

[22] 333 *H. C. Deb.* 617

court, of course, was bound by the decision of the political branch of the Government; consequently Judge Clauson dismissed the action for not having been brought by the liquidator's authority.[23]

During the year 1937 the Ethiopian delegation did not participate in the sessions of the Assembly. In notifying the Secretary General to this effect, the Emperor of Ethiopia never failed to stress the continuing membership of his country in the League of Nations.[24]

The action of the British Government was the prelude to the recognition of the Italian annexation by a series of other League Members.[25] On January 5, 1938, the Italian Government issued a semi-official statement boasting that already seventeen States, most of them League Members, had granted de jure recognition, and eleven, among them Great Britain and France, but not the Soviet Union, de facto recognition of the annexation.[26] The majority of the League Members, however, were still withholding it. Great Britain was not yet willing to take the last step. On February 21, 1938, the Prime Minister told the House of Commons that he had always taken the view "that the question of the formal recognition of the Italian position in Abyssinia was one that could only be morally justified if it was found to be a factor, and an essential factor, in a general appeasement." [27] But soon Mr. Chamberlain resolved to take further steps in order to appease the Italian dictator. The British Government entered into negotiations with Italy for a general "settlement" of their relations. By the beginning of April they were ready to sign an agreement including the grant of full recognition to Italian sovereignty in Ethiopia.

Opposition, however, was to be expected from certain League quarters. The British Government devised a plan to eliminate it. On April 9, 1938, the Foreign Secretary dispatched the following letter to the Secretary General of the League:

[23] J. Clauson's decision has since been subjected to vigorous criticism by Sir Arnold D. McNair (*Legal Effects of War*, 2 ed., 340-1)
[24] Letters of May 23 and September 10, 1937 (*LNOJ* 1937, 604 and 658)
[25] They were enumerated in a statement made by Mr. Butler in the House of Commons on June 29, 1938. (337 *H. C. Deb.* 1890)
[26] 32 *AJIL* 361
[27] 332 *H. C. Deb.* 58

I am directed . . . to inform you that His Majesty's Government in the United Kingdom have had under consideration the anomalous situation arising from the fact that many States Members of the League, including no less than five of the States represented on the Council, recognize that the Italian Government exercise sovereignty over Ethiopia or have taken action implying such recognition, whereas other States Members of the League have not done so.

His Majesty's Government in the United Kingdom are of opinion that this situation should be clarified, and I am therefore to request that you will include in the agenda for the forthcoming session of the Council the question of the "consequences arising out of the existing situation in Ethiopia." [28]

On April 16, 1938, a British-Italian Agreement was signed in Rome; [29] its stipulations implicitly amounted to the full recognition of Italian sovereignty over Ethiopia. Its details are not of interest for the subject of this work. Significant, however, was the following note of the same day from the British Ambassador in Rome to the Italian Foreign Minister:

I have . . . the honor to inform your Excellency that His Majesty's Government, being desirous that such obstacles as may at present be held to impede the freedom of Member States as regards recognition of Italian sovereignty over Ethiopia should be removed, intend to take steps at the forthcoming meeting of the Council of the League of Nations for the purpose of clarifying the situation of Member States in this regard. [30]

The League Council was convened for May 9. The British Government, in order to confront Geneva with a sort of fait accompli, submitted the Italian agreement at once to Parliament with the motion "that the House approve the results of the recent Anglo-Italian conversations as contained in the Agreement signed Rome April 16, 1938." [31] The debate in the House of Commons took place on May 2, and in the House of Lords on the following day. In the Commons the Prime Minister made a speech in which he purported to stand by the Covenant. After recalling his statement of February 21, 1938, he said:

[28] *LNOJ* 1938, 535
[29] *Doc. Int. Aff.* 1938, I 141
[30] *Ibid.* 150
[31] 335 *H. C. Deb.* 534

With regard to the question of recognition of the Italian conquest of Ethiopia, I would like to remind the House that a number of different States Members of the League whose loyalty to the League cannot be questioned, have taken a different view on this matter from that held by His Majesty's Government. They have taken the view that collective obligations in this matter were discharged on 4th July, 1936, when the League Assembly passed a resolution abolishing the sanctions. It is their view, therefore, that States Members were consequently free to take whatever action seemed good to them in the light of their own situation and what they considered to be their own obligations . . .

His Majesty's Government do not desire to criticize any States who have taken that view, but so far as they are concerned they, in common with many others, have held that this is not a question which concerns ourselves alone, but that it is one which requires consideration by the appropriate organ of the League. . . .

His Majesty's Government have taken the first step toward clarification by asking the Secretary General to place an item dealing with this question on the agenda of the forthcoming meeting of the Council. . . .[32]

The speakers of the opposition could not be appeased by the alleged loyalty to the Covenant. Said Mr. Morrison:

[The] Agreement includes the proposed recognition of Abyssinia as an Italian possession. . . . It really constitutes a double shame to the honor of our country, a double disgrace to the British name in the eyes of the world. It constitutes the ethics of the double cross. . . . It is a breach of the Covenant, in Article 10 . . . It is impossible to reconcile it with the previous decisions of the Council and the Assembly at Geneva. It is contrary to International Law accepted by the United States and other American States. It is unjustified by the facts of the situation in Abyssinia. . . . This is not an instrument of peace, but of moral dissolution.[33]

Sir Archibald Sinclair's opinion was that "unless the Assembly unanimously decide to withdraw recognition from Haile Selassie, he will remain Emperor of Abyssinia in the eyes of the League." [34]

The speeches of the opposition accomplished nothing; both Houses approved the agreement. After this prelude in Westminster the scene shifted to Geneva. The Council met on May 9, 1938. Already on April 21, 1938, the Emperor

[32] *Ibid.* 542
[33] *Ibid.* 555
[34] *Ibid.* 572

of Ethiopia, having learned that the Ethiopian question would be on the agenda of the session, had announced that his country would be represented; his communication was duly acknowledged by the Secretary General of the League.[35]

The first meeting and part of the second (May 9 and 10) were private.[36] During the public part of the latter—the Ethiopian delegates not being present as yet—the British representative, Foreign Secretary Lord Halifax, made a statement regarding the Anglo-Italian Agreement.[37] He called it a step toward the aim of the Covenant, namely, the maintenance of peace in this distracted world. The name of Ethiopia was not even mentioned; on the contrary, Lord Halifax asserted that the agreement "might be said to deal solely with Anglo-Italian affairs." The representatives of France, Rumania, Belgium, and Poland paid their tribute to the noble cause embodied in the agreement. Less optimistic was the representative of the U.S.S.R., Mr. Litvinov. He cautioned that

In dealing with bilateral pacts we have to take into consideration, not only their effect upon the relationship between the two parties concerned, but also upon the relations between those parties and the rest of the world. We have also to take into consideration the effect which such agreements may have on those problems which are still before the League and which are still to be dealt with. We therefore reserve our final judgment upon the importance of the Anglo-Italian Agreement from this point of view. . . .[38]

The Ethiopian question was officially taken up by the Council on May 12. What was schemed cannot be seen from its minutes; but it can be surmised from the subsequent debates in the House of Commons. What really happened was, according to the minutes, this: At the opening of the meeting the Ethiopian delegation, headed by Emperor Haile Selassie, came to the Council table, and was duly admitted. Lord Halifax spoke first. After rehearsing the content of the letter of April 9, 1938, and repeating what Mr. Chamberlain had told the Commons on May 2, 1938, he said:

[35] *LNOJ* 1938, 535
[36] Dell's book *The Geneva Racket* claims to give an account of these private meetings and their antecedents.
[37] *LNOJ* 1938, 305
[38] *Ibid.* 306

His Majesty's Government appreciates that it was open to Members of the League to regard the Assembly resolution of July 4, 1936, as closing the question in so far as they were concerned, and having regard to the action taken by so many States which are perfectly loyal to the League, His Majesty's Government does not think that the various steps which the League has taken in the course of the Italo-Ethiopian dispute can be held to constitute any binding obligation upon Member States to withhold recognition until a unanimous decision has been taken.

Accordingly, I think it right plainly to state the view of His Majesty's Government that the situation is one in which Members of the League may, without disloyalty, take such action at such time as may seem to them appropriate.[39]

From the wish for "clarification" expressed in the letter of April 9 to the Secretary General, in the note of April 16 to Count Ciano, and in Mr. Chamberlain's speech of May 2, one might have anticipated that the British Council member would move that some definite step be taken. Instead, Lord Halifax announced that he was not asking for decisions on questions of principle, nor suggesting that the Council should impose on any Member of the League a particular course of action. Why, then, had the British Government asked the Secretary General of the League to place the Ethiopian question on the agenda? Lord Halifax gave for this the following explanation:

My Government hopes . . . that Members of the Council will share its opinion, that the question of the recognition of Italy's position in Ethiopia is one for each Member of the League to decide for itself in the light of its own situation and its own obligation.[40]

The ensuing discussion was inaugurated by the Emperor of Ethiopia.[41] In a dramatic appeal, read in his place by Mr. Ato Taezaz, he predicted with almost prophetic vision the events of the following years. In strong words he denounced those League Members who had granted recognition to the Italian conquest.

Since 1935, Ethiopia has observed with sorrow how, one after another, the signatures affixed to the Covenant have been denied. A number of Powers, themselves threatened by aggression and realizing their own weakness, have abandoned Ethiopia. Their cry

[39] *Ibid.* 334
[40] *Ibid.* 335
[41] *Ibid.*

has been "Sauve qui peut," the cry of the panic-stricken and de-moralized. They have torn up the treaties which ensured their independence—Non-Aggression Treaties, the Covenant of the League of Nations, the Pact of Paris. By what right can they ever invoke such undertakings, if they treat the agreements they have signed as mere scraps of paper.[42]

Then the Emperor proceeded to discuss the intentions of the British Government: He asserted that the real purpose of its action was to ensure the execution of the note of April 16, 1938, by asking the Council to set aside "the protective rule" laid down by the Assembly of the League of Nations on March 11, 1932, and confirmed by the Assembly on July 4, 1936. He continued:

That is how it is proposed to treat the principles of international law and Article 10 of the Covenant. . . .

Yet non-recognition of a conquest by aggression is the least onerous way of observing Article 10, since it calls for nothing more than a passive attitude requiring no national sacrifice on the part of Member States, involving them in no risk of war or reprisals.

But it would seem that even this passive attitude has become too exacting for the Governments which, in order to resume with Rome what they describe as normal diplomatic relations, have felt impelled to protest—in varying forms, but always unsatisfactorily—their fidelity to the principle of non-recognition of territorial gains acquired by force. Today it is the callous abandonment of that principle which is contemplated and, apparently, even urged by the powerful British Empire. . . .

To attenuate this flagrant violation of the Covenant, the suggestion today before the Council is based on the de facto situation at present prevailing in Ethiopia.

Even were it true—which it is not—that the invader has broken my people's resistance; even if he were effectively occupying and administering the territory of my Empire—and he does not—even in such circumstances, the proposal before the Council should be unhesitatingly rejected. Was not the principle proclaimed by the United States of North America some years ago—namely, its refusal to grant legal recognition to the results of aggression—hailed throughout the world as one of the most important advances in the realm of international law and as a signal contribution to the organization of peace between the nations? . . .

It is unhappily true that my people cannot at present expect any material assistance from the States Members of the League.

[42] The day before (May 11, 1938), Mr. Butler, when questioned by Miss Rathbone, had informed the House of Commons of the status of recognition of the Ethiopian conquest. (335 H. C. Deb. 1607)

But I am at least entitled to ask that the rights of my people should continue to be recognized, and that, while awaiting the hour of divine justice, Ethiopia should remain in your midst as the living symbol of violated right. . . .

Concluding, the Emperor denied the competence of the Council in the matter, asserting that the competent body was none but the League Assembly. On this point, he invoked the authority of the statement Mr. Eden had made in the Commons on December 16, 1936,[43] and protested "against any procedural subtlety designed to evade the definite rules on the subject of competence embodied in the Covenant."

The speaker who followed, Mr. Bonnet, associated himself with the British Government in expressing "the desire for general recognition of the fact that circumstances henceforward entitle every State Member to judge for itself as to the decision to be taken." [44]

The plans of the British Government were disturbed by the representative of the Soviet Union. His remarks on non-recognition are highly significant. Said Maxim Litvinov:

Among the means for combating aggression and defending its Members which the League has at its disposal, non-recognition does not by any means play a conspicuous part. It is improbable that anyone would assert that the mere threat of non-recognition may avert aggression, or that non-recognition itself might free the victim of aggression from the grip of the conqueror. . . .

It would be quite wrong, however, to assert that resolutions on non-recognition are in themselves devoid of any particular value. While such resolutions have in every case a certain moral significance, and give satisfaction to public opinion, they also cause the aggressor some preoccupations and inconveniences, as is evidenced by the efforts which aggressors usually make to obtain recognition of their conquests, if only in an indirect way.

But, according to circumstances, non-recognition may be of vast importance, not only morally, but also politically—particularly when the victim of aggression itself continues to fight for its independence and for the integrity of its territory. In such cases, the recognition of the results of acts of violent aggression, or the abandonment of the policy of non-recognition, would be equivalent to abetting the aggressor directly, and to stabbing his victim in the back by discouraging and demoralising him. We have to reckon,

[43] Above, 136
[44] *LNOJ* 1938, 339

not only with the question whether any struggle between the aggressor and his victims has come to an end, but also—should that have occurred for the time being—whether there are chances of the struggle being renewed, and likewise we have to reckon with other circumstances which may bring about a change in the situation created by aggressive acts of violence.[45]

Then Mr. Litvinov turned to the legal aspect of the question:

Whatever the decision on the question before us, and whatever the conclusions which individual States will think it necessary to draw, on their own responsibility, from our discussion, one thing must be clear: The League of Nations has not changed its view of those actions which resulted in an Ethiopian problem arising within the League, and none of the condemnations of such activities adopted by the League is withdrawn. It must be made even more clear that the League of Nations has not changed its opinion on the general principle of non-recognition of the accomplished fact produced by aggression, and on the appropriate resolutions adopted by the League in other cases. The latter particularly applies in cases where the States which have been the victims of attack have aroused the amazement and admiration of the world by the valiance of their citizens who continue to fight the aggressor with unweakening energy, obstinacy and fortitude. It must be clear that the League of Nations has no intention of changing its attitude, whether to the direct seizure and annexation of other people's territory, or to those cases where such annexations are camouflaged by the setting-up of puppet "national" governments, allegedly independent, but in reality serving merely as a screen for, and an agency of, the foreign invader.

I have still to remark briefly on the other aspects of the question which I have mentioned. When the United Kingdom Government puts forward its motion to grant freedom of action to all League Members, it bases its principal argument on the fact that many Members of the League, in violation of League resolutions, have already taken steps towards recognizing the annexation of Ethiopia, and therefore the same opportunity should be afforded to others. This may be fair from the standpoint of equality of obligations, but equality at such a low level can hardly be an ideal of the League. If we once admit that principle, we may expect that it will be sufficient for one or a few Members of the League to break one of its decisions—and that may easily happen, in the present state of international morality—for all other Members of the League, one by one, to follow them.

We cannot admit that breaches of international obligations are examples to be followed. The League of Nations and its individual

45 *Ibid.* 840

Members have made mistakes, errors and blunders; they have not always fulfilled their obligations. We should recognize and condemn such failures and take measures to prevent their repetition in future, but on no account must we legalize them, or lower the collective responsibility of the League of Nations to their level. Of course, the League's decisions are not eternal, and can always be reviewed and corrected by the League, at the request of individual League Members, but it is the League collectively which has to recognize such decisions as being out of date and invalid, not the individual Members, when they think it required, or when it seems to be required, by their national interests at the time. The League Council should leave no room for doubt that it not only does not approve such anarchic activities, or erect them into a virtue, but severely condemns those of its Members who are the first to set the example of engaging in them.

Mr. Litvinov concluded:

If we had before us any resolution or résumé of our discussion, I should insist on its reflecting the considerations I have laid before you. To neglect them will not allow the League to remain in existence much longer, and I should like to think that its preservation answers to the interests of peace and to the wishes of the vast majority of States.

These words fittingly characterized the aimlessness of the debate, which, as Lord Halifax had announced in advance, was under no conditions to lead to a vote.

Most of the Council Members fell in line with the British Government and emphasized the sovereign freedom of action of their countries. Among them was the representative of Poland who denounced the principle of non-recognition even in its application to Manchuria. Said Mr. Komarnicki:

My Government believes that all the activities of the League of Nations should be animated by a just appreciation of political realities, a condition indispensable to all effective international collaboration. If the League continues to confine itself to rigid procedure, serving only to perpetuate sources of conflict—as was the case, for instance, in the "Manchukuo" affair—it is to be feared that its role as an organ of international co-operation will inevitably be diminished.[46]

Only the representatives of China and New Zealand joined Mr. Litvinov in the defense of the principles of the Covenant. Mr. Wellington Koo stressed that the existing situation in Ethiopia was only a question of fact, but that

[46] *Ibid.* 343

The question of principles is fundamentally important and should not escape our attention. As Members of the League of Nations dedicated to the maintenance of the rule of law as opposed to the rule of force in international relations, we cannot overlook it. The principle of non-recognition of territorial changes effected by force is implicit in the Covenant. It is the foundation upon which we hope to build a new and better world order wherein nations will be able to live in peace and security under the reign of law, and wherein political disputes and economic needs will be resolved by peaceful negotiation and amicable adjustment. . . .

The Chinese Government attaches the greatest importance to the safeguarding of this principle. . . .[47]

Mr. Jordan (New Zealand) did not mince words in denouncing the whole procedure:

In our view, the League of Nations should not divest itself of responsibility by leaving the issue to individual governments, each to choose for itself, for that is a direct denial of the collective responsibility which is fundamental.

The League, in its Assembly, agreed to sanctions. The Assembly condemned Italy's aggression in Ethiopia. Now, the Council is considering the question of allowing any who wish to do so to take their own line of action. It cannot be right to go back on the principles of the Covenant, or to condone acts of aggression, and while that is neither stated nor intended, yet our action might be so interpreted. It was the Assembly which recommended the lifting of sanctions, at the same time reaffirming its attachment to the principles of the Covenant. It is the League acting collectively, and not governments acting separately, which should have dealt with the matter.

My Government holds the view that, if recognition were ever to be afforded, it should have been in accordance with a general resolution of the League and not by separate decisions by individual Members. . . .

The proceedings in which we are engaged, however they may be disguised, will only be regarded as a stage further in the surrender to aggression. The suggestion of today is a compromise between leaving the League and remaining loyal to the Covenant. According to this suggestion any nation may remain in the League and, at the same time, disregard the terms of the Covenant. It seems illogical to retain the Covenant and decide that any Member State that wishes may disregard it. The New Zealand Government cannot support any proposal which would involve, either directly or by implication, approval of a breach of the Covenant.[48]

[47] *Ibid.* 344
[48] *Ibid.* 355

Mr. Jordan's statement was the only possible answer to Lord Halifax' assertion "that it was open to Members of the League to regard the Assembly resolution of July 4, 1936, as closing the question in so far as they were concerned." For this resolution had only terminated the sanctions, but neither did it end the Covenant nor repeal the League Resolution of March 11, 1932. The President of the Council, Mr. Munters (Latvia), however, hastened to endorse Lord Halifax' thesis. He stated that

The Latvian Government holds the view that, since collective action in the Italo-Ethiopian dispute was explicitly abandoned, the question of the consequences arising out of the existing situation in Ethiopia is one for each Member of the League to decide for itself.[49]

In summing up the results of the debate Mr. Munters repeated the formula, "the great majority of the Members of the Council feel, so far as the question we are now discussing is concerned, it is for the individual Members of the League to determine their attitude in the light of their own situation and their own obligations." According to plan, no vote was taken.

The Council session, however, had an epilogue in the House of Commons. On May 20, 1938, Mr. Noel-Baker vigorously criticized the attitude of the British Government. He said:

It is not for me to cite the terms of the resolutions which were adopted in February, 1932, by twelve Members of the Council on the Manchurian question, and unanimously by the Assembly a few weeks later, on 11th March 1932. Those resolutions are well known. They declare that it is incumbent upon Members of the League, as a result of the provisions of Article 10, not to recognize changes of territorial status or sovereignty brought about by Covenant-breaking war. That is precisely what we are intending now to do, and since we are intending to do it, the Government said: "Oh, well, we must cover ourselves in some way. We are setting aside a most important, indeed a fundamental principle of international law, what President Wilson called the heart of the Covenant, and therefore, we must have the approval of the League." They have not got the approval of the League. What happened in Geneva about Abyssinia? Before they went there the Government were extremely reluctant to tell us what proposals they were going to put forward. But everybody knows that they wanted to have a resolution of the

49 *Ibid.* 346

Council. In my view, if they had got a resolution of the Council, unanimously adopted, it would still not have been sufficient to set aside Article 10. It could not have wiped out the unanimous resolution of the Assembly of 1932. But when they got to Geneva, having wanted a resolution, they found that they could not get it, and so they fell back on the device of having a discussion, a series of isolated and detached declarations by different Members of the Council.[50]

The foregoing seems in fact to be the "inside story" of the Council session.[51] The circumstances certainly lend support to Mr. Noel-Baker's narrative, while his legal position that even a unanimous resolution of the Council could not have been able to set aside Article 10 nor the Assembly Resolution of March 11, 1932, appears unanswerable.

Following the Council meeting, a number of additional League Members granted recognition of the Italian annexation in various forms, mostly by issuing letters of credence accrediting their envoys to "His Majesty the King of Italy, Emperor of Ethiopia." [52]

The Protocol signed at Rome on April 16, 1938, provided that the instruments in which the accord was embodied were to take effect on such date as the two governments should jointly determine. Before making them operative, the British Government laid them before Parliament with a motion, in-

50 336 H. C. Deb. 785

51 On May 14, 1940, Professor Herbert W. Briggs delivered at a session of the American Society of International Law a lecture on "Non-Recognition of Title by Conquest and Limitations of the Doctrine." (34 ASIL 72) In the ensuing discussion Professor Malbone W. Graham revealed what had been behind the scenes of the League Council proceedings of May, 1938. He said (Ibid. 95): "The specific fate of the doctrine [of non-recognition] in the hands of the League of Nations was, I think we must openly and candidly admit, a function of the policy of appeasement. His Excellency, Mr. Munters, President of the League of Nations Council in the May meeting 1938, had the rather distasteful task of salvaging something for the British Government by allowing the 'decentralization' of policy, as regards non-recognition. Therefore the action was pushed through—I believe it is not in excess to say that this was done at the suggestion of Lord Halifax—and release of League members from the obligation to pursue a policy of non-recognition was held to be a desirable thing. Mr. Munters engineered that policy straight through the League Council. He told me so personally. In consequence, we must lay responsibility for the present status of the doctrine of non-recognition on the doorstep of the Council of the League of Nations, as one of the sacrificial pre-Munich tidbits laid on the altar of appeasement."

52 On June 29, 1938, Mr. Butler gave the House of Commons a complete list of the States Members of the League of Nations which had hitherto granted de jure or de facto recognition to the Italian annexation of Ethiopia. (337 H. C. Deb. 1890)

troduced by Prime Minister Chamberlain in the House of Commons on November 2, 1938, to the effect "that this House welcomes the intention of His Majesty's Government to bring the Anglo-Italian Agreement into force." [53] Speaking in support of the motion, Mr. Chamberlain said:

> Of all the countries in Europe there are only two, namely ourselves and the Government of Soviet Russia, which have restricted themselves to de facto recognition. The latest country to recognize formally Italian sovereignty in Ethiopia is France, and their new Ambassador is to be accredited to the King of Italy, Emperor of Ethiopia. We propose to follow the same course . . . thereby according legal recognition to Italian sovereignty.[54]

In the debate Mr. Noel-Baker took up the cudgels for the rule of law. He said:

> The League Assembly resolution of March 11, 1932, was perfectly precise, and it simply declared what was the existing law of the Covenant.
> It is very doubtful whether a unanimous resolution of the Assembly could set it aside. But in any case, we never tried to get such a resolution. . . . If we recognize Italian sovereignty over Abyssinia today, whatever other Governments may have done, we are in fact setting aside the Covenant and we are doing it without any approval of any organ of the League.[55]

As was to be expected, the House voted with overwhelming majority for the motion, and so did the House of Lords on the following day.[56] Accordingly, the agreement was put into effect by a joint British-Italian declaration, signed at Rome on November 16, 1938.[57] Thus "de jure" recognition was granted to the Italian annexation by the Great Powers of the League, with the exception of the Soviet Union.

Nevertheless, the agencies of the League did not draw the last consequences from this attitude of the "Western Democracies." Ethiopia was kept on the official lists of the League

[53] 340 *H. C. Deb.* 207
[54] *Ibid.* 210
[55] *Ibid.* 313
[56] *Ibid.* 331; 110 *H. L. Deb.* 1678
[57] *Doc. Int. Aff.* 1938, I 173. In a case tried before the Chancery Division of the High Court on December 6, 1938 (Haile Selassie v. Cable & Wireless Ltd.), the Foreign Secretary issued a certificate, dated Nov. 30, 1938, to the effect that H. M. Gvt. no longer recognized the plaintiff as de jure Emperor of Ethiopia, but now recognized the King of Italy as such. (*Ann. Dig.* 1938–40, No. 37, 94)

Members.[58] The subsequent meetings of Council and Assembly, however, were not attended by Ethiopian delegates.[59]

The attitude of the United States is easily described. The American Government never recognized the Italian annexation of Ethiopia. It is true that after the conclusion of the British-Italian Agreement of April 16, 1938, the President of the United States made a statement (released on April 19, 1938) to the effect that "this Government has seen the conclusion of an agreement with sympathetic interest because it is proof of the value of peaceful negotiations." But he added the proviso that the American Government "does not attempt to pass upon the political features of accords such as that recently reached between Great Britain and Italy." [60]

A few weeks later the Secretary of State, Mr. Hull, emphasized once again that the principles governing the foreign policies of the United States had undergone no change.[61] In token of this, a birthday telegram from President Roosevelt to Victor Emmanuel III, dispatched on November 11, 1938, styled the latter merely "King of Italy." [62]

In June, 1940, the policy of appeasement which the so-called Western Democracies had practiced toward Fascist Italy for years, led to the inevitable result: On June 11, 1940, King Victor Emmanuel III made war on his allies of 1915, as he had in that year made war on his former partners of the Triple Alliance. The British Government was presently confronted with the Ethiopian issue: On June 19, 1938, a Member of the House of Commons, Mr. Mander, asked the Under-Secretary of State for Foreign Affairs

whether, in view of the declaration of war by Italy against this country, the British Government any longer feels itself bound to recognize in the future Italy in connection with Ethiopia . . . and whether he will make it clear that, under present conditions, the British Government in no way recognizes Italian sovereignty over Abyssinia.[63]

58 *League Documents, Members of the League and Composition of the Council*, Sept. 21, 1938, 2
59 *LNOJ* 1938, 669; *LNOJ* 1939, 8
60 18 *D. S. Press Rel.* 527
61 *Ibid.* 575 (Statement of May 12, 1938, text, below, 166)
62 19 *D. S. Press Rel.* 331
63 362 *H. C. Deb.* 139

The Under-Secretary of State, Mr. Butler, replied:

In view of Italy's unprovoked entry into the war against this country, His Majesty's Government hold themselves entitled to reserve full liberty of action in respect to any undertaking given by them in the past to the Italian Government concerning the Mediterranean, North or East Africa or Middle East areas.[64]

On July 3, 1940, Mr. Butler implemented this statement by announcing that the British Government no longer recognized the Italian King as Emperor of Ethiopia.[65, 66] This, however, did not yet constitute recognition of Emperor Haile Selassie I as the rightful sovereign. On July 11, 1940, Col. Wedgwood asked in the House of Commons "whether the Emperor's Government will be recognized as the lawful Government of Ethiopia and admitted to the full status of an ally in the present war." [67] Mr. Butler's reply was evasive as was his reply to a question put by Mr. Mander on July 24, after the Emperor had returned to Africa.[68] Not until February 4, 1941, did the British Foreign Secretary, Mr. Eden, when questioned by Mr. Mander, announce that "His Majesty's Government would welcome the reappearance of an independent Ethiopian State and recognize the claim of Emperor Haile Selassie to his throne." [69]

The Emperor returned to his liberated capital on May 5, 1941.[70] The British Government, however, was still not prepared to take final steps. On August 6, 1941, Mr. Mander asked the Foreign Secretary "whether in view of the fact that fighting in East Africa has virtually come to an end, it is intended fully to recognize an independent Ethiopia." [71] Mr. Eden replied:

[64] *Ibid.*
[65] *Ibid.* 814
[66] In a case tried before the Palestine Supreme Court on December 11, 1940 (Azazh Kebbeda Tesema v. Italian Government. *Ann. Dig.* 1938–40, No. 36, 93), the High Commissioner of Palestine informed the court by letter of November 30, 1940, as follows: "I have been acquainted by the Secretary of State for Colonies that the de jure recognition by His Majesty's Government of the Italian conquest of Ethiopia has been withdrawn." The language is noteworthy in view of the assertion of many textbook-writers that de jure recognition is irrevocable. (Above, 113)
[67] 362 *H. C. Deb.* 1359
[68] 363 *H. C. Deb.* 761
[69] 368 *H. C. Deb.* 804
[70] 18 *Bull. Int. News* 648
[71] 373 *H. C. Deb.* 1921

Yes, Sir. His Majesty's Government have made abundantly clear their intention to recognize an independent Ethiopia as soon as the military situation permits. Such recognition would be followed by the establishment of diplomatic relations.[72]

On February 3, 1942, however, the Foreign Secretary announced in the House of Commons that an agreement had been signed on behalf of His Majesty's Government with the Emperor of Ethiopia on January 31, 1942, at Addis Ababa, and added: "This agreement restores our normal diplomatic relations with the Emperor." [73]

[72] *Ibid.*
[73] 377 *H. C. Deb.* 1052

CHAPTER XXII

AUSTRIA

The annexation of Ethiopia led to the seizure of Austria, also a League Member, by the German Reich. For the resistance which the Western Powers had initially exerted against Italy's Ethiopian schemes had prompted the government of King Victor Emmanuel III to accept the assistance which German diplomacy was clever enough to offer. In turn Italy had to pay the price which the Reich exacted for such assistance—a free hand in Austria—and she was willing to do it, although about four years earlier, in July, 1934, she had thwarted the same plans by the threat of immediate mobilization. Having bought off Italy's opposition, Germany felt strong enough to strike her first blow against the territorial order established at Versailles in 1919. Strong military reasons caused the Austrian Republic to be the first victim of renewed Teutonic aggression. With Austria in control of the Wehrmacht, Czechoslovakia was hopelessly outflanked, and her formidable natural defenses turned. Again, the destruction of the Czechoslovak Republic was the precondition for further German undertakings against eastern and southeastern Europe. Austria, it is true, was a Member of the League of Nations. Yet the political strategists of the German Reich anticipated that the military and political weakness of the Western Great Powers would prompt them to acquiesce in the results of German aggression. Without Great Britain and France, however, neither the smaller League Powers nor the Soviet Union would be in a position to take action.[1]

In February, 1938, the Austrian Chancellor, Dr. Schuschnigg, who for four years had carried on the struggle for the independence of his country, was tricked by the German Ambassador in Vienna, Mr. von Papen, into meeting the head of the German Government at Berchtesgaden. There

[1] The following narrative is mainly based on the source material in *Survey of International Affairs*, 1938, I 179 ff., and *Doc. Int. Aff.* 1938, II 86 ff.

he was subjected to the most ignominious abuse, and finally informed that the Wehrmacht was prepared to invade Austria unless he acquiesced in the demands presented by the "Fuehrer." These included the appointment to cabinet posts of two traitors to the Austrian cause, Dr. Seyss-Inquart, who was to become Minister of the Interior and Public Safety, and Dr. Guido Schmidt, a man who was posing as Schuschnigg's most devoted friend and was to be given the portfolio of Foreign Affairs. Despairing of help from the outside world, the Austrian Government yielded. The two traitors took office, and their underhand activities caused a rapid deterioration of the domestic situation in Austria. The country was swamped with noisy demonstrations and riots staged by elements infected with National Socialism.

On March 9, 1938, Dr. Schuschnigg announced in his Tyrolean home town, Innsbruck, that on the following Sunday a nation-wide plebiscite would be held. All Austrians who had completed the twenty-fourth year of age were to cast their votes on the question whether or not they backed their government's struggle for the independence of their country. The following day the head of the German Government deliberated at Potsdam with his political and military advisers. In the early afternoon of Friday, March 11, a German ultimatum was dispatched to the Austrian Government, demanding that the plebiscite be postponed indefinitely. It was rejected. Thereupon a second ultimatum was delivered, reiterating the first demand and further asking for Dr. Schuschnigg's resignation and the appointment of Dr. Seyss-Inquart in his place. At 6:15 P.M., Dr. Schuschnigg yielded to the first, but not to the second ultimatum. Soon thereafter, at 6:45 P.M., a third ultimatum was presented by a special representative of the German Chancellor. It repeated the demands of the second ultimatum, backing them by the threat that in case of non-compliance by 8 P.M., the German army would invade Austria.

At 7:50 P.M., Dr. Schuschnigg yielded; he announced his decision over the radio in the following words:

The Government of the German Reich has presented to the Federal President an ultimatum, with a fixed time-limit, demanding the appointment of a candidate of its own choice for the post of

Chancellor and the formation of a Government in accordance with the proposals of the German Reich Government. In the event of a refusal, it is intended that German troops shall march into Austria at this hour.

The Federal President instructs me to inform the Austrian people that we are yielding to force. . . .

A few minutes later, Dr. Seyss-Inquart announced to the Austrian people that he was still holding office, and warned them that there must be no resistance against the approaching German army. At the same time he sent a request to Hitler in which he styled himself and his accomplices as "the provisional Austrian Government," and asked the German Government to dispatch at once German troops to Austria.

In the course of the night, the invasion started according to plans obviously prearranged long before, since the German troops were already lined up along the Austrian border. While this was happening, a leader of the Austrian National Socialists announced that the Federal President had appointed Dr. Seyss-Inquart as Federal Chancellor. On March 12, Hitler entered Austria, and was greeted at Linz by Dr. Seyss-Inquart. In his welcoming address the latter declared that Article 88 of the Treaty of St. Germain was no longer effective.[2]

On Sunday, March 13, the Seyss-Inquart "Government" promulgated a "Federal Constitutional Law," [3] which proclaimed in Article 1 that "Austria is a land of the German Reich," while Article 2 provided that on April 10, 1938, a plebiscite would be held on the question of the reunion with the German Reich.[4]

On March 14, 1938, Prime Minister Chamberlain informed the House of Commons of the events that had led to the annexation of Austria.[5] His account was in keeping with the foregoing narrative. He added that on March 10, 1938, the Foreign Secretary, Lord Halifax, had addressed to the German Minister, von Ribbentrop, who was then in London,

---

[2] "The independence of Austria is inalienable otherwise than with the consent of the Council of the League of Nations."

[3] *Reichsgesetzblatt* 1938, I 237

[4] See *Survey Int. Aff.* 1938, I 188-213; Professor Herbert Wright's memorandum *The Attitude of the United States towards Austria* (House Doc. No. 477, 78th Congress, 2d Session) ; the same author's article "Legality of the Annexation of Austria" (38 *AJIL* 621)

[5] 333 *H. C. Deb.* 45-52

a grave warning regarding the Austrian situation; that he had repeated his representations on March 11, and that later on that day the British Ambassador in Berlin had registered with the German Government a protest in strong terms "against such use of coercion, backed by force, against an independent state in order to create a situation incompatible with its national independence." Similarly, the Foreign Secretary, Lord Halifax, addressing the House of Lords on March 16, 1938, characterized the invasion and annexation of Austria as a "ruthless application of power politics." [6]

Exactly the same view was taken by the Soviet Government. On March 17, 1938, Mr. Maxim Litvinov, People's Commissar for Foreign Affairs, made the following statement to the foreign press:

The violations of international undertakings ensuing from the League Covenant and from the Paris (Briand-Kellogg) Pact . . . have provided occasions for the Soviet Government to demonstrate not only its negative attitude toward these international crimes, but also its readiness to take an active part in all measures aiming to organize a collective rebuff to the aggressor, even disregarding the inevitable aggravation of its relations with the aggressor. At the same time, the Soviet Government voiced the warning that international inaction and the impunity of aggression in one case would inexorably lead to the repetition and multiplication of similar cases.

Unfortunately, international developments have justified these warnings. They received a new confirmation in the armed invasion of Austria and in the forcible deprivation of the Austrian people of their political, economic and cultural independence.[7]

Two days later, on March 19, 1938, the American Secretary of State, Mr. Cordell Hull, said at his press conference:

The day before yesterday I discussed fully the principles governing peaceful and orderly international relations and their application to present conditions in European and other world areas.

The extent to which the Austrian incident, or any similar incident, is calculated to endanger the maintenance of peace and the preservation of the principles in which this Government believes is of course a matter of serious concern to the Government of the United States.[8]

[6] 108 *H. L. Deb.* 179
[7] *Doc. Int. Aff.* 1938, I 314
[8] 18 *D. S. Press Rel.* 375

At the time of the annexation, the Council of the League of Nations was not in session. The Secretary General of the League, Mr. Avenol, received from the German Government a letter, dated March 18,[9] bringing to his notice the text of the reunion law of March 13, 1938. The letter concluded: "On the date of the promulgation of this law the former Federal State of Austria ceased to be a Member of the League of Nations." Among all the League Members, only one, Mexico, took the trouble of communicating with Mr. Avenol on the Austrian case. On March 19, 1938, the Mexican delegation sent him a note which stressed the duties of the League Members in case of aggression and called for action under the Covenant in the following terms:

In view of the suppression of Austria as an independent State as the result of armed foreign intervention, and since the Council of the League has not as yet been convened with a view to the application of Article 10 of the Covenant, which requires the Members of the League to respect and preserve as against external aggression the territorial integrity and political independence of all members, I have the honour, acting on the instructions of the Mexican Government, to transmit to you the following declarations, and to request you to be good enough to bring them to the knowledge of the States Members of the League.

The political extinction of Austria, in the form and circumstances in which it has taken place, constitutes a serious infringement of the League Covenant and the established principles of international law. . . .

The fact that the Vienna authorities handed over their powers to the invader is no excuse for the aggressor's action, and the League should not accept the fait accompli without the most vigorous protests or without taking the action provided for by the articles of the Covenant.

Moreover, the authorities who relinquished executive power are in no sense representative of the Austrian people, who undoubtedly regard the death of their country as a tragedy of evil omen; the very authorities who were obliged to "yield to force" were not acting of their own free will, since *voluntas coacta voluntas non est.* Consequently, the States Members of the League should not regard the action and words of these authorities as the free and lawful expression of the will of the nation subjected to military force.

The Mexican Government, which has always upheld the principles of the Covenant and in accordance with its consistent international policy refuses to recognize any conquest made by force, enters the most emphatic protest against the external aggression of

[9] *LNOJ* 1938, 237

which the Austrian Republic has just been the victim. It informs the public opinion of the world that in its view the only means of securing peace, and preventing further international outrages such as those that have been committed against Ethiopia, Spain, China, and Austria, is for the nations to carry out the obligations laid upon them by the Covenant, the treaties they have concluded and the principles of international law. Otherwise it will not be long before the world is overwhelmed by a far worse conflagration than that which it is sought to avoid by attempted action outside the League system.[10]

Mr. Avenol took no action on this note and merely acknowledged receipt of the German note.[11]

The British Government hastened to make clear its position regarding the events in Austria. On March 16, 1938, the British Foreign Secretary made in the House of Lords the following statement:

The problem of Austria . . . has been with us always ever since the War ended with the break-up of the Austro-Hungarian Monarchy. . . . I assert that, faced with it, the attitude of successive British Governments has been quite consistent. They . . . have never supposed that the status quo in Austria could necessarily be maintained for all time. They have been perfectly willing to recognize the special interest of the German Government in the relations between Germany and Austria. Therefore they have been perfectly willing to contemplate revision of the Peace Treaties.

The framers of the Treaties . . . stipulated . . . that the change, if desired, should only be brought about after the Council of the League had carefully considered the difficulties and the dangers that were involved, and had decided that those could be surmounted without endangering the paramount interest of European peace and European stability. Events have, of course, moved very differently. . . .

It was suggested by Lord Snell that the matter might usefully be referred to the League of Nations. I have, of course, had to give some thought before this debate to that suggestion. The juridical position of Austria as she existed up to a few days ago was, of course, that of an independent State which was bound by treaty not to alienate that independence without the consent of the Council of the League. That independence, in complete disregard of treaty provisions, has disappeared overnight, and the world, therefore, has been presented with a fait accompli in a fashion and in a setting of accompanying circumstances for which I can recall no parallel in history. But none the less . . . nothing that the League can do can undo what has been done and . . . I confess that I can

10 *Ibid.* 239
11 *Ibid.* 238

see no good to be gained at this juncture for the League or for any of the great purposes the League represents, by bringing this matter before the League tribunal. Nothing short of war can put back the clock, and States Members of the League are not prepared to go to war on this issue.

Those facts, I suggest, must be perfectly squarely faced, and the conclusion that I reach is that the League, though it has a perfect legal right to interest itself in the question, cannot conceivably do anything at this moment which would compel Nazi Germany to turn back from the course on which she has now embarked. His Majesty's Government are therefore bound to recognize that the Austrian State has now been abolished as an international entity and is in process of being entirely absorbed into the German Reich, and that is happening indeed without waiting for the plebiscite, the result of which, in view of the circumstances in which it is going to be held, is a foregone conclusion.[12]

Within a short time, the foreign embassies and legations in Vienna were either closed or converted into consulates general. The Austrian diplomatic and consular officers abroad partly resigned; some were dismissed; some accepted service for the German Reich. Not a single one tried to maintain himself as an officer of the invaded Austrian State, nor was any of the Powers willing to enable the continuance of Austrian diplomatic or consular agencies in exile.

The first official statement of the United States Government on the events in Austria was a press release of March 15, 1938.[13] It announced that the Secretary of State had received from the German Embassy a letter, dated March 14, informing his Government of the reunion of Austria with Germany, and that the former Austrian diplomatic representatives in foreign countries had received the order to place themselves, along with their personnel, under the German representatives. On March 19 the following statement was issued:

On March 17, 1938, the Minister of the Republic of Austria, Mr. Edgar L. G. Prochnik, informed the Department of State that, as a result of the developments which have occurred in Austria, that country has ceased to exist as an independent nation and has been incorporated in the German Reich; that therefore the Austrian mission to this country, of which he has been the head, has been abolished; and that the affairs of the mission have been taken over

[12] 108 *H. L. Deb.* 177
[13] 18 *D. S. Press Rel.* 374

by the Embassy of Germany. The German Ambassador has informed the Department of State that he has assumed the functions hitherto performed by the Minister of Austria.

The events pertaining to the changes which have taken place in the status of the Austrian Republic will necessitate, on the part of the Government of the United States, a number of technical steps, which are now being given appropriate consideration.[14]

Shortly thereafter, on April 6, 1938, the United States Ambassador in Berlin delivered to the German Foreign Minister the following two notes: [15]

[1]

Excellency:

I am directed by my Government to inform Your Excellency as follows:

On March 17, 1938, the Minister of the Republic of Austria, Mr. Edgar Prochnik, informed the Department of State that, as a result of the developments which had occurred in Austria, that country had ceased to exist as an independent nation and had been incorporated in the German Reich; that therefore the Austrian mission to this country, of which he had been the head, had been abolished; and that the affairs of the mission had been taken over by the Embassy of Germany. The German Ambassador has informed the Department of State that he has assumed the functions hitherto performed by the Minister of Austria.

The Government of the United States finds itself under the necessity as a practical measure of closing its Legation at Vienna and of establishing a Consulate General. In the circumstances I am directed by my Government to request provisional consular status for Mr. John C. Wiley, Consul General. . . .

[2]

Excellency:

In view of the announcement made to the Government of the United States by the Austrian Minister on March 17, 1938, my Government is under the necessity for all practical purposes of accepting what he says as a fact and accordingly consideration is being given to the adjustments in its own practices and procedure in various regards which will be necessitated by the change of status of Austria.

The note then proceeded to notify the German Government that the Government of the United States would look to it for the discharge of certain types of indebtedness of the Austrian Government, and concluded:

14 *Ibid.* 375
15 *Ibid.* 465

This Government will expect that these obligations will continue to be fully recognized and that service will be continued by the German authorities which have succeeded in control of the means and machinery of payment in Austria. . . .

A few days later, the Government of the United States was compelled to take another step regarding the Austrian situation. Since Austria and Germany were now de facto within one custom boundary, it was impossible to accord imports from the territory of Austria preferential treatment as against those from Germany. Consequently the President sent on April 6, 1938, the following letter to the Secretary of the Treasury:

I refer to my letter addressed to you on March 15, 1938 [16] concerning the application of duties proclaimed in connection with trade agreements concluded under the authority of the Act to Amend the Tariff Act of 1930, approved June 12, 1934 (48 Stat. 943), as extended by the Joint Resolution approved March 1, 1937 (50 Stat. 24).

You are hereby directed to delete the word "Austria" from numbered section 2 of my letter under reference, such deletion to be effective on and after May 6, 1938. The proclaimed duties shall cease to be applied to products of Austria entered for consumption or withdrawn from warehouse for consumption on and after such date.

The above mentioned letter of March 15, 1938, is hereby modified accordingly and you will please cause notice of such modification to be published in an early issue of the weekly Treasury decisions.[17]

The language of the foregoing documents, it is believed, reveals the desire of the United States Government to make it clear that it was merely taking measures to deal with a situation of fact. It would, therefore, be unwarranted to see in the respective measures acts extending recognition to the German annexation of Austria.[18]

[16] *Ibid.* 871
[17] *Ibid.* 474
[18] Similar views were expressed by Professor Quincy Wright in "The Denunciation of Treaty Violations" (32 *AJIL* 526), and by Professor Herbert Wright in the memorandum cited above, n. 4. Professor Quincy Wright wrote: "The care of the United States in confining its recognition of the German assumption of control in Austria to 'necessity' and 'facts' and in limiting the consequences of this assumption to 'practical measures' and 'practical purposes' suggests that the possibility of a breach of the Pact [of Paris] and a consequent applicability of the non-recognition doctrine remains open, a suggestion borne out by the explicit reaffirmation of the non-

In May, 1938, the League Council met in ordinary session. Only two delegates, the Chilean, Mr. Edwards,[19] and the Spanish, Mr. del Vayo,[20] mentioned on May 11 the Austrian case in short remarks. A resolution, adopted on May 14, expressed the desirability of extending the authority of the High Commissioner for Refugees from Germany to cover refugees coming from the territory "which formerly constituted Austria." [21] In September, 1938, a roster of the League Members was published on which Austria was not listed.[22] In the same month the League Assembly met in its ordinary session. By that time, the seizure of Austria was already producing its inevitable consequence, the dismemberment of the Czechoslovak Republic. Again the League Assembly, dominated by the "Western Democracies," was unwilling to take any action. Two delegates, however, recalled its failures. On September 19, the Spanish Delegate, Mr. del Vayo, said:

We have seen a free and independent State which a year ago was enjoying the prerogatives of a Member of the League and was regularly collaborating in our work, disappear over night from our midst. You will not find in the whole of the Secretary-General's report one word of farewell or of sympathy for its fate.

recognition doctrine by the Secretary of State on May 12, 1938." Professor Herbert Wright commented on the press release of March 15, 1938, as follows: "This reference to the 'changed status of the Austrian Republic,' far from constituting recognition of the legal annexation of Austria by Germany is an affirmation of the continued recognition of the 'Austrian Republic,' whose 'changed status' consists in de facto occupation by Germany, which fact 'necessitates' certain technical steps on the part of the Government of the United States. This interpretation is borne out by subsequent statements and actions of President Roosevelt, Secretary Hull, and other officials and agencies of the Government."

[19] *LNOJ* 1938, 323: "The events which have been occurring in the world for some time prove more adequately than any argument that may be advanced that the Covenant of the League of Nations . . . remains a dead letter. There is no need to mention particular cases. All the Members of the Council are familiar with them. Need I remind you that nothing has been said at the League of Nations about certain events which quite recently led to the disappearance of a State Member who was regarded as of vital importance in the political system of the old continent?"

[20] *Ibid.* 326: "There exist in Europe two countries impelled by an irresistible force of expansion, two countries whose very political regimes lead them to use those expansive forces in a violent and aggressive manner. They have devoured Austria. They are trying to reduce Spain to ashes; they menace the very existence of Czechoslovakia. . . ."

[21] *Ibid.* 367

[22] *League Documents, Members of the League and Composition of the Council,* Sept. 21, 1938, 2

The aggressors know, therefore, that a State Member of the League may be swallowed up with impunity, and that in the annals of the supreme institution of peace such disappearance will not even be recorded among the list of international crimes. May the Spanish delegation be at least permitted to cast a glance of indignant protest towards the seats formerly occupied by the Austrian delegation.[23]

Two days later, the statesman who had carried on for years an unsuccessful struggle for collective security denounced the betrayal of Austria. Said the delegate of the U.S.S.R., Mr. Maxim Litvinov:

It must not be forgotten that the League was created as a reaction to the world war; that its object was . . . to safeguard all nations against aggression, and to replace the system of military alliances by the collective assistance to the victim of aggression. In this sphere the League has done nothing. Two States—Ethiopia and Austria—have lost their independent existence in consequence of violent aggression. . . . The League of Nations has not carried out its obligations to these States. . . .

.   .   .   .

Such an event as the disappearance of Austria passed unnoticed by the League of Nations. Realizing the significance of this event for the fate of the whole of Europe, and particularly of Czechoslovakia, the Soviet Government immediately after the Anschluss, officially approached the other European Great Powers with a proposal for an immediate collective deliberation on the possible consequence of that event, in order to adopt collective preventive measures. To our regret, this proposal, which, if carried out, could have saved us from the alarm which all the world now feels for the fate of Czechoslovakia, did not receive its just appreciation.[24]

The measures of persecution inflicted by the occupant forced tens of thousands of Austrian nationals to seek a haven in foreign countries. The United States Government was faced with a new problem. The Austrian immigration quota was far smaller than the number of Austrians seeking admission to the United States. The German quota was many times larger, moreover it was filled only to a small extent. The Government, in order to grant relief, resolved to combine the two quotas. To this effect on April 29, 1938, a Presidential Proclamation was issued,[25] providing for the

[23] *LNOJ*, Spec. Suppl. 183, 61
[24] *Ibid.* 74 and 77
[25] No. 2283, 3 *Fed. Reg.* 997

increase of the German quota by the Austrian figure, while dropping the latter from the list. The proclamation, however, added:

The immigration quotas assigned to the various countries and areas are designed solely for the purposes of compliance with the pertinent provisions of the Immigration Act of 1924 and are not to be regarded as having any significance extraneous to this object.

In view of this caveat, it would appear unwarranted to construe the content of the proclamation as an act implying recognition of the German annexation. In fact, shortly thereafter, on May 11, a press release was issued which explicitly mentioned Austria as distinct from Germany.[26] On the following day, May 12, Secretary Hull was asked at his press conference about the non-recognition policy of the United States. He answered: "There is nothing new to be said in that connection. Our policy remains unchanged." [27]

On June 7, 1938, the United States Ambassador in Berlin dispatched to the German Government a note following up the question of the Austrian public debt.[28] The note recalled that the assets and revenues of Austria had been "taken over by the German Government." It continued:

It is believed that the weight of authority clearly supports the general doctrine of international law founded upon obvious principles of justice that in case of absorption of a state, the substituted sovereignty assumes the debts and obligations of the absorbed state, and takes the burdens with the benefits. . . . There appears no reason why American creditors of Austria should be placed in any worse position by reason of the absorption of Austria by Germany than they would have been in had such absorption not taken place.

The term "absorption," also used in two subsequent notes on the same subject,[29] is certainly somewhat ambiguous. Again, however, it would appear unwarranted to see in these notes more than an attempt to deal with a situation of fact.

A more serious deviation from the conduct which a consistent application of non-recognition is believed to require,

[26] 18 D. S. Press Rel. 575 (. . . to facilitate the emigration from Austria and from Germany of political refugees. . . .")
[27] Ibid.
[28] 18 D. S. Press Rel. 694
[29] 19 D. S. Press. Rel. 875 (note of Oct. 19, 1938) and 20 D. S. Press. Rel. 53 (note of Jan. 20, 1939)

took place in the late fall of 1939. On November 11, 1939, the United States Government made the following announce- ment: [30]

> By a note dated July 22, 1939, the German Chargé in Washing- ton, on behalf of his Government, requested that this Government agree to the proposal that the operation of the Extradition Treaty between the United States and Germany, signed on July 12, 1930,[31] shall now extend also to the territory in which the former Extradi- tion Treaty between the United States and Austria (Treaty Series No. 822) was effective.
>
> The proposal was accepted by this Government and the notice thereof was given to the German Chargé on November 2, 1939.
>
> The proposal as stated in the above-mentioned note of July 22, 1939, is quoted in translation as follows:
>
> "The Government of the German Reich considers the Extradition Treaty between the Republic of Austria and the United States of America, of January 31, 1930,[32] to have ceased to exist in conse- quence of the reunion of Austria with the German Reich. Since that time, the German extradition law has been introduced into the state of Austria by the Order of April 26, 1939, (Reichsgesetzblatt 1939, I, p. 844).
>
> "The Government of the German Reich therefore proposes that the operation of the Extradition Treaty of July 12, 1930, between the German Reich and the United States of America (Reichsgesetz- blatt 1931, II, p. 403), shall now extend also to the territory in which the former Austro-American Treaty was effective.
>
> "I should be greatly obliged to you for the favor of a statement whether the United States Government agrees to this proposal of the Government of the German Reich."

In concluding this agreement, the United States Govern- ment took a step hardly reconcilable with the principles set forth in the second part of this work.[33] It is true that it was under no legal obligation to pursue a different course. In ac- cepting the German proposal, however, the United States Government should at least have added that this acceptance did not imply recognition of the German annexation, if it was not in its plans to grant it.

Of paramount importance, because affecting the personal fate of tens of thousands of people, was the question of the status of nationals of Austria. On July 3, 1938, the German

[30] 1 D. S. Bull. 546
[31] USTS 836; 4 U. S. Treaties 4216
[32] USTS 822; 4 U. S. Treaties 3946
[33] Above, 103

Minister of the Interior issued a decree [34] containing the following provisions:

(1) The hitherto existing Austrian federal citizenship and the citizenship in the former Austrian federal provinces are abolished.

(2) There is only the German nationality. . . .

The practice of the immigration agencies of the United States was at first not uniform. Some required the immigrants from Austria to state their nationality as "German," others accepted its registration as "Austrian." On September 12, 1940, however, the Department of Justice issued instructions regarding the general registration of alien residents under the Alien Registration Act of 1940.[35] These instructions [36] authorized "alien Austrians" to register "as 'Austrians' in the same manner as 'alien Czechs, Poles, Dutch, Norwegians, Danes, French, Albanians, Manchukuoans, and Luxembourgers.' " By according to Austrians, for the purposes of the registration, the same treatment as to nationals of countries whose change of status the United States Government refused to recognize, the latter, it is believed, made sufficiently clear its position regarding the non-recognition of the German annexation of Austria. An even stronger manifestation of this position may be seen in the following provision of the Executive Order of June 14, 1941,[37] issued for the purpose of freezing assets of nationals of Axis and Axis-occupied countries:

Sec. 3. The term "foreign country" designated in this Order means a foreign country included in the following schedule, and the term "effective date of this Order" means with respect to any such foreign country, or any national thereof, the date specified in the following schedule: . . . (j) June 14, 1941 . . . Austria, Czechoslovakia.

A press release of the same date added to this provision the following comment:

[34] Verordnung über die deutsche Staatsangehörigkeit im Lande Österreich, *Reichsgesetzblatt* 1938, I 790

[35] Act of June 28, 1940, Public No. 670, 76th Congress, 3d Session; *AJIL*, Suppl., 203

[36] Commerce Clearing House, *War Law Service*, 8514. 12, p. 8515. (The listing of "Manchukuoans" was obviously due to a slip, since it was incompatible with the non-recognition of Manchukuo.)

[37] 6 *Fed. Reg.* 2897

In view of the unlimited emergency declared by the President, he has today issued an Executive Order freezing immediately all German and Italian assets in the United States. At the same time the order also freezes the assets of all invaded or occupied European countries not previously frozen. These include Albania, Austria, Czechoslovakia, Danzig, and Poland.[38]

Administrative practice, however, was not rectilinear. Thus a Draft Board Release of August 1, 1941, provided that

Registrants will be permitted to state their nationality as of the country of their nativity without regard to the fact that, as a consequence of the present wars, such country has been annexed, occupied, or is dominated by another country through armed conquest or forced or invited peaceful means.

The provisions of this release shall apply to the natives of Austria, although the German annexation of Austria was officially recognized by the Government of the United States.[39]

The question of the status of the Austrians assumed increased importance when war broke out between the United States and Germany in December, 1941. Under the Act of April 16, 1918, as incorporated in the Code of Laws of the United States:

Whenever there is a declared war between the United States and any foreign nation or government, or any invasion of predatory incursion is perpetrated, attempted or threatened against the territory of the United States by any foreign nation or government, and the President makes public proclamation of the event, all natives, citizens, denizens, or subjects of the hostile nation or government, being of the age of fourteen years or upward, who shall be within the United States and not actually naturalized, shall be liable to be apprehended, restrained, secured, and removed as alien enemies.[40]

On December 8, 1941, the President issued a Proclamation [41] to the effect that "an invasion or predatory incursion is threatened upon the territory of the United States by Germany." This proclamation made all "natives, citizens, denizens, or subjects" of the German Reich enemy aliens. At once the question arose whether or not the Austrians were included in this enumeration.

[38] 4 D. S. Bull. 718
[39] Local Board Release No. 17
[40] USCA, Title 50, c. 3, §21
[41] No. 2525, 6 Fed. Reg. 6323

The Federal district attorneys, who had the task of putting into effect the above quoted rules of the Enemy Alien Act, issued regulations in which the categories of persons affected were defined. These regulations, however, were not uniform. In many districts the enumeration of persons who were to be regarded as enemy aliens included the Austrians, either in the wording, "Germans and Austrians" or in that, "Germans including Austrians." [42]

The Austrians in the United States felt utterly aggrieved. In numerous petitions to the Executive Departments of the Government they pointed out that to classify them as Germans, and consequently, as enemy aliens, was hardly reconcilable with the non-recognition policy of the United States. The Government tried to find a compromise solution of the question. On February 9, 1942, the United States Attorney General announced that Austrians who had stated their nationality as "Austrian" in the alien registration of 1940 were exempted from the restrictions provided for enemy aliens, and that those who had involuntarily or mistakenly stated their nationality as "German" would be given an opportunity to correct their alien registrations following suitable investigation.[43] He added, however, that the exemption was only conditional and that the respective persons remained subject to arrest and detention as enemy aliens "if at any time their apprehension is regarded as necessary to maintain the national security." [44] This meant that the Austrians, although relieved of the most cumbersome restrictions, legally still remained enemy aliens, subjected to the special rules decreed for the latter in many respects. Thus, Section 326 of the Nationality Act of 1940 established for the naturalization of enemy aliens stricter requirements than for other applicants. As regards Austrian public and private property located in the United States, it was treated as

[42] Information obtained from the United States District Attorney for the Southern District of New York.

[43] *New York Times* of Feb. 9, 1942

[44] The announcement included not only Austrians, but also Austro-Hungarians and Koreans; the opportunity of reclassification extended to persons belonging to any of these categories if they had registered as "Germans, Italians or Japanese." The term "Austro-Hungarians" obviously covered residents who had been nationals of the former Austrian Empire or the pre-1919 Kingdom of Hungary and had neither acquired the nationality of one of the successor States nor American citizenship.

German property and consequently placed under the control of the Enemy Alien Property Custodian.

This situation prompted a correspondent to remark at the Secretary of State's press conference of July 27, 1942, "that there appeared to be some confusion with respect to the view of this country as to the present status of Austria" and to ask for clarification on this point. Mr. Cordell Hull replied:

It is probable that such confusion, if it exists, has arisen from administrative steps which may have been taken by this Government in pursuance of its own laws designed to afford adequate protection to this country's interests in dealing with the situation presented by the imposition of military control over Austria and residents of Austria by Germany. This Government very clearly made known its opinions as to the manner in which the seizure of Austria took place and the relation of that seizure to this Government's well-known policy toward the taking of territory by force. This Government has never taken the position that Austria was legally absorbed into the German Reich.[45]

In spite of this statement, doubts survived as to whether or not the United States had recognized the annexation of Austria. They are reflected in certain judicial decisions.[46]

[45] 7 *U. S. Bull.* 660

[46] For judicial views interpreting in various ways the attitude of the American Government see the following cases: Johnson v. Briggs, Inc., 12 N. Y. Supp. (2d) 60; Anninger et al. v. Hohenberg et al., 18 N. Y. Supp. (2d) 499; Land Oberoesterreich v. Gude, 109 F. (2d) 635; U. S. ex rel. Zdunic v. Uhl, 137 F. (2d) 858; U. S. ex rel. Schwarzkopf v. Uhl, *ibid.* 898; U. S. ex rel. d'Esquiva v. Uhl, *ibid.* 903. The last mentioned decision deserves extensive quotation, for it contains a detailed analysis of the documents bearing on the question whether or not the United States Government had recognized the German annexation of Austria. The facts underlying the case at bar were the following: Mr. d'Esquiva, a native-born Austrian citizen, had resided in France at the time of the German invasion of Austria, had thereafter been admitted to the United States, had subsequently been taken into custody as an alien enemy, instituted habeas corpus proceedings and appealed from the decision of the Federal District Court which dismissed his writ, to the United States Circuit Court of Appeals. The court held that if the United States had recognized the annexation, appellant was to be considered a "native" of Germany. The opinion continued:
"The district court, therefore, properly considered the acts of the Department of State taken with reference to the Austrian Anschluss of 1938.
"In its able opinion, the court refers particularly to the photostatic copy of a letter of May 9, 1942, from the Secretary of State to the Attorney General in response to the latter's inquiry as to what diplomatic recognition was given by the United States Government to the incorporation of Austria into the German Reich. The Secretary referred the Attorney General to two notes which had been delivered to the German Foreign Minister on April 6, 1938, by the American Ambassador to Berlin pursuant to instructions from the Department of State. In substance these notes stated that the Government of the United States was obliged to close its legation in Vienna and

Nor did the United States Government take all the administrative steps which a consistent application of nonrecognition policies would have warranted. The Austrian nationals legally remained in the status assigned to them on February 9, 1942. In practice, however, their situation was improved. Thus, the Department of Justice issued on May 15, 1943, a ruling to the effect that natives and citizens of

to establish in place thereof a Consulate General because the Minister of the Republic of Austria had informed the Department of State on March 17, 1938, that Austria had ceased to exist as an independent nation and had been incorporated into the German Reich, and further that the Government of the United States was under the necessity for all practical purposes of accepting the announcement of the Austrian Minister and that thereafter this Government would look to the German Government for the payment of the Austrian debts. The district court thereupon said:

The action taken by the Department of State, as reflected in the letter to the Attorney General and the two notes delivered to the German Minister, is some evidence tending to show that the United States recognized the consolidation of Austria with Germany. Such action took place only after the Austrian Government had formally notified the Department of State that that country had ceased to exist as an independent nation. Further evidence of such recognition is this action taken by the President, on April 28, 1942, when he abolished the Austrian quota allowed under the Immigration Act of 1924 (43 Stat. 153) and at the same time increased the German quota by the number formerly allowed Austria. (Proclamation No. 2283, 52 Stat. 1544.) In the absence of any proof to the contrary it must be assumed, therefore, that this government has officially recognized the consolidation of Austria with Germany.

"This conclusion, therefore, led to its judgment of dismissal of the writ. It should be said that on a somewhat different issue we had earlier reached a similar conclusion as to the action of the State Department, in Land Oberoesterreich v. Gude, 2 Cir., 109 F. 2d 635, 637, certiorari denied, 311 U. S. 670.

"Appellant, however, relies on other representations from the State Department, referred to in United States ex rel. Schwarzkopf v. Uhl, supra, which now constitute 'proof to the contrary.' In particular a press release of the Secretary of State, No. 386, July 27, 1942, after the decision below had been rendered, is quoted and relied on. Here, after referring to the confusion with respect to the view of this country 'as to the present status of Austria' and speaking of the 'situation presented by the imposition of military control over Austria, and residents of Austria, by Germany,' the Secretary says: 'This Government very clearly made known its opinions as to the manner in which the seizure of Austria took place and the relation of that seizure to this Government's well-known policy toward the taking of territory by force. This Government has never taken the position that Austria was legally absorbed into the German Reich.' Since courts are bound by the action of the Executive, and where necessary address their own inquiries to it, it is held that further clarification made by the Executive, even after the decision below has been made, is to be considered by the appellate court. . . .

"But even if we give all proper weight to this statement, we cannot find in it anything absolutely decisive. The word 'legally' can hardly be given the same content with reference to intercourse between nations as it has in domestic law. Whether this statement was intended as a definite nonrecognition of the inclusion of Austria in Germany, thus making the situation of Austria comparable to that of Czechoslovakia (the country of which

Austria who had never voluntarily acquired German nationality should henceforth be treated as Austrians and not Germans, and, therefore, not as alien enemies under Section 326 of the Nationality Act of 1940. The ruling also directed the officers of the Immigration and Naturalization Service that in the preparation of declarations and petitions for naturalization for such persons, their nationality should be shown as Austrian rather than German.[47] On the other hand, a Local Board Memorandum of June 3, 1943,[48] listed among enemy countries "Germany including Austria and Danzig." Nor did any change take place regarding the classification of Austrian public and private property. Nevertheless, the situation of the Austrians in the United States was incomparably better than in all the other countries, no matter whether or not they were League Members. Everywhere the nationals of Austria were for a long time regarded and treated as nationals of Germany, and consequently, in the States which became involved in war with the latter, as enemy aliens. Only very gradually did a change of attitude

---

Schwarzkopf, in the companion case, was a native), or of other governments in exile, or whether it was merely a condemnation of the means by which the result was accomplished, is not clear.

"There appear to be other governmental regulations tending to throw some further doubt on the matter. Thus, the Immigration and Naturalization Service of the Department of Justice has issued new instructions dated May 14, 1943, and June 8, 1943, pertaining to the proper classification for naturalization purposes of aliens of Austrian nativity and nationality and holding that they are not now to be considered natives of Germany for the purposes covered by the instructions. And recent instructions of the Treasury Department dealing with reports to be made of property owned in foreign countries are cited to us as distinguishing between Austria and Germany. How far these various regulations and instructions have been made in the light of, and in conformity with, the present view of the Department of State is not disclosed. At any rate, we think the ends of justice require a further inquiry into the recognition accorded the Austrian absorption into Germany by our Department of State. We might address our inquiries to the Department, but we think the better course is to remand the proceedings to the district court, since a hearing and the taking of testimony may prove desirable.

"The judgment is, therefore, reversed and the case remanded for further proceedings consistent with this opinion."

The inquiry ordered by the court of review, however, was never carried out, for before the district court was able to ascertain the views of the Department of State, the United States District Attorney dropped the proceedings against Mr. d'Esquiva subsequent to the Moscow Declaration of November 1, 1943.

[47] Letter of the Immigration and Naturalization Service, dated May 18, 1943, file No. 3913.

[48] Local Board Memorandum No. 112

take place. Even countries such as New Zealand, which had taken a courageous stand regarding non-recognition of the Italian annexation of Ethiopia, or Mexico, which had entered a solemn protest to the League in the very case of Austria, formed no exceptions.[49]

The treatment meted out to citizens of Austria by the British Government was in keeping with the statement made by Viscount Halifax in the House of Lords on March 16, 1938, to the effect that "His Majesty's Government are bound to recognize that the Austrian State has now been abolished as an international entity." This, unfortunately, is not only true of the Government of Mr. Neville Chamberlain, but also of that of Mr. Winston Churchill. The attitude of the Government, however, remained not unopposed by British public opinion and gave rise to frequent debates in the House of Commons, touching not only upon the personal fate of the Austrians residing in Great Britain, but also upon the general aspects of the recognition of the annexation of Austria.

From the day of the recognition by the British Government of the incorporation of Austria—that is, since March 16, 1938—the Austrians residing in or admitted to Great Britain were regarded and treated by the British authorities as Germans. It is true that those who left their homeland prior to October, 1938, were allowed to register as "Austrians," but this had no influence on their treatment when the war broke out. The controlling statute was the Aliens Order of 1920 [50] as amended on September 1, 1939.[51] Its Article 6 distinguishes between "aliens, not being enemy aliens" and "enemy aliens," the latter being subjected to special restrictions. Article 20 (2) defines the term "enemy alien" as follows: "The expression 'enemy alien' means a person who, not being either a British subject or a British protected person, possesses the nationality of a state at war with His Majesty." Although it is hard to see how Austria, whose very existence Great Britain did not recognize at that

[49] According to information obtained from the New Zealand Legation at Washington under date September 13, 1943, "de facto recognition of the annexation is implied in the treatment of such questions as alien control, visa requirements and commercial treaties and has been given since 1939."

[50] *S. R. & O.* 1920, I 138 (No. 448)
[51] *S. R. & O.* 1939, I 121 (No. 994)

time, could possibly be regarded as a "State at war with His Majesty," the British Government made in the application of the statute no distinction between persons registered as Austrians and such registered as Germans. On September 4, 1939, the Home Secretary, Sir John Anderson, made in the House of Commons the following announcement:

An Order in Council has been made amending the peace-time Aliens Order in a number of respects. The new Order requires all enemy aliens (that is, Germans and Austrians) who are over the age of 16 . . . to report to the police. . . . A large proportion of the Germans and Austrians at present in this country are refugees, and there will, I am sure, be a general desire to avoid treating as enemies those who are friendly to the country which has offered them asylum. At the same time care must be taken to sift out any persons who, though claiming to be refugees, may not, in fact, be friendly to this country.

To avoid risks, I propose that there shall be an immediate review of all Germans and Austrians in this country. . . . I am also arranging for a similar review, by a special tribunal, of all Czechoslovaks. Citizens of the former Republic of Czechoslovakia will not be treated as enemy aliens [At this point the Member Mr. Dallon interjected: This is reparation for Munich] although there may be among them certain individuals who will be subjected to restrictions similar to those applicable to enemy aliens.[52]

This statement prompted a Member of the House, Miss Rathbone, to the question:

Has the right honourable gentleman considered the possibility of drawing a distinction between Austrians and Germans and placing the Austrians in the same category as Czechoslovaks, seeing that their country was taken from them without their consent? Is he aware that there is a very strong feeling to that effect among the Austrian community, who are only too anxious to serve this country?[53]

The reply was:

I can give the House the assurance that there will be every desire, while keeping considerations of security paramount, to show sympathy for the kind of case that the Hon. Lady has in mind, but sweeping distinctions of the kind she suggested, automatically applied, will not be compatible with the public interest.

The issue was taken up again on September 21, 1939, by Mr. Mander, who asked the Home Secretary

[52] 351 *H. C. Deb.* 866
[53] *Ibid.* 369

whether he will consider the advisability of withdrawing the description "enemy alien" now placed on every registration card of Austrians and other refugees, in view of the fact that nearly all these persons are friendly aliens, and the victims of aggression.[54]

Sir John Anderson replied:

I am in sympathy with the Hon. Member's suggestion. Under the Aliens Order, nationals of a state with which this country is at war are subject to certain provisions which are not applicable to aliens of other nationality. These provisions are explained in two printed slips, of which one is attached to the registration certificate of Germans and Austrians, and the other to the certificates of other aliens. I find that, in order to prevent mistakes in the use of the two prints, there were added at the foot of the first print the words: "enemy alien." All these cases are, however, to be reviewed by the tribunals which I am appointing, and wherever the tribunal decides that a German or Austrian can be relieved from the special restrictions applicable to enemy aliens, this slip will be cancelled, and a more appropriate endorsement stamped on the certificate.

Thereupon Mr. Noel-Baker asked:

Does the answer which the Right Hon. Gentleman has just given and for which we are very grateful mean that Austrians will in future be treated in approximately the same way as the Czechs?[55]

The reply was:

That point is covered in the general answer which I made when I explained rather carefully about the various categories.

Thereupon the question of the status of Austria was at rest for several months, as was the war on the western front. The military events of the early spring, 1940, however, caused a wholesale spy-scare in the British Isles. Stern measures against the "enemy aliens" were demanded and adopted. In connection with this, the issue of the status of the Austrians was raised again.

On May 28, 1940, a Member of the House of Commons, Mr. Sorensen, asked the Under-Secretary of State for Foreign Affairs

whether he is aware that Austrian opponents of the Nazi Government regret the frequent identification of Austria with the German State; that Austrian refugees from Nazi oppression desire that their country shall be classified as being essentially in the

[54] *Ibid.* 1047
[55] *Ibid.*

same category as other States invaded or annexed by the German Government; and whether he is sympathetically considering representations recently made to him to this effect by representative friendly Austrian refugees.[56]

In his reply, Mr. Butler limited himself to referring to a statement which he had made on May 7 in replying to a question of the Member, Mr. Parker. The reference, however, was by no means to the point. For Mr. Parker had merely asked the Prime Minister "whether His Majesty's Government have pronounced in favor of allowing the Austrian people to decide their own political future when the war ends." [57] Whereupon Mr. Butler had referred to the statement made by the Prime Minister in a broadcast address of November 25, 1939, in which the latter had said "that we sought to establish a Europe in which each country should have the unfettered right to choose its own internal form of Government."

On July 31, 1940, Mr. Wedgwood went a step further, asking

whether, now that Czechoslovakia has been recognized as an Allied State and Czechs as friendly aliens who may serve against the enemy, the Foreign Office will consider extending the privileges granted to Czechs also to Austrian citizens in view of the fact that under the treaty of St. Germain His Majesty's Government undertook that no alienation of the status of full independence of Austria would be recognized.[58]

Mr. Butler's reply was that

The same circumstances [as in the case of the Czechs] do not prevail in the case of Austrians, but the enlistment in the Pioneer Corps is open to all former Austrian citizens.

On November 9, 1940, Mr. Churchill made a speech at Mansion House in which he said that "Austria is one of the countries for whom we have drawn the sword and for whom our victory will supply liberation." Although this was a clear admission on the part of the head of the Government that Austria was a victim of aggression, no consequences regarding the status of the Austrians were drawn. On the con-

[56] 361 *H. C. Deb.* 420
[57] 360 *H. C. Deb.* 1059
[58] 363 *H. C. Deb.* 1207

trary, members of the British Government repeated over again that Austrians were nationals of Germany and consequently enemy aliens. On March 18, 1941, Captain Margesson stated for the Government that "Aliens of enemy nationality, including Austrians, are not eligible for enrolment." [59]

On March 5, 1942, Mr. Mander questioned the Secretary of State for Home Affairs regarding

the advisability of differentiations in treatment and status between Austrians and Germans in this country in view of the declared policy of the Allies to restore freedom to Austria, and in view of the action on these lines recently taken by the Government of the United States. [60]

Mr. Morrison gave the following reply:

I regret that I should not be prepared to grant these exemptions wholesale to all persons of former Austrian nationality. As regards status, the expression "aliens of enemy nationality" includes all persons who are nationals of a state at war with His Majesty, and I do not think any useful purpose would be served by attempting to differentiate between different classes of persons who possess enemy nationality. . . . Conditions in the United States are different. . . .

On September 9, 1942, the Foreign Secretary, Mr. Eden, made the following statement:

The policy of His Majesty's Government towards Austria was stated by my right honourable friend, the Prime Minister, at the Mansion House on November 9, 1940, when he said that Austria is one of the countries for whom we have drawn the sword and for whom our victory will supply liberation. While His Majesty's Government cannot of course commit themselves at this stage to recognize or support the establishment in the future of any particular frontier in Central Europe, I must make it plain that His Majesty's Government equally do not regard themselves as being bound by any change effected in Austria in and since 1938. [61]

This statement did not touch upon the question of the status of the Austrians. On October 15, 1942, Mr. Mander took up the question again by asking the Home Secretary whether he will consider the advisability of altering the present system of entry of nationality in the certificates of registration, so that those Austrians who left Austria after September, 1938, may be placed in the same position as those who left before, thus giving them Austrian and not German nationality.[62]

Mr. Morrison replied:

The change in present practice suggested by my hon.Friend would not bring about any change in an alien's status and treatment in this country, and that no matter whether an individual is regarded as an Austrian or as a German, he is in present circumstances an alien of enemy nationality.

On October 22, 1942, Mr. Morrison, when questioned by Colonel Cazalet, declared himself to be opposed to changing the designation of the nationality on the identity cards, for the reason that

We should get into complications. It does not follow because a person comes from Austria that he is more loyal than if he comes from Germany. It would be most unwise to give this sentimental concession, which would only land us into difficulties before we were much older.[63]

On November 18, 1942, Mr. Mander asked the Foreign Secretary

whether he will consult other members of the United Nations with a view to the treatment of Austrians on similar lines, in view of the fact that they are regarded as enemy aliens here and have been removed from the category in the United States of America.[64]

Mr. Eden limited himself to refer to the reply given by the Home Secretary on March 5. On May 13, 1943, Mr. Mander brought up the issue again, by asking the Home Secretary

whether he will now consider the advisability of permitting Austrians, now described as Germans, to be registered as Austrians in view of the declaration made on behalf of the British Government on September 9, 1942, concerning the non-recognition of any change effected in Austria since 1938, . . . and whether he is aware of the action taken on these lines in Canada, Palestine, and other countries.[65]

[62] *Ibid.* 1755
[63] *Ibid.* 2105
[64] 385 *H. C. Deb.* 384
[65] 389 *H. C. Deb.* 778

Mr. Morrison replied:

I have considered this matter carefully, but have not felt justified in altering the present practice as regards the registration of
Austrians here, whatever may be the practice outside of the United
Kingdom. As I have previously stated, the suggested change in registration would not alter the status and treatment in this country of
any of the aliens affected.

This time Mr. Mander retorted:

Will my right honourable friend take into consideration the action
of the Palestine authorities, who have recently, in view of statements made by the Government in regard of Austria in this House,
made arrangements to re-register Austrians as Austrians, and cannot we do the same here?

Mr. Morrison replied that "it would be inconvenient in
this country, and I do not think that I ought to engage
in it."

At this juncture, however, another Member, Mr. Silverman, took up the cudgels for Austria. He asked:

Does the right honourable gentlemen realize that his practice of
registering Austrians as Germans is in conflict with the declared
policy of His Majesty's Government not to recognize the German
conquest of Austria?

Mr. Morrison's reply was:

Not at all. I have to take the facts as they are. All Austrians
hold German passports, and they are subjects of the German Reich.

This statement met with opposition, for the minutes of
the debate register at this point: "Hon. Members: No."
Apparently somewhat irritated, Mr. Morrison continued:

The Austrians are at the moment subjects of the German Reich.
It is equally absurd to assume that every person who comes from
Austria is not a Nazi.

Thereupon another Member, Mr. Harris, remarked:

Could not the same kind of thing be said about Czechoslovakia?
Is not Austria in more or less the same category?

The reply was: "No, Sir."

The issue of the status of the Austrians was also raised in
the House of Lords. On February 2, 1943, Lord Sempill
asked the Government

whether in view of the agreed importance of the restoration of Austrian independence in the post-war settlement they will declare their determination to see this achieved and will take forthwith all steps to implement this policy by establishing a clear distinction between Austrians and Germans, in line with the policy already adopted by the Government of the United States which regards Austrians as friendly aliens.[66]

Commenting on the steps taken by the Canadian Government regarding reclassification of Austrians. Lord Sempill said:

The Government of the Dominion of Canada has but recently taken action very similar to that taken by the Government of the United States, and thus re-recognizes Austria's sovereign independence.[67]

The spokesman of the Government, Viscount Cranbone, answered in similar terms as had Mr. Morrison in the Commons.[68]

Such was the situation regarding the status of Austria and the Austrians when the Foreign Ministers of the United States, the United Kingdom, and the Soviet Union met in October, 1943, at Moscow in a Three Power Conference. On November 1, 1943, the results of their meeting were announced in form of a series of Declarations, among them the following "Declaration on Austria":

The Governments of the United Kingdom, the Soviet Union and the United States of America are agreed that Austria, the first free country to fall a victim to Hitler's aggression, shall be liberated from German domination.

They regard the annexation imposed upon Austria by Germany on March 15th, 1938, as null and void. They consider themselves in no way bound by any changes effected in Austria since that date. They declare that they wish to see reestablished a free and independent Austria, and thereby to open the way for the Austrian people themselves, as well as those neighboring states which will be faced with similar problems, to find that political and economic security which is the only basis for lasting peace.

Austria is reminded, however, that she has a responsibility which she cannot evade for participation in the war on the side of Hitlerite Germany, and that in the final settlement account will inevitably be taken of her own contribution to her liberation.[69]

[66] 125 H. L. Deb. 869
[67] Ibid. 873
[68] Ibid. 881-2
[69] 9 D. S. Bull. 310

The statement that the Conference Powers "regard the annexation imposed upon Austria by Germany on March 15th, 1938, as null and void" is a clear statement of law. What is null and void is by definition legally invalid from its inception.[70] The statement, therefore, can have no other meaning than that in the eyes of the Conference Powers the annexation of Austria by Germany had not the effect of establishing German sovereignty over the Austrian territory, nor, consequently, the effect of ending the legal existence of Austria, notwithstanding the fact that the German occupant had temporarily succeeded in imposing de facto control on that country and that no organs of Austrian sovereignty such as a government-in-exile or diplomatic representatives had remained in function abroad.

As to the last paragraph of the Declaration, it stands to reason that it was mainly written as an incentive to Austrian resistance against the occupant. (Incidentally, it has not yet been disclosed at whose suggestion the paragraph was inserted.) As a statement of law, it would be bound to invite serious objections. For it is hard to see how a country which had been subjugated by a foreign invader with the tacit assent of those who were under the legal duty to respect and preserve her political independence could legally "participate" in a war "on the side" of the occupant. The Austrians, it is true, were drafted by the invader into his army, their economy made to work for his war machine. Yet the same took place also in Allied countries, the use of manpower in all areas annexed during the war to the German Reich (as e.g. parts of Poland and Slovenia), the use of resources without exception in all German-occupied territories. Such happenings, it is submitted, constituted a mere situation of fact, and were not able to make Austria in its capacity as a legal entity a belligerent. For belligerency is the consequence of the decision of a nation to enter into a state of war with another nation. This decision presupposes the existence of an organized national government, able to act on behalf of its nation. Now, from the moment when Chancellor Dr. Schuschnigg resigned under the imminent threat of for-

[70] Above, 114

eign invasion Austria was deprived of a national government and was consequently thereafter unable to establish a state of war with any other nation. Nor could Austria, in the eyes of the Conference Powers, be considered as sharing Germany's belligerency as a part of the German Reich since those Powers had declared in the same breath that they regarded the annexation as null and void, and consequently— this conclusion is cogent—Austria as a legal entity of its own and not as a part of Germany. But, it might be asked, if Austria was not a belligerent, what was her status during the war? The reply to this question is that, strange as it may seem at first glance, Austria was a neutral. For there is no other alternative under international law. (The attempt, made during the Second World War, to introduce the concept of "non-belligerency" was discarded, since it was merely devised to veil the violation of neutral duties.) Austria's neutrality, of course, was of a peculiar kind: Not only was her territory occupied by a belligerent, but it was treated by him as a part of his own territory in every respect, in particular regarding manpower and resources, and became the theater first of aerial warfare, and finally of full-scale land warfare. In certain—not in all—respects the situation was similar to that prevailing in the Manchurian provinces of China during the Russo-Japanese War.

The Moscow Declaration, it is believed, should have prompted the Governments of the United States and of Great Britain to revise the measures taken regarding Austrian public and private property and the status of Austrian nationals. In the United States, however, the situation in these fields remained unchanged. In Great Britain no consequences were drawn from the Moscow Declaration regarding reclassification of Austrian property. The status of the Austrian nationals, however, was somewhat improved. On November 23, 1943, Mr. Mander asked the Home Secretary

whether in view of the decision of the Moscow Conference that the annexation of Austria by Germany on March 15, 1938, is null and void, it is now proposed to treat those at present in this country who were citizens of Austria before that date as Austrians, and not as German subjects.[71]

[71] 393 *H. C. Deb.* 1427

Speaking for the Government, the Under-Secretary of State for the Home Department, Mr. Peake, replied:

As my right honourable friend has explained on previous occasions, it makes no difference to the treatment of status of an alien in this country if his nationality is described as Austrian instead of German. His treatment depends upon whether or not he is wholeheartedly sympathetic with the allied cause and willing to assist our war effort. If he is, he can obtain exemption from the special restrictions applicable to aliens of enemy nationality.

Not satisfied with this answer, Mr. Mander retorted:

Is not the right honourable Gentleman aware that these Austrians feel deeply humiliated at being wrongly described as Germans? In the light of the Moscow Conference and what was decided there, will he give the matter further consideration?

Mr. Peake replied:

The honourable Member's question was read as dealing with the treatment of these people. As I have explained, it makes no difference whether they are described as Germans or Austrians. But as regards registration with the police, I will take note of the honourable Member's point.

On December 9, 1943, Mr. Mander asked the Home Secretary

whether he has now given consideration to the proposal that, in the light of decisions arrived at at the Moscow Conference, those who were Austrian subjects before the seizure of that country by Germany on March 15, 1938, shall in future be described in their passports as Austrian and not German subjects.[72]

Mr. Morrison's reply was that

This matter is receiving consideration, but I am not at present in a position to make any statement.

A week later, on December 16, 1943, Mr. Mander asked the Home Secretary

whether he is now in a position to announce his decision on the proposal that former Austrians shall in future be described in their police registration certificates as Austrians and not as Germans, or as Germans, formerly Austrians.[73]

This time Mr. Morrison answered:

[72] 395 H. C. Deb. 1120
[73] Ibid. 1677

Yes, Sir, I have decided that any alien now registered as German who can furnish to the police with whom he is registered satisfactory evidence that he possessed Austrian citizenship when Germany annexed Austria, on application, be registered as Austrian.

No further step, however, was taken by the British Government to redefine the status of the Austrians in the sense of "possessing the nationality of a state not at war with His Majesty," and consequently of being "aliens, not being enemy aliens" under the Aliens Order as amended.[74] Not even after the German surrender and the complete liberation of Austria were the British statesmen willing to draw from the Moscow Conference the legal and logical consequences regarding the status of the Austrians. As late as October 11, 1945, the Member of the House of Commons, Mr. Strauss, asked the new Home Secretary of the Labor Government, Mr. Ede, whether he would consider an alternative to the descriptions "enemy alien" for those Austrians and Germans who had proved by military service or in other ways their loyalty to England and to democratic principles.[75] Mr. Ede replied:

The expression "enemy alien" merely connotes a foreigner who is the subject of a State at war with His Majesty and has no neces-

[74] In a British case decided on July 26, 1944 (The King v. The Home Secretary, 1 K. B. 7 [1945]), the applicants, who were Jews within the meaning of the German laws and decrees, and who had been nationals of Austria prior to the German invasion, left Austria in 1938, went first to France, and boarded in 1941 a ship which sailed to South America via the Port of Spain in Trinidad. When the ship reached that port, an Order of Detention was issued against them and they were apprehended and brought to the United Kingdom. They applied for a writ of habeas corpus on the ground that they were no longer nationals of Germany under a German decree of November 25, 1941, under which Jews who had their ordinary residence outside of Germany were deprived of their German nationality, and that consequently they could no longer be considered enemy aliens. The court rejected the application on the ground that "the courts of this country will not in time of war recognize any change of nationality brought about by a decree of an enemy state, which purports to turn any of its subjects into a stateless person . . . wherefore an alien enemy who in consequence of such decree has become a stateless person, still retains, in law, his enemy status, and if interned in this country, cannot move for a writ of habeas corpus." The court further stated that "the applicants were at one time Austrian nationals, but became German nationals in consequence of a German decree of July 3, 1938, the effect of which was recognized by His Majesty's Government; and therefore, when war broke out, they became enemy aliens as subjects of Germany. . . ." The question whether the Moscow Declaration, to which the British Government was a party, had not possibly affected the recognition of the effect of the German decree of July 3, 1938, was not raised during the whole proceedings, nor taken up by the court ex officio.

[75] 414 H. C. Deb. 392

sary reference to the political sympathies of those so described. . . .
Except in a few cases . . . all the Germans and Austrians who have
proved their loyalty to the cause of the United Nations have been
exempted from the special restrictions applicable to aliens of
enemy nationality.

This statement did not satisfy the Member, Mr. Driberg.
He asked:

Even though it is a technical definition, is it not grossly unfair to
the Austrians who were among Hitler's first victims, and is it not in
effect recognizing the Anschluss and recognizing Hitler's seizure of
Austria?

Mr. Ede's reply was in about the same vein as the previous statements of his predecessor, Mr. Morrison. Said Mr.
Ede:

It recognizes the facts of the situation at the time we went to
war.

Regarding another question equally connected with the
non-recognition of the German annexation of Austria, British practice moved ahead of that of the United States. The
Prisoners of War Convention, concluded at Geneva on July
27, 1929,[76] provides in Article 9, paragraph 3, that

Belligerents shall, so far as possible, avoid assembling in a single
camp prisoners of different races or nationalities.

To this convention the United States as well as Great Britain and Austria became parties. During the recent war,
tens of thousands of Austrians who had been forced to serve
in the German army were captured by British and American
troops. The question arose whether they should be separated
from the German prisoners of war. From the non-recognition
of the German annexation of Austria by the United States
and since the Moscow Declaration also by Great Britain it
would appear to follow that these two Powers were bound to
regard the Austrians as being of "different nationality"
than Germans, and that the failure to separate prisoners of
these different nationalities was hardly in keeping with the
spirit of the convention. The military authorities of the
United States, however, rejected all pleas for such separation. In Great Britain the practice was different, as evi-

[76] *USTS* 846; 4 *U. S. Treaties* 5224

denced by the following: On May 17, 1944, Lord Vansittart
asked in the House of Lords "what steps have been taken to
segregate Austrian . . . prisoners of war from the ordinary
Teuto-Prussians." [77] Speaking for the Government, Lord
Croft replied:

The joint Declaration issued at the Moscow Conference made it
clear that it was the desire of the three signatory Governments to
see reestablished a free and independent Austria. His Majesty's
Government have considered it a logical consequence of the Declaration to segregate Austrian from German prisoners of war.

The military events of the summer months of 1944 made
it likely that before long Allied armies would enter Austrian
territory. Early in September, 1944, newspaper reports
from London predicted that Austria would be occupied by
the Allies after Germany's defeat, but that the Allies' occupation of Austria would serve different purposes than Germany's, that it would be designed for rehabilitation rather
than for punishment.[78] These rumors were confirmed by an
official statement of the British Government. On October 24,
1944, the War Secretary, Sir J. Grigg, was asked in the
House of Commons by Mr. Strauss to give an assurance
that currency to be issued to Allied forces in Austria would
not be the same as the currency issued to troops in Germany. He replied that "the financial consequences of the
Moscow Declaration to separate Austria from Germany had
not been overlooked in making plans for the occupation of
Austria." [79]

From February 4 to 11, 1945, President Roosevelt, Marshal Stalin, and Prime Minister Churchill met in another
Big Three Conference at Yalta, Crimea. The report released
at the close of the conference [80] made no mention of Austria.
It contained, however, in Article V the following "Declaration on Liberated Europe":

The Premier of the Union of Soviet Socialist Republics, the
Prime Minister of the United Kingdom and the President of the
United States of America have consulted with each other in the
common interest of the peoples of their countries and those of

[77] 131 *H. L. Deb.* 805
[78] *New York Times* of Sept. 5, 1945 (Report MacCormac)
[79] 404 *H. C. Deb.* 12-13
[80] 12 *D. S. Bull.* 213

liberated Europe. They jointly declare their mutual agreement to concert during the temporary period of instability in liberated Europe the policies of their three governments in assisting the peoples liberated from the domination of Nazi Germany and the peoples of the former Axis satellite States of Europe to solve by democratic means their pressing political and economic problems. . . .

The establishment of order in Europe and the rebuilding of national economic life must be achieved by processes which will enable the liberated peoples to destroy the last vestiges of nazism and fascism and to create democratic institutions of their own choice. This is the principle of the Atlantic Charter—the right of all peoples to choose the form of government under which they will live— the restoration of sovereign rights and self-government to those peoples who have been forcibly deprived of them by the aggressor nations. . . .

When, in the opinion of the three governments, conditions in any European liberated State or any former Axis satellite State in Europe make such action necessary, they will immediately consult together on the measures necessary to discharge the joint responsibility set forth in this declaration. . . .

On March 1, 1945, the Member of the House of Commons, Mr. Strauss, while commenting on this Declaration, made the following remarks:

There is one question I want to ask about this part of the Agreement. . . . I am most anxious to know what the position of Austria is. Does Austria, in the first place, come under this section at all? Is Austria considered either a liberated State—and we hope she is going to be liberated very shortly now—or a former Axis satellite? . . . The difference is really very important indeed. It seems to me that, in the ordinary meaning of the English language, she should not be considered a satellite nation because at no time did she have a Government which consented to go to war with Germany. It seems to me just that when the Nazis and the German army are driven out of Austria, she should be considered a liberated nation and not an Axis satellite country.[81]

This statement would appear unanswerable. The Foreign Secretary, Mr. Eden, however, replied:

Now may I say a word about Austria? On November 1, 1943, at Moscow we agreed on a joint Declaration with the Soviet Government and the United States Government that Austria, the first victim of Nazi aggression, should be liberated from the German yoke. The position of Austria, though she waged war as an integral part

[81] 408 *H. C. Deb.* 1654

of Germany, is none the less rather a special one. It is not conceivable in our judgment that she can be placed on an equal footing with liberated territory, or Allied territory, or any arrangement of that kind. On the other hand, it has been repeatedly made clear that in the final settlement account must be taken of Austria's own contribution, if any, to the overthrow of the Nazi regime. So perhaps I might take this opportunity to remind the Austrian people that time is running short. It remains the wish of His Majesty's Government that a free and independent Austria should be reestablished.[82]

Mr. Eden's statement that Austria had waged war as an integral part of Germany is hardly reconcilable with the announcement of the Moscow Conference that the signatories regarded the German annexation of Austria as "null and void." The main object of the statement, however, apparently was to spur the Austrian underground to more strenuous efforts. The same was also the purpose of an appeal by the American Acting Secretary of State, Mr. Grew, broadcast to the Austrian people on March 10, 1945.[83]

In the meantime the Allied armies forged ahead from the east, west, and south, and it became obvious that at least part of Austria would be cleared of the occupant within a few weeks. Yet no official announcement was forthcoming regarding the steps the Allied governments intended to take in order to restore the independent life of the Austrian State. Unofficially, however, it was reported early in March, 1945, that Austria would not only be occupied by the Allied armies, but also be divided into several zones of occupation, and that this system would even be applied to the capital, Vienna.[84]

In the second half of March the Red Army reached the Austrian border, broke through the defenses east of Vienna, and invested the capital in the first days of April. On April 8, 1945, the Soviet Government broadcast from Moscow the following statement:

In contrast to the Germans in Germany, the Austrian population is resisting the evacuation carried out by the Germans, is remaining in its place and meeting hospitably the Red Army as liberator of Austria from the yoke of the Hitlerites.

[82] *Ibid.* 1665
[83] 12 *D. S. Bull.* 397
[84] *New York Times* of March 8, 1945 (Report MacCormac)

The Soviet Government is not pursuing the aim of acquiring any part of Austrian territory or of changing the social system in Austria. The Soviet Government adheres to the point of view of the Allied Moscow Declaration on the independence of Austria. It will carry out this declaration. It will facilitate the liquidation of the regime of the German Fascist invaders and the restoration of a democratic order and institutions in Austria.[85]

By April 13 Vienna was completely liberated. Again, a broadcast from Moscow commended the Austrian population. Addressing the Viennese, it said:

Having thus assisted in the liberation of the city, you have earned immortal merit by saving cultural monuments and vital installations and, more important, you have saved the honor of the Austrian nation.

Draw new strength from the joy of liberation of your capital and fight shoulder to shoulder with the Red Army to give the knockout blow to the vile Nazi oppressors.[86]

It was about that time that the Allies' plans regarding Austria were first officially announced. On April 18, the Member of the House of Commons, Captain Gammans, asked the Foreign Secretary "if an inter-Allied Commission is to be set up to implement the promise of independence made to the Austrian people." [87] Speaking for the Government, Mr. Law answered in the affirmative. The subject was followed up on April 25 by Mr. Morrison, who asked the Foreign Secretary whether he had any information as to the contribution the Austrian people had made themselves toward their own liberation.[88] Mr. Law replied that he had no precise information, but he referred to the Moscow broadcast of April 8.

On April 29 another Moscow broadcast announced that the day before an Austrian Provisional Government had been formed with the veteran Austrian statesman, Dr. Renner, as Chancellor.[89] The matter was instantly taken up in the House of Commons. On May 2, 1945, Mr. Strauss asked the Foreign Secretary whether the British Government had been consulted about the formation of the Renner Govern-

85 *New York Times* of April 9, 1945
86 *New York Times* of April 14, 1945
87 410 *H. C. Deb.* 187
88 *Ibid.* 837
89 22 *Bull. Int. News* 446

ment, and whether Austria and Vienna had been divided into zones of occupation. Mr. Law replied:

Yes, Sir. On 26th April the Chargé d'Affaires in Moscow was informed by the Soviet Government that on the entry of the Red Army into Austrian territory the Soviet Commandant had been approached by Dr. Karl Renner, a past Chancellor of the Austrian Republic, with a suggestion for the formation of a provisional Austrian Government. His Majesty's Chargé d'Affaires was at once instructed to inform the Soviet Government that His Majesty's Government would require time to consider the matter, which was of equal concern to all the Four Powers who are to participate in the occupation and control of Austria. However, on 29th April, a broadcast from Moscow announced that a provisional Government had been established under Dr. Renner.

The whole question is being taken up with the Soviet Government, both by His Majesty's Government and the United States Government, with whom we are in complete agreement, and I should prefer to say nothing further at the present.

As regards the occupation of Austria, this will be effected by British, American, Soviet, and French forces and the zones of Austria as a whole have been agreed. The precise delimitation of zones in Vienna itself is under active consideration by the four Powers.[90]

On May 2, 1945, the German armies in Italy surrendered.[91] This opened to the British and American forces in the southern European theater the way into Austria from the south, while the complete surrender of Germany on May 8, 1945, enabled the four Allied Powers to occupy the last portions of the country still held by the enemy. On the very next day, May 9, Captain Gammans asked the Foreign Secretary what agreement had been reached at the Crimea Conference concerning the occupation of Austria by the various Allied armies, and the nature and methods of selection of the Provisional Government. Mr. Law replied that these subjects had not been discussed at the Crimea Conference.[92]

One of the first acts of the Austrian Provisional Government was the issuance, on May 1, 1945, of a "Proclamation on the Independence of Austria." [93] The document, dated April 27, 1945, invoked in the preamble the Moscow Decla-

---

[90] 410 *H. C. Deb.* 1386
[91] 12 *D. S. Bull.* 865
[92] 410 *H. C. Deb.* 1881
[93] *Staatsgesetzblatt für die Republik Österreich* 1945, 1

ration on Austria of November 1, 1943, and stated that

Article I   The democratic Republic of Austria is restored and shall be organized in the spirit of the constitution of 1920.

Article II   The annexation which was forcibly imposed on the Austrian people in the year 1938 is null and void.

Article III   To carry this Declaration into effect, a Provisional State Government is being formed with the participation of all anti-fascist parties, and shall be vested with full legislative and executive power, subject to the rights of the occupying Powers.

For a long time, however, no recognition of the Renner Government was forthcoming. Its activities were limited to the parts of Austria which were occupied by the Red Army. There it was able to exercise governmental functions subject to the supervision of the Soviet Commander. In the portions of the country which were in control of American, British, and French forces its very existence was completely ignored, and these areas subjected to exactly the same regime which international law has developed for conquered enemy territory. Thus, on May 24, 1945, the Supreme Allied Commander in the Mediterranean theater, Field Marshal Sir Harold Alexander, announced the establishment of a Military Government to exercise supreme legislative, judicial, and executive authority and powers within the Austrian territory occupied by the British army.[94] The proclamation added:

The Allied forces enter Austria as victors inasmuch as Austria has waged war as an integral part of Germany against the United Nations.

To this proclamation applies what has been said regarding the irreconcilability of Mr. Eden's statement of March 1 with the assertion of the Moscow Declaration that the Allies regarded the German annexation of Austria as null and void. The martial language of the British Field Marshal, however, was soon toned down in statements made in the House of Commons by Members of the British Government. On May 30, 1945, Sir Geoffrey Mander asked the Foreign Secretary to state his position regarding the Austrian Provisional Government.[95] Mr. Eden replied:

[94] 22 *Bull. Int. News* 521; *New York Times* of May 25, 1945 (Report Clifton Daniel)
[95] 411 *H. C. Deb.* 193

It is not recognized by His Majesty's Government. Our attitude is that we cannot recognize the Government until such time as our part of the Allied Commission has a full opportunity to see for itself.

On the same day, the War Secretary, Sir J. Grigg, when questioned by Mr. Strauss, stated:

It is the policy of His Majesty's Government that in all parts of Austria occupied by British forces democratic Austrian institutions should be allowed and encouraged to function wherever practicable. . . . Austria should be, as soon as possible, severed from all parts of Germany and treated as a separate entity.[96]

In the same vein Sir J. Grigg replied on June 5 to a question of Mr. Rhys Davies as follows:

The non-fraternization order applies to Austria. Its detailed application is left to the discretion of the local commander, who will interpret the order in the light of the Moscow Declaration.[97]

For many weeks neither the British nor the Americans nor the French were able "to see for themselves" whether the Renner Government was merely a Soviet puppet, as they suspected, or a government spontaneously formed by Austrian patriots in the hour of liberation of their country. For the entry of the forces of the Western Allies into Vienna suffered considerable delay. In the meantime each of them carried on in its individual zone of occupation.

To the Commander in Chief of the American zone, Lieutenant General Mark Clark, the Joint Chiefs of Staff of the United States issued on June 27, 1945, a detailed directive regarding the American Military Government of Austria.[98] The following portions of the directive—which was not made public until October 28—deserve extensive quotation:

1. The Purpose and Scope of This Directive

. . . .

c. In the event that recognition is given by the four governments to a provisional national government of Austria, such government should be delegated authority in appropriate matters to conduct public affairs in accordance with the principles set forth in

[96] *Ibid.* 236
[97] *Ibid.* 725
[98] 13 *D. S. Bull.* 661

this directive or agreed upon by the occupying powers. Such delegation, however, shall be subject to the authority of the occupying powers and to their responsibility to see that their policies are in fact carried out.

d. Any provisional national government of Austria which is not recognized by all of the four Governments of the occupying powers shall not be treated by you as possessing any authority. . . .

PART I.   GENERAL AND POLITICAL

2.   The Basis of Military Government

a. The rights, powers and status of the military government in Austria prior to the unconditional surrender and total defeat of Germany, were based upon the military occupation of Austria and the decision of the occupying powers to reestablish an independent Austrian state. Thereafter the rights, powers and status are based, in addition, upon such surrender or defeat. . . .

b. Subject to the provisions of paragraph 3 below, you are, by virtue of your position, clothed with supreme legislative, executive, and judicial authority in the areas occupied by forces under your command. . . .

c. You will issue a proclamation continuing in force such proclamations, orders and instructions as may heretofore have been issued by Allied Commanders in your zone, subject to such changes as you may determine. . . .

3.   The Allied Council and Zones of Occupation

a. The four Commanders in Chief, acting jointly, will constitute the Allied Council which will exercise supreme authority in Austria. . . . For purposes of administration of military government, Austria will be divided into four zones of occupation. . . .

b. The authority of the Allied Council to formulate policy and procedures and administrative relationships with respect to matters affecting Austria as a whole will be paramount through Austria. This authority shall be broadly construed to the end that, through maximum uniformity of policy and procedures throughout Austria, the establishment of an independent Austrian Government may be accelerated. . . .

c. The Allied Council shall cooperate with the Control Council in Germany in effecting the severance of all political and administrative connections between Austria and Germany, and the elimination of German economic and financial influences in Austria. . . .

4.   Basic Objectives of Military Government in Austria

a. You will be chiefly concerned in the initial stages of military government with the eliminaton of German domination and Nazi influences. Consistently with this purpose, you will be guided at every step by the necessity to ensure the reconstruction of Austria as a free, independent and democratic state. . . .

12. Reconstitution of an Administrative System

. . . .

b. The formal abrogation of the Anschluss (Act of March 13, 1938) will not be considered as reestablishing the legal and constitutional system of Austria as it existed prior to that event. . . . In so far as it may prove desirable to utilize constitutional laws for Austrian administration, suitable provisions of the Austrian Constitution of 1920, as amended in 1925 and 1929, should be applied.

14. Establishment of Independent Austrian Government

The Allied Council should, and in your zone you will, make it clear to the Austrian people that the Allied Powers do not intend through military government to appoint or establish a national government for Austria but will aid the Austrian people themselves to prepare for the election of a national assembly by democratic means. The Austrian people will be free to determine their own form of government provided the new regime be democratic in character and assume appropriate internal and international responsibilities and obligations.

15. Political Activity and Civil Rights

. . . .

d. For purposes of military government you may consider as Austrian citizens all persons who held Austrian citizenship on or before March 13, 1938. . . . German laws purporting to affect Austrian citizenship should be ignored.

PART II. ECONOMIC

Agriculture, Industry and Internal Commerce

32. In order to supplement the measures taken by the Control Council in Germany for the industrial disarmament of Germany and pending final decision as to the steps necessary in Austria to eliminate Germany's war potential, you should, in cooperation with the other zone commanders, take steps to. . . .

c. take an inventory of all German-owned plant and equipment regardless of ownership erected or expanded in Austria subsequent to Anschluss, in the following industries: . . . ; in order that the Allied Council may determine what portion of it is redundant to the development of a sound peacetime Austrian economy and make recommendations to the governments of the occupying powers regarding the treatment of these industries; . . .

33. Without prejudice to the possible eventual transfer of equipment or production on reparation account in accordance with any Allied agreements which may be reached, the Allied Council should facilitate the conversion of industrial facilities to non-military production.

Reparation and Restitution

39. As a member of the Allied Council and as zone commander you will ensure that the programs of reparation and restitution embodied in Allied agreements are carried out in so far as they are applicable to Austria. You should urge the Allied Council to an agreement that, until appropriate Allied authorities formulate reparation and restitution program for application in Austria,

a. no removals should be permitted on reparation account, and

b. restitution to other countries should be confined to identifiable looted works of art, books, archives and other cultural property.

Part III. Financial

Property Control

55. Subject to any agreed policies of the Allied Council, you will impound or block all gold, silver, currencies, securities accounts in financial institutions, credits, valuable papers, and all other assets falling within the following categories: . . .

b. Property which has been the subject of transfer under duress, or wrongful acts of confiscation, disposition or spoliation, whether pursuant to legislation or by procedures purporting to follow forms of law or otherwise.

An interesting feature of this Directive is that it undertook to analyze the title of the occupation of Austria by inter-Allied forces. This title hinged on the legal status of Austria in the light of the Moscow Declaration. As explained above, her status was that of an enemy-occupied neutral country. The entering and occupation of such a territory by the armed forces of the opponent while the war is still in progress may be considered inherent in the customary rights of a belligerent. The situation, however, changes as soon as hostilities have come to an end. Thereafter the occupation of neutral territory by one of the belligerents can hardly rely for its justification on any accepted rule of international law, since it no longer can be regarded as belligerent occupation, and no general law of non-belligerent occupation has developed as yet.[99] The justification of such an occupation, especially if the latter is extended over a considerable period, can only be found in specific circumstances. In the Austrian case such circumstances may be seen in the fact that the country had been deprived for many years of the exercise of its sovereignty, and that the liberating Powers had the task of assisting her in its restoration. Therefore, the statement in the Directive is believed to be sound that prior to the unconditional surrender and total defeat of Germany as well as thereafter the rights, powers and status of the military government in Austria were based on the military occupation of Austria and the decision of the occupying Powers to re-establish an independent Austria; the sentence that follows this statement, it is true, in stating that thereafter they were also based on such surrender and defeat, may appear questionable. For it is hard to see how the surrender of a belligerent is apt to create rights of occupation against a neutral. But otherwise the legal basis of the inter-Allied occupation of Austria appears well-founded. Nor could it be denied that the efforts of the Directive were concentrated upon the goal of the earliest possible restoration of full Austrian sovereignty, and that the provisions of Part I of the document were pertinent and adequate in this respect. The same cannot be said unreservedly of the provisions of Part II which concern the fate of certain assets located in Austria, and reparations. The wording of paragraph 33: ". . . transfer of equipment or production on reparation account . . ." and of paragraph 39: ". . . the programs of reparation and restitution embodied in Allied agreements should be carried out in so far as they are applicable to Austria . . ." would appear to lack precision since it could seem doubtful whether these provisions referred to reparations to be exacted from Austria, or to reparations from Germany. In fact, it was not until August 13, 1945, that the doubts were dispelled by an announcement of the American Assistant Secretary of State, Mr. Clayton, made at a United Nations Relief and

[99] See on this subject Robin, *Des Occupations Militaires en dehors des Occupations de Guerre.*

Rehabilitation Administration Conference, held at London, to the effect that the United States, the United Kingdom, and the Soviet Union had decided against asking reparations of Austria.[100] This was confirmed by a statement, made on August 23, 1945, in the House of Commons by Mr. McNeil on behalf of the British Government.[101] It is hard to see how a different decision could have been reached in the light of the Moscow Declaration.

Yet referring, as they did, to German reparations, the provisions of paragraphs 33 and 39 could only mean reparations to be paid out of German-owned assets located in Austria. In this sense they were clearly connected with paragraph 32-c (". . . an inventory of all German-owned plant and equipment . . ."). But no definition of the term "German-owned assets" was given. German ownership, however, hinged in many cases on the question of the validity of transfers of property effected during the German occupation of Austria, and this question, in turn, is to a large extent bound to be affected by the application of non-recognition policies, as explained in the second part of this work.[102] In view of the importance of the matter it would have been advantageous if the Directive had undertaken to define the term "German-owned assets" or at least inserted a proviso after the pattern of the Inter-Allied Declaration of January 5, 1943.[103]

The Potsdam Declaration of August 2, 1945,[104] contained a series of provisions concerning Austria. Article VIII announced that

The Conference examined a proposal by the Soviet Government on the extension of the authority of the Austrian Provisional Government to all of Austria.

The three governments agreed that they were prepared to examine this question after the entry of the British and American forces into the City of Vienna.

While this article was essentially a statement of policy, other provisions contained important statements of law. Article IV ("Reparations from Germany") stated that

[100] *New York Times* of August 14, 1945
[101] 413 *H. C. Deb.* 808
[102] Above, 108 ff.
[103] Above, 109
[104] Above, 128

8. The Soviet Government renounces all claims in respect of reparations to shares of German enterprises which are located in the western zones of occupation in Germany, as well as to German assets in all countries, except those specified in paragraph 9 below.

9. The Governments of the United Kingdom and the United States of America renounce their claims in respect of reparations to shares of German enterprises which are located in the eastern zone of occupation in Germany, as well as to German foreign assets in Bulgaria, Finland, Hungary, Rumania and Eastern Austria.

Again, as in the American Directive, no definition of the term "German foreign assets" was given although by that time the question of the nationality of assets transferred to German property during the German occupation of Austria and other invaded countries had already assumed considerable proportions in public discussion. The question, it is believed, can only be properly solved in the light of a consistent application of the non-recognition doctrine.

The military occupation of Austria itself was only mentioned in passing in Article II, last paragraph, of the Declaration.[105] On August 8, 1945, detailed statements were issued announcing two agreements, reached on that subject by the Governments of the United States, the United Kingdom, the Soviet Union, and the French Republic.[106] One agreement provided for the establishment of a control machinery in Austria, to consist of an Allied Council, an Executive Committee, and staffs appointed by the four governments concerned, the whole organization to be known as "Allied Commission for Austria."

The primary task of the Commission was defined as follows:

to achieve the separation of Austria from Germany;
to secure the establishment, as soon as possible, of a central Austrian administrative machine;
to prepare the way for the establishment of a freely elected Austrian Government;
meanwhile to provide for the administration of Austria to be carried on satisfactorily.

[105] "The Conference . . . has noted with satisfaction that the [European Advisory] Commission has ably discharged its task by the recommendations that it has furnished for the terms of Germany's unconditional surrender, for the zones of occupation in Germany and Austria, and for the inter-Allied control machinery in these countries. . . ."
[106] 13 *D. S. Bull.* 221

The agreement further provided that

The Allied Council will consist of four Military Commissioners who will jointly exercise supreme authority in Austria in respect of matters affecting Austria as a whole. Subject to this, each Military Commissioner in his capacity as Commander in Chief of the forces of occupation furnished by his Government will exercise full authority in the zone occupied by those forces.

Under the second agreement "On Zones of Occupation in Austria" the country was to be divided into four zones, one to be allotted to each of the four Powers; the same arrangement was to be devised for the city of Vienna. In the following weeks, the agreements were put in operation. On September 11, 1945, the Allied Council held its first session, and soon took up the question of extending the authority of the Renner Government to the whole of Austria. Recommendations to this effect were made by the Council toward the end of September, and on October 15, 1945, the Allied Governments announced their approval.[107] On October 20, 1945, the decision was handed to Dr. Renner by the Allied Council together with a memorandum setting forth the conditions attached to the extension of authority of his government.[108] The memorandum provided that control over the ministries and departments of government would be exercised through the machinery of the Allied Commission, that certain functions of government—not specified in the document—would be reserved to the Allied Council, that the Provisional Government would now be empowered to make laws for all Austria, but that these laws would first have to be submitted to the Allied Council, and that the latter would also have to ratify the previously enacted legislation of the Provisional Government. Such ratification was granted to the bulk of that legislation; among others, the Proclamation on the Independence of Austria was approved on November 10, 1945.

On November 25, 1945, general elections were held in the whole country on the basis of the constitutional and electoral system that had been in force prior to the abolition of the democratic constitution in 1934. The new Parliament elected

[107] *Ibid.* 612
[108] *New York Times* of Oct. 21, 1945 (Report MacCormac)

on December 20, 1945, Dr. Renner President of the Republic. The Provisional Government was replaced by a parliamentary government under the leadership of Mr. Figl as Chancellor. On January 7, 1946, the occupying Powers extended to this government formal recognition.[109] The American announcement, however, stated that

The recognition of the Austrian Government by the United States in no way affects the supreme authority of the Allied Council. The Council will continue to operate in carrying out the Allied objectives in Austria. As the Council proceeds with its task of eliminating Nazi influences and institutions in Austria, and assisting in the reconstruction of democratic life, it is hoped that a large-scale reduction may be made in the number of occupation troops of the four states and that Austria may progressively acquire the status of an independent state. The United States Government also hopes that an Austrian agent will arrive soon in Washington to discuss matters of mutual interest which do not affect the supreme authority of the Allied Council.

Two days later, on January 9, 1946, the United States Department of State announced that Austrian refugees in the United States who wished to return to their homeland could now apply for exit permits. The text of the document is noteworthy. It read:

The United States did not recognize the German annexation of Austria in 1938 and provided a haven for many Austrians who escaped religious and political persecution by the Nazis. They have made many contributions to American democracy and to the war against fascism.

Those who return will be able to contribute to the reconstruction of Austria and to assist in the completion of Allied objectives as stated in the Moscow Declaration as well as to bring to the Austrian people the assurance that the United States is fulfilling its pledge to create an independent and democratic Austria.[110]

Less satisfactory was the attitude of another organ of the international community regarding the non-recognition of that annexation. On previous pages of this chapter it has been described how after the German invasion Austria was deprived of her rights as a Member of the League of Nations. Now, by the end of 1945 the League was legally still in existence although its organization and activities had

[109] 14 *D. S. Bull.* 81
[110] *Ibid.* 73

been adapted to wartime conditions and, in particular, the Assembly had not been in session since December, 1939. The years 1944 and 1945 had been filled with discussions how to dispose formally of the League and its agencies and assets once the pact of the United Nations had come into force. Finally, it was decided to convene the League Assembly for a last session in which the formal dissolution of the League was to be voted. Accordingly, the acting Secretary General of the League, Mr. Lester, issued on February 4, 1946, letters of invitation whereby the League Assembly was convoked to meet in Geneva on April 8, 1946.[111] This prompted the Austrian Government to send to Mr. Lester under date April 1, 1946, the following communication, signed by the Austrian Federal Minister for Foreign Affairs, Dr. Gruber:

Sir,

I have the honour to communicate to you the following:

By your letter dated February 4th, 1946, A.1.1946, you summoned the Assembly to meet in Geneva on April 8th, 1946, at 11 A.M.

My Government is of opinion that Austria continues to be a member of the League of Nations.

It is true that, after the forcible occupation of the Austrian territory by the German Army, the German Government, in a letter dated March 18th, 1938, brought to your knowledge the German law of March 13th, 1938, concerning "the return of Austria to the German Reich", which, for its part, adopted the Austrian Law of March 13th, 1938, which has been imposed by the occupants and according to which Austria would be a country of the German Reich. This letter concluded with the allegation that "on the date of the promulgation of this Law, the former Federal State of Austria ceased to be a Member of the League of Nations."

This occupation by force was, however, subsequently deemed to be null and void by the declaration of November 1st, 1943, signed in Moscow by Great Britain, the U.S.S.R. and the United States, which placed on record the fact that Austria was the first victim of Hitlerite aggression and was to be liberated from the German yoke.

Further, I would draw your attention to the fact that long before this declaration, the statesmen of Great Britain and of the United States had expressed their opinion in the same sense. Thus, the English Prime Minister, Mr. Churchill, proclaimed in his speech of November 9th, 1940, that his country was fighting for the cause

[111] *LNOJ* 1946, document A.1.1946

of all peoples "with whom or for whom it had drawn the sword, namely Austria, Czechoslovakia, . . ." (See also the closely similar speeches of Mr. Churchill on August 24th, 1941, in the House of Commons on returning from his interview with President Roosevelt after the signature of the Atlantic Charter, and of the Minister for Foreign Affairs, Mr. Eden, on September 10th, 1942.) On July 28th, 1942, the Secretary of State of the United States, Mr. Cordell Hull, also recalled the fact that the United States have never recognized the annexation of Austria by Germany.

In conformity with these facts the Declaration of Independence of Austria, of April 27th, 1945 (Bulletin of the Austrian Laws, Nr. 1 of the year 1945), states: "The Union imposed in 1938 on the Austrian people is null and void" and this annulment was ratified by the Allied Council on November 10th, 1945.

It may perhaps be useful to observe that the attitude of the Allied Powers in regard to this question has not changed. Thus, on the occasion of the session of the U.N.R.R.A. in London in August, 1945, the American Secretary of State, Mr. Clayton, proposed that U.N.R.R.A. should give its aid and the necessary relief to the population of Austria without having to change its statute for that purpose, in view of the fact that "Austria must not be considered as an enemy country but as a liberated country."

The Austrian Federal Government therefore considers that the aforementioned declaration of the German Reich of March 18th, 1938, concerning the situation of Austria in regard to the League of Nations must, for its part, be deemed to be null and void, and accordingly considers Austria to be a Member of the League of Nations.[112]

The foregoing communication was referred by the President of the Assembly to the General Committee of the latter regarding the answer to be given to the Austrian Foreign Minister. The General Committee proposed the adoption of the following draft resolution:

The Assembly

Takes note of the communication addressed to the Secretary General on the 1st April 1946 by the Foreign Minister of Austria;

Recalls that Austria, which for many years gave her loyal cooperation to the League of Nations, was the first victim of Nazi aggression;

Heartily welcomes the liberation of Austria and notes with satisfaction the desire she expresses to collaborate with the free peoples of the world;

Invites the representatives of the Austrian Government to be present as observers at the present Assembly of the League.[113]

[112] *Ibid.*, Document A.22.1946
[113] *Ibid.*, Annex to A.22.1946

The Assembly adopted the resolution on April 12, 1946. The Austrian Government was informed accordingly and accepted the invitation.[114] Thus a half-way solution was resorted to, possibly in view of the fact that Austria, although liberated from the occupant, had not yet recovered her status as an independent state.

As this book goes to press, the Allied occupation of Austria is still in progress and is likely to continue for a certain period of time until the Allied objectives appear fully attained. Yet recent developments point to a growing understanding, at official quarters, of the legal implications of the non-recognition doctrine in its application to the Austrian case. The question of the so-called German assets in Austria has assumed considerable proportions and will have to be solved by a multilateral agreement implementing the Potsdam Declaration. More and more the public discussion of the issue revolves around the question of the validity of acts of a non-recognized occupant, and it is therefore to be hoped that the final settlement of the issue will be based on a consistent application of the non-recognition principle.

In the United States, at least, considerable progress has been made in this direction during the past few months. At the beginning of the year 1946 property belonging to nationals of Austria was still regarded and treated as enemy alien property, as witnessed by the following letter, dated January 16, 1946, from the Alien Property Custodian to a prominent New York law firm:

Gentlemen:
I am in receipt of your letter requesting information as to whether Austrian assets in the United States heretofore vested by the Alien Property Custodian have been segregated from German assets and whether said assets are still deemed by the Alien Property Custodian to be alien enemy property.

Assets vested by the Alien Property Custodian are being or have been liquidated and separate accounts for each property have been maintained. Austrian assets were vested as property of nationals of designated enemy alien country as defined by Executive Order No. 8389. Assets once vested by the Custodian, but not already liquidated, are still deemed to be vested and have not been divested by political changes.[115]

114 *Ibid.,* document A.29.1946
115 According to personal information.

In June, 1946, however, the Office of the Alien Property Custodian, in its Annual Report for the Fiscal Year Ending June 30, 1945, announced that

Property of residents of Austria, Sudetenland, or Danzig, other than citizens of Germany or Japan, is no longer vested except upon the finding that such persons have acted for or on behalf of the enemy. The State Department has determined that these areas are not parts of Germany and that they constitute liberated rather than enemy territory.[116]

It is not amiss to see in this statement an important contribution to the application of the non-recognition doctrine. Of equal importance was the following letter, written on July 9, 1946, by the head of the American occupation in Austria, Gen. Mark Clark, to the Austrian Federal Chancellor, Mr. Figl: [117]

I take pleasure in informing you that the President of the United States, as one of the signers of the Potsdam Agreement, has directed me to inform the Austrian Government that the United States Government is now prepared to enter negotiations with other Allied Governments and the Austrian Government looking towards the renunciation of the United States share of German assets in Austria as part of the general settlement of German assets in Austria.

While these negotiations are under way the United States Government now agrees to turn over to the Austrian Government, as trustees, all German assets now physically located in the United States zone. It assures the Austrian Government such assets may be immediately used for purposes of reconstruction in Austria without fear of removal of the plants and equipment from the United States zone in Austria, but with the question of ownership to be resolved later.

The United States Government also wishes to make it clear that it will recognize no physical transfer of property as conforming to the terms of the Potsdam Agreement which does not also conform to the terms of the United Nations Declaration on forced transfers of January 5, 1943,[118] and which does not leave to Austria the sovereign control of an independent country over the resources within its borders which was envisaged in the Moscow Declaration of 1943.[119]

---

[116] *Annual Report, Office of Alien Property Custodian, Fiscal Year Ending June 1945,* Washington, D. C., 1946
[117] *New York Times* of July 11, 1946 (Report MacCormac)
[118] Above, 109
[119] Above, 181

In making the foregoing statement, the United States Government took the position that the Declaration of January 5, 1943, applies not only to belligerent occupation, but also to other non-recognized seizures of territory.[120]

[120] Above, 109

CHAPTER XXIII

CZECHOSLOVAKIA

O<small>N</small> March 16, 1938, the British Foreign Secretary, Viscount Halifax, told the House of Lords the following:

I would like to say something about Czechoslovakia. No one who looks at the map can be blind to the new position that has been created for that country by what has passed, or the significance that in certain circumstances these tenets might hold for that country and for Europe.[1]

He was seconded by the Prime Minister, who addressed the House of Commons on March 24, 1938. Said Mr. Chamberlain:

His Majesty's Government have expressed the view that the recent events in Austria have created a new situation. . . . We have already placed on record our judgment upon the action taken by the German Government. I have nothing to add to it. But the consequences still remain. There has been a profound disturbance of international confidence. In these circumstances the problem before Europe, to which in the opinion of His Majesty's Government it is their most urgent duty to restore this shaken confidence, is how to maintain the rule of law in international affairs, how to seek peaceful solutions to questions that continue to cause anxiety. Of these the one which is necessarily most present in our minds is that which concerns the relations between the Government of Czechoslovakia and the German minority in that country; and it is probable that a solution of this question, if it could be achieved, would go far to re-establish a sense of stability over an area wider than that immediately concerned.

Accordingly, the Government have given special attention to this matter, and in particular they have fully considered the question whether the United Kingdom, in addition to those obligations by which she is already bound by the Covenant of the League and the Treaty of Locarno, should, as a further contribution towards preserving peace in Europe, now undertake new and specific commitments in Europe, and in particular such a commitment in relation to Czechoslovakia. I think it is right that I should here remind the House what are our existing commitments, which might lead to the use of our arms for purposes other than our own defence. They

[1] 108 *H. L. Deb.* 181

are, first of all, the defence of France and Belgium against unprovoked aggression in accordance with our existing obligations
under the Treaty of Locarno. . . .

There remains another case in which we may have to use our
arms, a case which is of a more general character, but which may
have no less significance. It is the case arising under the Covenant
of the League of Nations which was accurately defined by the
former Foreign Secretary when he said:

> In addition, our armaments may be used in bringing help to a
> victim of aggression in any case where in our judgment it would
> be proper under the provision of the Covenant to do so.

The case might, for example, include Czechoslovakia. The ex-
Foreign Secretary went on to say:

> I use the word "may" deliberately, since in such an instance
> there is no automatic obligation to take military action. It is
> moreover right that it should be so, for nations cannot be ex-
> pected to incur automatic military obligations save for areas
> where their vital interests are concerned.

His Majesty's Government stand by these declarations. They
have acknowledged that in present circumstances the ability of the
League to fulfil all the functions originally contemplated for it is
reduced; but this is not to be interpreted as meaning that His
Majesty's Government would in no circumstances intervene as a
member of the League for the restoration of peace or the maintenance of international order if circumstances were such as to make
it appropriate for them to do so.[2]

From this statement it is obvious that already at that
early date—March 24, 1938—Prime Minister Chamberlain
was under no illusions regarding the mortal threat which the
annexation of Austria had created for the Czechoslovak
Republic; but that he toyed already at that time with the
idea of sacrificing the latter is indicated by his words about
the solution of the question of the German minority.

A fitting accompaniment to this tune was a speech made
in the House of Lords by Lord Ponsonby of Shulbrede on
March 29, 1938:

> If the Government had committed us to fight for Czechoslovakia,
> who in this country would have had any sort of enthusiasm for
> a war of that description, when there is not one person in a hun-
> dred who knows where Czechoslovakia is?[3]

[2] 333 *H. C. Deb.* 1403
[3] 108 *H. L. Deb.* 461

The destruction of the Czechoslovak Republic was effected by two stages. The first, taking place in September and October, 1938, comprised the cession of large areas of Bohemia and Moravia-Silesia to Germany, of parts of Slovakia to Hungary, of the Těšin district to Poland, and the transformation of the remaining area of the Republic into a Federal State made up of Bohemia-Moravia, Slovakia, and the Carpatho-Ukraine as constituent parts. The second stage was carried out in March, 1939. It consisted in the complete suppression of the Republic, the incorporation of Bohemia-Moravia into the German Reich under the guise of a protectorate, the erection of Slovakia into an allegedly independent State, being in reality a German puppet state, and finally the annexation of the Carpatho-Ukraine to Hungary.

Encouraged by the military and moral conditions then prevailing in the so-called Western Democracies, the Government of the German Reich decided to strike in September, 1938, the second blow at the territorial order established in 1919.

Already a few weeks after the invasion of Austria the Hitlerite party in the Czechoslovak Republic, camouflaged as yet under the name of "Sudeten German Party" had formulated demands for the full self-government of the "German" areas of the Republic; these demands became known as the Eight Points of Karlsbad.[4] The Government of the Republic entered into negotiations which dragged on for many months amidst a steadily rising tension and to the accompaniment of a series of violent incidents. During these negotiations a number of "plans" were drafted, only to be rejected one by one by the Hitlerites, who were obviously under orders from the German Government to procrastinate until certain military measures of the Reich would be completed. By the second week of September Germany felt strong enough to resort to overt action, heralded by a speech delivered by the German Chancellor at the close of the National Socialist Party Congress at Nuremberg on September 12, 1938.[5] He gave a lurid description of the

[4] *Int. Conc.* 344, 401
[5] *Ibid.* 411, 413, 416; *Doc. Int. Aff.* 1938, II 191 ff.

"tortures" to which the "Germans" living in the Czechoslovak Republic were subjected, and announced that

> If these tortured creatures can of themselves find no justice and no help, they will get both from us. . . . If the democracies, however, should be convinced that they must in this case protect with all their means the oppressors of Germans, then this will have grave consequences.

The following day the Sudeten German Party served on the Government of the Republic an ultimatum [6] in which it asked for the withdrawal, within six hours, of the State Police from all districts containing a German majority; failing the acceptance of the ultimatum the party vowed to refuse all responsibility for further disorders. On September 14, the leader of the party, Mr. Henlein, declared the negotiations with the Government ended,[7] and the next day he issued a proclamation demanding the "return" of the Sudetan German area to the German Reich.[8]

In the meantime the British Government had decided to take action in order to "save the peace." On September 15, Mr. Chamberlain arrived in Berchtesgaden [9] and was told by the German Chancellor that the latter

> had made up his mind that the Sudeten Germans must have the right of self-determination and of returning, if they wished, to the Reich. If they could not achieve this by their own efforts, he said, he would assist them to do so, and he declared categorically that rather than wait he would be prepared to risk a world war.

The further course of the Berchtesgaden meeting was described by Mr. Chamberlain as follows:

> So strongly did I get the impression that the Chancellor was contemplating an immediate invasion of Czechoslovakia that I asked him why he had allowed me to travel all that way, since I was evidently wasting my time. On that he said that if I could give him there and then an assurance that the British Government accepted the principle of self-determination he would be quite ready to discuss ways and means of carrying it out; but, if, on the contrary, I told him that such a principle could not be considered by the British Government, then he agreed that it was of no use to continue our conversations. I, of course, was not in a position to give there

---

[6] *Int. Conc.* 344, 417
[7] *Doc. Int. Aff.* 1938, II 198
[8] *Int. Conc.* 344, 418
[9] See Mr. Chamberlain's statement of Sept. 28, 1938 (**339** *H. C. Deb.* 5-26)

and then such an assurance, but I undertook to return at once to consult with my colleagues if he would refrain from active hostilities until I had time to obtain their reply. That assurance he gave me. . . . That assurance has remained binding ever since. I have no doubt whatever now, looking back, that my visit alone prevented an invasion, for which everything was ready. It was clear to me that with the German troops in the positions they then occupied there was nothing that anybody could do that would prevent that invasion unless the right of self-determination were granted to the Sudeten Germans and that quickly. That was the sole hope of a peaceful solution.

Thereupon Mr. Chamberlain returned to London; the next day (September 16) the Cabinet met; the meeting was attended by Lord Runciman, who had been dispatched some weeks before to Prague as an independent investigator of the Sudeten German dispute. Lord Runciman recommended that the districts with a Sudeten German majority be given at once the full right of self-determination. The Government agreed, but deemed it necessary to consult the French Government before they replied to Hitler. Accordingly, the French Prime Minister, Mr. Daladier, and his Foreign Minister, Mr. Bonnet, were invited to fly to London on September 18 for conversations with the British Ministers. The result of their trip was laid down in a communiqué which read:

After a full discussion of the present international situation, the representatives of the British and French Governments are in complete agreement as to the policy to be adopted with a view to promoting a peaceful solution of the Czechoslovak question. The two Governments hope that thereafter it will be possible to consider a more general settlement in the interests of European peace.[10]

As Mr. Chamberlain explicitly admitted on September 28, during these conversations "the representatives of the two Governments were guided by a desire to find a solution which would not bring about a European War, and, therefore, a solution which would not automatically compel France to take action in accordance with her obligations."

The decisions taken at the Anglo-French conference were intimated to the Czechoslovak Government on September 19, 1938, in a note delivered by the French and British Ambassadors in Prague, stating:

[10] Doc. Int. Aff. 1938, II 213

We are both convinced that, after recent events, the point has now been reached where the further maintenance within the boundaries of the Czechoslovak State of the districts mainly inhabited by Sudetan Deutsch cannot, in fact, continue any longer without imperilling the interests of Czechoslovakia herself and of European peace. In the light of these considerations both Governments have been compelled to the conclusion that the maintenance of peace and the safety of Czechoslovakia's vital interests cannot effectively be assured unless these areas are now transferred to the Reich.[11]

Lest there should be any mistake about the ultimative character of the démarche, the last paragraph of the note said:

The Prime Minister must resume conversations with Herr Hitler not later than Wednesday, and earlier if possible. We therefore feel we must ask for your reply at the earliest possible moment.

The reply of the Czechoslovak Government was made on September 20, 1938.[12] It stressed that

These proposals were made without consultation with the representatives of Czechoslovakia. They were negotiated against Czechoslovakia, without hearing her case, though the Czechoslovak Government has pointed out that they cannot take responsibility for a declaration made without their consent.

The note proceeded to invoke the German-Czechoslovak Arbitration Treaty of October 16, 1925,[13] emphasized that this treaty could be applied, and asked that it should be done.

The answer from London was the following telegram of instructions, sent by Lord Halifax to the British Minister at Prague on September 21, 1938, at 1:20 A.M.

You should at once join with your French colleague in pointing out to the Czech Government that their reply in no way meets the critical situation which the Anglo-French proposals were designed to avert, and if adhered to would, when made public, in our opinion lead to an immediate German invasion. You should urge the Czech Government to withdraw this reply and urgently consider an alternative that takes account of realities. Anglo-French proposals remain in our view the only chance of avoiding immediate German attack. On the basis of the reply now under consideration I would have no hope of any useful result ensuing from a second visit to

11 *Ibid.; Cmd.* 5847; *Int. Conc.* **344, 430**
12 *Doc. Int. Aff.* 1938, II 214
13 54 *LNTS* **341**

Herr Hitler, and Prime Minister would be obliged to cancel arrangement for it. We therefore beg Czech Government to consider urgently and seriously before producing a situation for which we could take no responsibility. We should of course have been willing to put Czech proposal for arbitration before the German Government if we had thought that at this stage there was any chance of its receiving favourable consideration. But we cannot for a moment believe that it would be acceptable now, nor do we think that the German Government would regard the present proposition as one that is capable of being settled by arbitration as the Czech Government suggest. If on reconsideration Czech Government feel bound to reject our advice, they must of course be free to take action that they think appropriate to meet the situation that may thereafter develop. Please act immediately on receipt at whatever hour.[14]

The envoys acted immediately. At 2 A.M. they drove up to Hradčany castle and presented President Beneš with the second ultimatum from the Governments of two fellow Member States of the League of Nations.

The Czechoslovak Government accepted. It notified the Ambassadors of the so-called Western Democracies of its capitulation by a note of September 21, 1938, reading:

The Czechoslovak Government, forced by circumstances, yielding to unheard-of pressure and drawing the consequences from the communication of the French and British Governments of September 21, 1938, in which both Governments expressed their point of view as to help for Czechoslovakia in case she should refuse to accept the Franco-British proposals and should be attacked by Germany, accepts the Anglo-French proposals with feelings of pain. . . . It notes with regret that these proposals were elaborated without previous consultation with the Czechoslovak Government. . . .
In the opinion of the Czechoslovak Government, the Franco-British proposals imply that all details of the practical realization of the Franco-British proposals will be determined in agreement with the Czechoslovak Government.[15]

In a broadcast to the nation, delivered at 7 P.M., the Government was more explicit than in the diplomatic parlance of the note of acceptance:

The British and French Governments, during a common démarche made last night before the President of the Republic by their diplomatic representatives, intimated to the Czechoslovak Government that this solution [i.e. negotiations regarding arbitration] would not prevent a conflict, and that Great Britain and France would be

[14] *Doc. Int. Aff.* 1938, II 216
[15] *Ibid.* 217

unable to afford any help to Czechoslovakia in the event of her being attacked by Germany, which would happen if Czechoslovakia did not immediately agree in principle to the cession of the territories with German population to the Reich.

Since the Soviet Union could afford us military help only in company with France, or, alternatively, if France would not act, until Germany had been declared an aggressor by the League of Nations, we found ourselves faced with a threat of war, which would endanger, not merely the present boundaries of our state, but even the very existence of the Czechs and Slovaks as one indivisible nation. . . . The President of the Republic, therefore, together with the Government, could not do anything but accept the plan of the two Great Powers as the basis of further negotiations. We had no other choice, because we were left alone.[16]

The details of the settlement had to be negotiated between the British Prime Minister and the German Chancellor. The ultimate result of Mr. Chamberlain's negotiations was the conclusion of the following Agreement, signed at Munich on September 29, 1938:

Germany, the United Kingdom, France and Italy, taking into consideration the agreement which has been already reached in principle for the cession to Germany of the Sudeten German territory, have agreed on the following terms and conditions governing the said cession and the measures consequent thereon, and by this agreement they each hold themselves responsible for the steps necessary to secure its fulfillment.

1. The evacuation will begin on the 1st October.
2. The United Kingdom, France and Italy agree that the evacuation of the territory shall be completed by the 10th October. . . .
3. The conditions governing the evacuation will be laid down in detail by an international commission composed of representatives of Germany, the United Kingdom, France, Italy and Czechoslovakia.
4. The occupation by stages of the predominantly German territory by German troops will begin on the 1st October. The four territories marked on the attached map will be occupied by German troops in the following order: . . . The remaining territory of preponderantly German character will be ascertained by the aforesaid international commission forthwith and be occupied by German troops by the 10th of October.
5. The international commission referred to in paragraph 3 will determine the territories in which a plebiscite is to be held. . . .

[16] *Ibid.*

6. The final determination of the frontiers will be carried out by the international commission. . . .[17]

An Annex to the Agreement laid down that

His Majesty's Government in the United Kingdom and the French Government have entered into the above agreement on the basis that they stand by the offer, contained in paragraph 6 of the Anglo-French proposals of the 19th September, relating to an international guarantee of the new boundaries of the Czechoslovak State against unprovoked aggression.

When the question of the Polish and Hungarian minorities in Czechoslovakia has been settled, Germany and Italy for their part will give a guarantee to Czechoslovakia.

The agreement was concluded without consulting the Czechoslovak Government. Nothing was left to the latter but to accept. On September 30, 1938, the Czechoslovak Foreign Minister, Dr. Krofta, announced in the presence of the French, British and Italian Ministers that "in the name of the President of the Republic and in the name of the Czechoslovak Government we accept the decisions taken at Munich without us and against us." [18] The nation was notified by a communiqué of the same day which said:

. . . .

The decision of this [the Munich] Conference was communicated to the Czechoslovak Government this morning. . . .

After thoroughly weighing and examining from all points of view all the urgent recommendations which were communicated to the Government by the British and French Governments, . . . the Czechoslovak Government . . . has resolved to accept the decisions adopted by the four Great Powers at Munich.

It has done this in the knowledge that the nation will be preserved, and that no other decision is possible today.

In adopting this resolution, the Government of the Czechoslovak Republic at the same time registers its protest before the world against this decision, which was taken unilaterally and without its participation.[19]

On October 5, 1938, President Beneš announced his resignation.[20] On the same day the International Commission, set up under Article 3 of the Munich Agreement, began its

[17] *Ibid.* 289; *Cmd.* 5848; *Int. Conc.* 344, 462.
[18] *Cz. Y. Bk.* 25
[19] *Doc. Int. Aff.* 1938, II 326
[20] *Int. Conc.* 344, 476; *Doc. Int. Aff.* 1938, II 329

work. On October 13 it announced its decision to refrain from any plebiscite,[21] and on November 21 the new frontier was determined.[22]

In the course of the September crisis also Poland and Hungary had advanced territorial claims against the Czechoslovak Republic. Immediately after the conclusion of the Munich Agreement, Poland delivered to Czechoslovakia a note, dated September 30, demanding with a twenty-four-hour time limit the cession of the Tĕšin district.[23] The Czechoslovak Government acceded to the demand. A communiqué motivated this decision as follows:

> In consideration of the grave international situation, and under stress of the circumstances arising out of the Munich decision, the Government could not do other than decide to accept the Polish propositions. This grave decision was taken by the Government with the full consent of the responsible representatives of the political parties. It did so, knowing that any other decision would have led to new and serious complications.[24]

The Hungarian claims were not pressed in the form of an ultimatum, but asserted by means of diplomatic correspondence. Finally the Governments of Hungary and Czechoslovakia agreed upon joint arbitration by Germany and Italy. The award, handed down at Vienna on November 2, 1938, transferred to Hungary considerable parts of the Slovak and Carpatho-Ruthenian territories, including the cities of Košice and Užhorod.[25] Soon thereafter the constitutional structure of the Czechoslovak Republic was changed. Two Acts of the Czechoslovak Parliament, promulgated on November 22, granted autonomy on a federal basis to Slovakia and the Carpatho-Ruthenian territory, henceforth called Carpatho-Ukraine. On November 30, 1938, Dr. Hácha was elected President of the Republic.[26]

At the session of the League Assembly which opened on September 12, 1938, Czechoslovakia was not represented, nor was any of the League bodies invoked to deal with the

21 *Ibid.* 339; *Int. Conc.* 344, 477
22 *Doc. Int. Aff.* 1938, II 341
23 *Ibid.* 324
24 *Ibid.* 343
25 *Ibid.* 325 and 351
26 *Ibid.* 323, 325

Sudeten crisis. Only Mr. Litvinov stated at the Assembly meeting of September 21 that the Assembly

should consider desirable that the question be raised at the League of Nations if only as yet under Article 11, with the object, first, of mobilizing public opinion, and secondly, of ascertaining the position of certain other States, whose passive aid might be extremely valuable.[27]

All the Assembly accomplished was the adoption, on September 29, of the following resolution:

Representatives of forty-nine States meeting as delegates to the Assembly of the League of Nations have watched with deep and growing anxiety the development of the present grave situation in Europe.

The Assembly is convinced that the existing differences are capable of being solved by peaceful means. . . .

The Assembly, therefore, . . . expresses the earnest hope that no Government will attempt to impose a settlement by force. . . .[28]

The attitude of the Members of the League was in keeping with that of the League bodies. All of them acquiesced in a settlement which Mr. Anthony Eden characterized on October 3, 1938, in the following words:

War has been averted, for which the world is immeasurably grateful; but let it be remembered, it has been averted, not at our expense, nor at the expense of any Great Power, but at the cost of grave injustice to a small and friendly nation. Czechoslovakia was not even heard in her own defense.[29]

On the same day, however, Viscount Cecil recalled in the House of Lords the commitments under the Covenant. He said:

What about our own Government? The Lord Archbishop said just now that we were under no obligation to Czechoslovakia. That is not so. It is quite true we were under no special obligation, but we were under the very precise obligation of the Covenant of the League. Let me read the words, they are very short. We solemnly undertook that we would "respect and preserve as against external aggression" the political independence and territorial integrity of Czechoslovakia.[30]

[27] *LNOJ*, Spec. Suppl. 183, 78
[28] *Ibid.* 94
[29] 339 *H. C. Deb.* 82
[30] 110 *H. L. Deb.* 1327

The Government of the Soviet Union, whose suggestion that the League Powers should consult on collective measures had been as little successful in the case of the Sudeten area as it had been in the case of Austria, kept aloof and remained silent. It did not issue a declaration of non-recognition, but on the other hand took no measure that could be construed as an act of recognition of the Munich settlement.

As to the Government of the United States, it issued no declaration of non-recognition, nor did it otherwse clarify its attitude regarding the first phase of the dismemberment of the Czechoslovak Republic (which, it will be remembered, had, like the United States, become a party to the Anti-War Treaty of October 10, 1933 [31]). Much later, however, on January 4, 1940, the Assistant Secretary of State, Mr. Berle, informed the United States diplomatic and consular officers abroad that "the United States accepted as a fact the transfer of Sudetenland to Germany, and the transfers of parts of Slovakia and Ruthenia to Hungary, and of Tĕšin to Poland." [32]

Less than six months after the Munich settlement, the German Government proceeded to the second phase of the destruction of Czechoslovakia. On March 15, 1939, Prime Minister Chamberlain gave the House of Commons the following account of the respective events:

On 10th March the President of the Czechoslovak Republic dismissed certain Members of the Slovak Government including the Prime Minister Tiso. . . . On 11th March a new Slovak Government was appointed, under the Premiership of Minister Sidor. . . . Dr. Tiso appealed to Herr Hitler and received an official invitation to go to Berlin. He had an interview with Herr Hitler on 13th March, after which he returned to Bratislava to attend a special session of the Slovak Diet, which had been called for 14th March. At the conclusion of this session the independence of Slovakia was proclaimed, with the approval of the Diet, and a new Government was constituted under Mr. Tiso.[33]

The British Prime Minister added that Slovakia had placed herself under the protection of the German Reich. Furthermore he informed the House that

[31] Above, 77
[32] 5 Hackworth 372
[33] 345 H. C. Deb. 435

Yesterday afternoon the President of the Czechoslovak Republic and the Foreign Minister left for Berlin. They had an interview with Herr Hitler and Herr Ribbentrop, at the conclusion of which a signed communiqué was issued.

After rehearsing the content of that document, Mr. Chamberlain added:

The occupation of Bohemia by German military forces began at 6 this morning. The Czech people have been ordered by their Government not to offer resistance.

The communiqué had the following text:

The Fuehrer today, in the presence of the Reich Minister for Foreign Affairs, Herr von Ribbentrop, received the Czechoslovak President, Dr. Hácha, and the Czechoslovak Minister for Foreign Affairs, Dr. Chvalkovsky, at their request in Berlin. At the meeting the serious situation which had arisen as a result of the events of the past week on what was hitherto Czechoslovak territory was closely and frankly examined. Both sides gave expression to their mutual conviction that the aim of all efforts in this part of Central Europe should be the safeguarding of calm, order and peace. The Czechoslovak President declared that in order to serve this purpose, and in order to secure final pacification, he placed the destiny of the Czech people and country with confidence in the hands of the Fuehrer and the German Reich.

The Fuehrer accepted this declaration and expressed his determination to take the Czech people under the protection of the German Reich and to guarantee to it an autonomous development of its national life in accordance with its particular characteristics.[34]

What really happened in Berlin on that night was described on March 20, 1939, by Lord Halifax in the House of Lords in the following way:

It is not necessary, I think, to say much upon the assertion that the Czecho-Slovak President really assented to the subjugation of his people. In view of the circumstances in which he came to Berlin, and of the occupation of Czech territory which has already taken place, I think most sensible people must conclude that there was little pretence of negotiation, and that it is more probable that the German representations were presented with an ultimatum under the threat of violence, and that they capitulated in order to save their people from the horrors of a swift and destructive aerial bombardment.[35]

[34] *Cz. Y. Bk.* 223
[35] 112 *H. L. Deb.* 311-3

Summarizing the whole process the Foreign Secretary said:

We are confronted with the arbitrary suppression of an independent sovereign state by force.

On March 16, 1939, the German Government issued a decree providing that

(Article I) The areas of the former Czechoslovak Republic occupied by the German troops in March, 1939, belong from now on to the domain of the Greater German Reich and come under its protection as the Protectorate of Bohemia and Moravia.

(Article II) The German inhabitants of the Protectorate become nationals . . . of the Reich. . . . The other inhabitants become nationals of the Protectorate of Bohemia and Moravia. . . .[36]

The same day the former President of the Czechoslovak Republic, Dr. Beneš, sent to President Roosevelt, Prime Minister Chamberlain, and Premier Daladier the following telegram:

The Czech and Slovak people are victims of a great international crime. The people of Czechoslovakia cannot protest today, and because of happenings of the last months cannot defend themselves. Therefore, I, as ex-president of Czechoslovakia, address this solemn protest to you.

Last September the Franco-British proposals and a few days afterwards the Munich decision were presented to me. Both these documents contained the promise of guarantee of the integrity and security of Czechoslovak territory. Both these documents asked for unheard-of sacrifices by my people in the interest of European peace. These sacrifices were made by the people of Czechoslovakia.

Nevertheless, one of the great powers who signed the agreement of Munich is now dividing our territory, is occupying it with its army and is establishing a "protectorate" under threat of force and military violence.

Before the conscience of the world and before history I am obliged to proclaim that the Czechs and Slovaks will never accept this unbearable imposition on their sacred rights and that they will never cease their struggle until these rights are reinstated for their beloved country, and I entreat your Government to refuse to recognize this crime and to assume the consequences which today's tragic situation in Europe and in the world urgently requires.[37]

Simultaneously, Dr. Beneš notified the Secretary General

[36] *Reichsgesetzblatt* 1939, I 485
[37] *Cz. S. & D.* II 15

of the League of Nations of the dispatch of these telegrams, adding the following:

I herewith submit this telegram to the President of the Council of the League of Nations and invoke such articles of the League of Nations Covenant as are involved, especially Article Ten. I am convinced that no League of Nations' Member will recognize this crime and hope that all Members of the League of Nations will, in due time, do what their commitments under the League of Nations Covenant impose upon them.[38]

The League Council was at that time not in session, nor did its President, Mr. Sandler, take action. Yet when the Council met in May, 1939, its new President, Mr. Maisky (U.S.S.R.), raised the issue of Dr. Beneš' telegram. He was opposed by the Secretary General, Mr. Avenol, and by Lord Halifax on the ground that the telegram was not a "communication from a government," and the issue was shelved.[39] But at least Czechoslovakia was not dropped from the roster of the League Members, as had been Austria, and she appeared until 1945 on the list of the membership contributions.[40]

This time, however, declarations of non-recognition were issued by several Great Powers.

On March 17, 1939, the French Ambassador to Germany handed the German Foreign Minister the following note:

. . . .

The French Ambassador has the honor to convey to the Minister of Foreign Affairs of the Reich the formal protest made by the Government of the Republic against the measure referred to in Count von Welczeck's communication.

The Government of the Republic considers itself, through the action taken against Czechoslovakia by the German Government, confronted with a flagrant violation of both the letter and the spirit of the agreement signed in Munich on September 29, 1938.

The circumstances in which the agreement of March 15 was imposed on the leaders of the Czechoslovak Republic could not, in the view of the Government of the French Republic, legalize the state of affairs registered in this agreement.

The French Ambassador has the honor to inform His Excellency the Reich Minister of Foreign Affairs that the Government

[38] *Ibid.* 16
[39] *LNOJ* 1939, 248
[40] League of Nations Document C. L. 1944 X-Annex (Geneva, October 31, 1944)

of the Republic cannot in the circumstances recognize the legality of the new situation brought about in Czechoslovakia by the action of the Reich.[41]

The following day the People's Commissar for Foreign Affairs of the U.S.S.R., Maxim Litvinov, dispatched to the German Ambassador in Moscow the following letter:

I have the honor to confirm the receipt of your note of the 16th March, as well as that of 17th March, in which you inform the Soviet Government of the incorporation of Bohemia in the German Reich and of the creation of a protectorate over it.

The Soviet Government does not consider it possible to pass the above-mentioned notes in silence and thus create a false impression of its allegedly indifferent attitude to Czecho-Slovak events, and therefore finds it necessary, in answer to above notes, to express its real attitude to the aforesaid events.[42]

The note then proceeded to refute the attempts of the German Government to justify its action on historical and political grounds, further stressed the invalidity of the Berlin Agreement under Czechoslovak constitutional law, and continued:

In the absence of any expression of the will of the Czech people, the occupation of the Czech provinces by German troops and the subsequent actions of the German Government cannot but be considered as arbitrary, violent and aggressive.

The above remarks also refer in their entirety to the change in the status of Slovakia, subordinating the latter to the German Empire, which was not justified by any expression of the will of the Slovak people.

The actions of the German Government served as a signal for the gross invasion of Carpatho-Ukraine (Ruthenia) by Hungarian troops and for the violation of the elementary rights of its population.

In view of the above, the Soviet Government cannot recognize the inclusion of the Czech provinces and also, in one form or another, of Slovakia in the German Empire to be legitimate and in conformity with the generally accepted rules of international law and justice or the principle of self-determination of nations.

The attitude of the British Government was different. Already on March 15, 1939, the Prime Minister had declared in the House of Commons that the guarantee of the integrity of Czechoslovakia promised by the British and

---

[41] *Cz. Y. Bk.* 226; *Cz. S. & D.* II 23
[42] *Cz. Y. Bk.* 227; *Cz. S. & D.* II 23

French Governments in September, 1938, in no case applied to the events in Slovakia. For, said Mr. Chamberlain,

in our opinion the situation has radically altered since the Slovak diet declared the independence of Slovakia. The effect of this declaration put an end by internal disruption to the State whose frontiers we had proposed to guarantee and His Majesty's Government cannot accordingly hold themselves any longer bound by this obligation.[43]

This attempt to characterize the events in Slovakia as the result of "internal disruption" was partly disowned by Lord Halifax in the House of Lords on March 20, 1939. He said:

The independence of Slovakia was proclaimed on 14th March, but at the request of Dr. Tiso, the head of the Slovak State, Herr Hitler has undertaken to place Slovakia under German protection, and the military occupation of the territory by German troops is now proceeding. . . .

There has always been a Party in Slovakia which advocated autonomy. That autonomy was in fact achieved after Munich in agreement between the various Slovak parties and the Central Government in Prague. The extremist elements, however, were not satisfied with these arrangements, but on all the evidence that is available to me I find it is impossible to believe that the sudden decision of certain Slovak leaders to break off from Prague, which was followed so closely by the appeal to the German Reich, was reached independently of outside influence.[44]

The issue of non-recognition was taken up in the House of Commons. On March 20, 1939, Mr. Henderson asked the Prime Minister

whether His Majesty's Government contemplated granting de jure recognition to the German Government's annexation and control of the territories formerly forming part of Czechoslovakia, namely Bohemia and Moravia.[45]

Mr. Chamberlain answered:

So far as I am aware, no written ultimatum was presented to Dr. Hácha prior to his acceptance of this [the Berlin] agreement. His Majesty's Ambassador to Berlin was instructed on the 17th March to inform the German Government that His Majesty's Government desire to make it plain to them that they could not but regard the

[43] 345 H. C. Deb. 436-7
[44] 112 H. L. Deb. 309-10
[45] 345 H. C. Deb. 885

events of the past few days as a complete repudiation of the Munich agreement. Sir Nevile Henderson was also instructed to say that His Majesty's Government must take this occasion to protest against the changes effected in Czechoslovakia by German military action, which are, in their opinion, devoid of any basis of legality.[46]

But in the same breath he declared:

His Majesty's Government will require to give full consideration, in concert with other Governments, to all the consequences of German action against Czechoslovakia before any statement can be made in the question of recognition.

On April 3, 1939, Mr. Mander asked the Prime Minister about the future intentions of the Government with regard to the maintenance of the British Legation at Prague and the recognition of German acts of aggression in Czechoslovakia and Memel.[47] In reply, Mr. Butler stated that no decision had been taken as yet regarding the Legation. As to the second part of the question, he referred to the Prime Minister's reply of March 20 to Mr. Henderson, which, he said, also applied to Memel.

On May 15, 1939, however, Mr. Butler informed the House that

In order to facilitate the conduct of normal business His Majesty's consul at Bratislava has, on my noble Friend's instruction, sought and obtained from the Slovak Government recognition as His Majesty's consul for Slovakia. The Slovak Government have been informed that His Majesty's Government regard this step as amounting to de facto recognition.[48]

At that time, the Czechoslovak Legation in London was still in function, and the British Government continued to grant it diplomatic status throughout the period during which no government representing Czechoslovak independence was recognized. The same was the case with the Czechoslovak mission in Paris.

Mr. Butler's announcement caused anxiety among the Members lest recognition of the Slovak puppet state might be the prelude to recognition of the German Protectorate in Bohemia-Moravia. On May 22, 1939, Mr. Adams asked the Prime Minister

[46] *Ibid.* 887
[47] *Ibid.* 2426
[48] 347 *H. C. Deb.* 961

whether in view of the refusal of the Nazi Government to grant continued extraterritorial rights to the diplomatic representatives in Prague, he will make it clear that the shutting of the British Legation in Prague does not imply recognition by His Majesty's Government of the forcible annexation by Germany of Czechoslovakia.[49]

Mr. Butler answered in behalf of Mr. Chamberlain that

The withdrawal of His Majesty's Legation does not affect the attitude of His Majesty's Government which was stated by the Prime Minister in the House on March 20.

Two days later the issue of recognition was again placed before the House by Sir Percy Harris, who asked the Prime Minister

whether it is proposed to appoint a British consul in Prague, and whether he is in a position definitely to state that His Majesty's Government will take no action which will involve de facto or de jure recognition of German sovereignty in Bohemia and Moravia.[50]

The Prime Minister answered:

On the departure of His Majesty's Chargé d'Affaires from Prague on May 25 British interests will be temporarily in charge of the British Vice-Consul. The question of the future representation of His Majesty's Government in Prague and its bearing on the question of recognition is being considered.

Thereupon Sir Archibald Sinclair asked:

Can the right honorable Gentleman assure the House that whatever decision may be taken about the appointment of a consul no action will be taken which might in any degree involve recognition of the German annexation of Bohemia and Moravia.

Mr. Sandys seconded him, asking the Prime Minister

whether he will make it quite clear that while the British consul remains in Prague to carry on certain work on behalf of British interests, we shall not ask the German Government to accord him consular status, thereby implying recognition of the German annexation.

Mr. Chamberlain repeated that the matter was being considered. Thereupon Mr. Sandys brought up another aspect of the issue. He asked the Prime Minister

[49] *Ibid.* 1891-2
[50] *Ibid.* 2268

(1) whether l.e will assure the House that His Majesty's Government will not enter into any formal discussions with the German Government on the subject of the release of Czecho-Slovak assets in this country unless they are satisfied that they will not thereby be according de facto recognition to the German annexation of Czecho-Slovakia;

(2) why Treasury officials have been permitted to enter into conversations with the German Foreign Office on the subject of the release of Czecho-Slovak assets in this country, in view of the fact that the German Government has no authority or status to negotiate in a matter solely concerning Czecho-Slovakia; and whether the Czecho-Slovak Legation in London was informed or consulted before the conversations began.[51]

The Prime Minister answered:

The informal conversations which have taken place did not imply de facto recognition of the new status of Bohemia and Moravia, and my hon. Friend will have appreciated . . . that the question of recognition is being considered in connection with the future of the representation of His Majesty's Government in Prague.

Mr. Sandys retorted:

First, may I ask whether it is not a fact that formal negotiations are contemplated, and that there is a danger that these formal conversations will in fact imply a de facto recognition? Secondly, is it not a fact that the Czecho-Slovak Legation still enjoys full diplomatic status, and would it not have been normal to consult or inform them before entering into negotiations with another Government about Czech affairs?

Thereupon Sir Archibald Sinclair asked:

Is it not quite inconsistent with the policy of collective resistance to aggression that His Majesty's Government should be considering the question of recognizing the German annexation of Bohemia and Moravia?

Mr. Sandys added:

In view of the fact that the Prime Minister told the House after the annexation of Czecho-Slovakia that the Government did not recognize the legality or the validity of this act—an announcement which was received with universal approval—may we not have the assurance that the House will be consulted before the policy is reversed?

Mr. Chamberlain's reply was very brief: "I cannot give such an assurance."

[51] *Ibid.* 2274

The anxiety of the Members did not subside. On May 26, 1939, Mr. Sandys asked the Prime Minister

whether, since the recognition by His Majesty's Government of the Government of Slovakia, the French Government have accorded similar recognition.[52]

Mr. Butler replied:

The French Government were approached before we took action for the de facto recognition of Slovakia, but their approval was not obtained.

Mr. Sandys continued his cross-examination. He asked

whether the Czecho-Slovak Legation in London was consulted about or have since been informed of the recognition by His Majesty's Government of the Government of Slovakia,

and, upon Mr. Butler's "No, Sir," he added:

Is it not almost without precedent for His Majesty's Government to recognize a new Government in a foreign country, and not to consult with or inform the accredited representatives of that country in London?

Mr. Butler tried to explain:

This step was taken in order to facilitate the conduct of normal business and to protect British interests. In the circumstances, my noble Friend did not consider it necessary to inform the Czecho-Slovak Legation . . . The status [of the latter] remains unaffected.

Now another member, Mr. Alexander, stepped in:

Why was it thought necessary to take action in this way in order to protect British interests in this case when it was not thought necessary to take similar action in the case of Manchuria? Why this distinction? [53]

Mr. Butler's reply was:

The procedure taken in this case was taken in order that His Majesty's consul would obtain an exequatur so that British business could be transacted and communication maintained with the Government in British interests. I think, therefore, the action was justified in this case.

The Government's replies being what they were, Mr. Alexander rose to discuss the issue of recognition in an ex-

[52] *Ibid.* 2686
[53] *Ibid.* 2688

haustive speech in which he gave much consideration to the
legal aspects of the problem. He said:

We submit today that not only should the Government not give
actual recognition to the annexation of Czecho-Slovakia, but ought
not even to consider it. . . .

I would go further and say that even from the point of view of
his own self-respect I should have thought the Prime Minister
would not have considered it. But after all, there is something at
stake far more important than the self-respect of the Prime Minister. Such recognition, if it would be given, would be, in our view,
entirely contrary to the principles of the League of Nations. . . .

The more one considers the actions of the Prime Minister in
these matters, the more they give ground for the gravest suspicion.

The right honourable Gentleman now seems to hanker after recognition of the Czecho-Slovak conquest. . . .

I ask the Chancellor of the Exchequer when he replies to this
debate to consider also the actual legal position. . . . It is plain from
such evidence as is available that if de facto recognition takes
place, the British courts thereafter will have to give recognition to
the validity of the action of the German authorities in Czecho-
Slovakia. For no other reason than that this House ought immediately to persuade the Government to refuse to consider de facto
recognition.

The other point I would bring to the notice of the Prime Minister
is that there has grown up in the last few years in international law
a clear recognition of a principle which has to be observed in these
matters, which is that in this so-called non-recognition there must
be a definite act taken by way of resolving not to recognize. This
is of fundamental importance in the post-war legal position of international relations. The statement that was made by Mr. Stimson
over the invasion of Manchuria by Japan was one of the precedents
which will no doubt be followed by other nations in such questions
where aggression has taken place.

The effect of the principle will be that nations who are signatories to the Covenant of the League, or signatories of the Pact of
Paris with the principles there laid down, must refrain from giving
de facto or de jure recognition.[54]

After referring to the Argentine Anti-War Treaty, Mr.
Alexander turned to the question how long in a given case
non-recognition could, and should, be applied. He said:

It may be admitted that in the course of time international law
may have to develop a rule corresponding to prescription in order
to validate a position which may have been wrong at its inception,
but which has been de facto accepted for a long time.[55]

54 *Ibid.* 2704
55 *Ibid.* 2707

Yet Mr. Alexander stressed that in municipal law the span of prescription was ten or even thirty years. Concluding his speech, he said:

In conclusion I would say that if the British Government were to grant recognition to Germany over the annexation of Czecho-Slovakia at this time, such an action would be inconsistent with the Covenant of the League. . . . Secondly, it would be impossible for such an action to be reconciled with the previous decisions of Council and Assembly. Thirdly, it is contrary to international law as accepted by the American States; and fourthly, it is impossible to justify on grounds of prescription. Such action will strike a very heavy blow indeed at the hopes we have of beginning to rebuild a proper recognition of international law. . . .

On behalf of the Government, the Chancellor of the Exchequer, Sir John Simon, replied. He said that he was familiar with the precedent. Then he continued:

I am, however, bound to say that I do not think anybody would agree that the everlasting exclusion of British consular assistance in an area would be in the interest of British trade. . . .
The case of Manchuria is an instance, the only instance so far as I know, of almost a general decision not to recognize a changed sovereignty which has been brought about by means contrary to the Covenant.[56]

It is interesting to compare with this statement the words which Sir John Simon had used some seven years earlier at Geneva in connection with the League Assembly Resolution of March 11, 1932.[57]

From the position taken by the British Cabinet Ministers in the House of Commons it was pretty clear what was to come. On June 19, 1939, Mr. Butler informed the House as follows:

His Majesty's Ambassador in Berlin has been instructed to make an application to the German Government for an exequatur for a Consul General in Prague. The practical reasons for which His Majesty's Government have taken this step were given by my right hon. Friend the Chancellor of the Exchequer in the debate on 26th May. I would refer for example to the importance of having an officer at Prague competent to grant visa, among others to refugees whom it is proposed to admit into this country. While, in His Majesty's Government's opinion the step taken implies de facto recogni-

[56] *Ibid.* 2757
[57] Above, 65

tion of the present position in Bohemia and Moravia, it does not involve any modification of the views already expressed by His Majesty's Government in this question.[58]

On July 31, 1939, however, Mr. Butler had to admit that the request for an exequatur had been refused by the German Government

on the ground that His Majesty's Government had declared that while their request for an exequatur constituted in itself the de facto recognition of the present position in Bohemia and Moravia they could not modify their views which they had already expressed as regards the legality of the manner in which that position had been brought about.[59]

Thus in the end Germany had British recognition of, but His Majesty's Government no consuls in, the Protectorate.

Another issue in which the problem of recognition was involved was the fate of the Czechoslovak assets located in Great Britain. Among them was an amount of gold which the Czechoslovak National Bank had deposited with the Bank for International Settlements, and the latter transferred to the vaults of the Bank of England. On May 19, 1939, the London newspapers reported that this gold reserve was to be retransferred to the BIS for release to the German Reichsbank, which now controlled the National Bank of Prague. These reports prompted Members of the opposition in the House of Commons to repeated attacks on the policies of the Government.[60] The details of the debates cannot be discussed in this work; suffice it to say that Sir John Simon tried to stave off these attacks by referring to the immunities granted the Bank for International Settlements under the Protocols of 1930 and 1936.[61] He asserted that

His Majesty's Government cannot accept responsibility for the actions of the BIS and the British Members of the BIS are not responsible to the British Government.[62]

The Government of the United States adopted a strict policy of non-recognition. On March 17, 1939, the follow-

[58] 348 *H. C. Deb.* 1786
[59] 350 *H. C. Deb.* 1932
[60] 345 *H. C. Deb.* 612; 347 *H. C. Deb.* 1813, 1831, 1917, 2079, 2531, 2718.
[61] *Ibid.* 2749
[62] 348 *H. C. Deb.* 2006

ing statement of the Acting Secretary of State, Mr. Welles, was released:

This Government, founded upon and dedicated to the principles of human liberty and of democracy, cannot refrain from making known this country's condemnation of the acts which have resulted in the temporary extinguishment of the liberties of a free and independent people with whom, from the day when the Republic of Czechoslovakia attained its independence, the people of the United States have maintained specially close and friendly relations.[63]

Already the day before, the Czechoslovak Minister at Washington, Colonel Hurban, had announced that the first secretary of the German Embassy had come to see him and had read to him an order from the German Foreign Office advising the German Embassy to take over the Czechoslovak legation and the consulates, and that Colonel Hurban had refused to comply with the demand.[64] This attitude was backed by the United States Government which continued to recognize Colonel Hurban as the Envoy of the Czechoslovak Republic.

On March 17, 1939, Mr. Welles also sent to the Secretary of the Treasury, Mr. Morgenthau, the following note:

My Dear Mr. Secretary:
In view of the recent military occupation of the Provinces of Bohemia, Moravia and Slovakia by German armed forces and the assumption of control over these areas by German authorities, the Department, while not recognizing any legal basis for the assumption of so-called "protection" over this territory, is constrained by force of the foregoing circumstances to regard the above-mentioned provinces as now being under de facto administration of the German authorities. The Department of State, therefore, perceives no objection to the Treasury, under such regulations as it may issue, regarding as German for customs purposes, including the application of rates of duties, goods coming from the Provinces of Bohemia, Moravia and Slovakia. You will be later advised as to the Province of Carpatho-Ukraine or Ruthenia.[65]

The Secretary of the Treasury acted at once in conformity with the instructions contained in the foregoing note.[66]

[63] 20 D. S. Press Rel. 199
[64] Cz. S. & D. II 15
[65] 20 D. S. Press Rel. 200; Cz. S. & D. II 21.
[66] 20 D. S. Press Rel. 200-1

In the meantime the Department of State had received from the German Chargé d'Affaires a note [67] notifying the American Government of the Decree of March 16, 1939, regarding the establishment of the Protectorate,[68] and adding that

Under Article 6 of this decree the German Reich takes charge of the foreign affairs of the Protectorate, in particular, of the protection of its nationals in foreign countries. The former diplomatic representatives of Czechoslovakia in foreign countries are no longer qualified for official acts.

The reply of the State Department was:

I acknowledge the receipt of your note of March 17. . . .
The Government of the United States has observed that the provinces referred to are now under the the de facto administration of the German authorities. The Government of the United States does not recognize that any legal basis exists for the status so indicated.[69]

On March 23, the Department made the following announcement:

The President today signed a proclamation terminating as of April 22, 1939, the rates of duty which he had previously proclaimed pursuant to the trade agreement with Czechoslovakia. The action taken by the President is based upon the fact that, although the trade agreement remains in effect, its operation has been been suspended as a result of the occupation of the Czechoslovak Provinces of Bohemia, Moravia, and Slovakia by the armed forces of Germany, and of the Province of Ruthenia by the armed forces of Hungary.[70]

This statement is highly significant in that it bears out the views taken in Part II of this work regarding the effect of non-recognition on the treaties between the non-recognizing and the dispossessed sovereign.[71]

The declaration of non-recognition was confirmed in the following letter, sent by President Roosevelt to Dr. Beneš on March 27, 1939:

[67] *Ibid.* 220
[68] Above, 220
[69] 20 *D. S. Press Rel.* 221
[70] *Ibid.* 241
[71] Above, 103

My dear Dr. Beneš:

I have received your telegram of March 16, 1939, regarding the tragic events of last week in Central Europe. I have followed these happenings with deep concern. While the United States Government has observed that the provinces of Bohemia and Moravia have been occupied by German military authorities and are now under the de facto administration of the German authorities, it has not recognized the legal status of that situation. . . .[72]

Prior to the outbreak of the Second World War, the puppet state of Slovakia was granted recognition not only by Great Britain, but also by the Vatican, Hungary, Spain, Switzerland, Poland, Japan, Manchukuo, and France.[73] On September 17, 1939, the Soviet Government received a minister from Slovakia,[74] thereby reversing its previous non-recognition policy as expressed in the note of March 18, 1939.

The issue of non-recognition was also involved in a diplomatic correspondence resulting from steps taken by the German occupant of the "Protectorate" and its Slovak puppet in the field of international administration.

On June 30, 1939, the Swiss Minister at Washington informed the Department of State [75] that the Minister of Foreign Affairs at Bratislava had notified the Swiss Government of the adherence, on June 17, 1939, of the Slovak State to the Universal Postal Convention, signed at Cairo on March 20, 1934.[76]

Furthermore, on October 25, 1939, the United States Department of State received from the Swiss Political Department a copy of a note from the German Legation at Bern.[77] In this note the Legation, referring to Article 5 of the International Telecommunications Convention, signed at Madrid on December 9, 1932,[78] advised the Swiss Government "that the acceptance, by Germany, of the said Convention and the four Regulations annexed thereto is valid for the territory of the Protectorate of Bohemia and Moravia."

[72] *Cz. S. & D.* II 38
[73] 33 *AJIL* 570 and 761
[74] 34 *AJIL* 133
[75] 1 *D. S. Bull.* 35
[76] 174 *LNTS* 171
[77] 1 *D. S. Bull.* 605
[78] 4 *U. S. Treaties* 5379; *USTS* 867

These communications were followed by a letter from the Swiss Legation at Washington, dated November 2, 1939, to the effect

that the Government of the Reich . . . has notified the Swiss Government that the adherence of Germany to the Universal Postal Union Convention, signed at Cairo March 20, 1934 . . . implies that of the Protectorate of Bohemia and Moravia.[79]

This time the American Government did not pass over in silence the Swiss communication as it had done before. On November 24, 1939, the Department of State sent to the Swiss Legation the following note:

In acknowledging the receipt of your note of November 2, 1939, . . . I have the honor to state that the Government of the United States does not recognize the claim of Germany to a protectorate over Bohemia and Moravia, perceiving the existence of no legal basis therefor.[80]

This correspondence is instructive, for it shows that the structure of international entities may afford opportunities for evading the consequences of non-recognition.

After the outbreak of the Second World War the governments of the Western Democracies took measures in order gradually to restore the legal status of Czechoslovakia. From the outset of the war nationals of Czechoslovakia residing in France or Great Britain were classified as friendly aliens.[81] As early as October 2, 1939, the French Government conceded to the Czechoslovak Ambassador in Paris the right to reconstitute on French soil a Czechoslovak national army.[82] On September 3, 1939, Dr. Beneš sent to the British, French and Polish Prime Ministers telegrams in which he expressed the desire of the Czechs and Slovaks to join in the struggle for a free Europe, adding: "We Czechoslovak citizens consider ourselves as being also at war with the German military forces. . . ."[83] The next step was the formation, in November, 1939, of a Czechoslovak National Committee in Paris. On November 17, 1939, the French Government recognized it as "qualified to represent the

79 1 D. S. Bull. 645
80 Ibid.
81 Cz. Y. Bk. 55
82 Ibid.; Cz. S. & D. II 64
83 Ibid. 41

Czechoslovak people and, in particular, to carry out the Accord of October 2nd, regarding the reconstruction of the Czechoslovak Army." [84] A similar statement was issued on December 20, 1939, by the British Foreign Office.[85]

When France fell, the Czechoslovak National Committee transferred its seat to England, and on July 21, 1940, it secured from the British Government a declaration to the effect that the British Government "are happy to recognize and enter into relations with the provisional Government established by the Czechoslovak National Committee to function in this country." [86]

On July 25, 1939, the Prime Minister of the Czechoslovak Provisional Government, Mgr. Jan Šrámek, broadcast to the Czechoslovak people the news of the obtained recognition, adding that

As a consequence, the Czechoslovak State, its sovereignty and its external attributes, in conformity with the Czechoslovak Constitution of 1920, continue to exist in the territory of this country on the basis of the declaration made by the British Government in Parliament.[87]

On July 18, 1941, the Czechoslovak Minister for Foreign Affairs was informed of the decision of the British Government "to accord full recognition to the Czechoslovak Government and . . . to accredit an Envoy Extraordinary and Minister Plenipotentiary to Dr. Beneš as President of the Czechoslovak Republic." [88] The same day a treaty was signed at London between the Czechoslovak and the Soviet Governments.[89]

From the United States Ambassador in London, Mr. Winant, Minister Masaryk received on July 30, 1941, the following note:

The American Government has not acknowledged that the temporary extinguishment of their liberties has taken from the people of Czechoslovakia their rights and privileges in international affairs, and it has continued to recognize the diplomatic and consular repre-

[84] *Ibid.* 44
[85] *Ibid.* 46
[86] *Ibid.* 49
[87] *Ibid.* 50
[88] *Ibid.* 54
[89] *Ibid.* 78

sentatives of Czechoslovakia in the full exercise of their functions. . . .

In furtherance of its support of the national aspirations of the people of Czechoslovakia, the Government of the United States is now prepared to enter into formal relations with the provisional government established at London for the prosecution of the war and the restoration of the freedom of the Czechoslovak people, under the presidency of Dr. Beneš. . . .[90]

On December 16, 1941, the President of the Czechoslovak Republic issued the following Proclamation:

In accordance with article 3, paragraph 1, of section 64 of the Constitutional Charter, I hereby proclaim that the Czechoslovak Republic is in a state of war with all countries which are in a state of war with Great Britain, the U.S.S.R. and the United States, and that the state of war between the Czechoslovak Republic on one side and Germany and Hungary on the other, has been in existence since the moment when the Governments of·these countries committed acts of violence against the security, independence and territorial integrity of the Republic.[91]

The clear implication of this proclamation is that in the eyes of the Czechoslovak Government the whole territory of Czechoslovakia was merely under belligerent occupation, but still under the sovereignty of the Czechoslovak Republic.[92] In keeping with this view is the fact that on December 19, 1941, the Czechoslovak Government issued a Proclamation [93] which invalidated transfers of public or private property, effected on the territory of the Republic since September 27, 1938, "under the pressure of enemy occupation or also under exceptional political circumstances."

In the following year the Czechoslovak Government took steps in order to secure from the Great Powers the acceptance of its legal position as defined above. In this it was not entirely successful.

On June 9, 1942, the People's Commissar for Foreign Affairs, Mr. Molotov, informed President Beneš "that the Soviet Government had taken no part in the Munich dis-

---

[90] *Ibid. 55;* 5 *D. S. Bull.* 88
[91] *Cz. S. & D.* II 84; 5 *D. S. Bull.* 543
[92] In an article, published on Feb. 1, 1940, in the *Central European Observer* (reprinted in *Cz. S. & D.* II 98) President Beneš had written: "Czechoslovakia has been at war with Germany since the summer of 1938."
[93] *Cz. S. & D.* II 117

cussions and never considered itself, and does not now consider itself, bound by any degree by what was agreed upon in Munich and by what took place in 1938 and 1939 in respect to Czechoslovakia." [94] Mr. Molotov's statement was followed on August 5, 1942, by an exchange of notes between the British Foreign Secretary, Mr. Eden, and the Czechoslovak Minister for Foreign Affairs, Jan Masaryk.

Mr. Eden wrote:

The Prime Minister had already stated in his message broadcast to the Czechoslovak people on September 30, 1940, the attitude of His Majesty's Government in regard to the arrangements reached at Munich in 1938. Mr. Churchill then said that the Munich Agreement had been destroyed by the Germans. This statement was formally communicated to Dr. Beneš on November 11, 1940. The foregoing statement and the formal act of recognition have guided the policy of His Majesty's Government in the United Kingdom, in regard to Czechoslovakia, but in order to avoid any possible misunderstanding I desire to declare on behalf of His Majesty's Government in the United Kingdom, that as Germany has deliberately destroyed the arrangements concerning Czechoslovakia, reached in 1938, in which His Majesty's Government in the United Kingdom participated, His Majesty's Government regard themselves as free from any engagements in this respect. At the final settlement of Czechoslovakia's frontiers to be reached at the end of the war, they will not be influenced by any changes effected in and since 1938.[95]

To this Minister Masaryk replied:

My Government accept your Excellency's note as a practical solution of questions and difficulties of vital importance for Czechoslovakia which emerged between our two countries as a consequence of the Munich Agreement, maintaining, of course, our political and juridical position with regard to the Munich Agreement and events which followed it as expressed in the note of the Czechoslovak Ministry of Foreign Affairs of December 16, 1941. We consider your important note of August 5, 1942, as a highly significant act of justice toward Czechoslovakia, and we assure you of our real satisfaction and of our profound gratitude to your great country and nation. Between our two countries the Munich Agreement can now be considered dead.[96]

On September 29, 1942—the fourth anniversary of the Munich Agreement—General Charles de Gaulle, in his ca-

[94] *Ibid.* 103
[95] *Ibid.* 93
[96] *Ibid.* 94

pacity as Chairman of the French National Committee, and the Czechoslovak Prime Minister, Mgr. Šrámek, signed the following document:

> The French National Committee, rejecting the agreements signed in Munich on September 29, 1938, solemnly declare that they consider these agreements null and void as also all acts accomplished in the application or in consequence of these same agreements. Recognizing no territorial alterations affecting Czechoslovakia effected in 1938 or since that time, they undertake to do everything in their power to ensure that the Czechoslovak Republic within the frontiers prior to September, 1938, obtains all effective guarantees for her military and economic security, her territorial integrity and her political unity.[97]

As regards the United States, President Beneš announced on November 12, 1942, that he had been informed by the representative of the United States Government "that the previous state of provisionality had been changed into a full and legal diplomatic recognition." [98]

Among all these declarations only that of the French National Committee clearly stated the position that Czechoslovak sovereignty over the territory of the Republic as constituted in 1920 was regarded as not having been terminated by the events of 1938 and 1939. The other statements lacked precision in this respect. The position of the Czechoslovak Government was made clear once again by President Beneš on May 23, 1943. Addressing an American delegation of Carpatho-Russian origin, he said:

> Sub-Carpathian Russia has never ceased legally to be a part of the Czechoslovak Republic; and this fact has been recognized by the United States, Great Britain, and the Soviet Union, as well as by the other United Nations.[99]

During the year 1943 a Czechoslovak unit was formed in the Soviet Union; it expanded later to a Czechoslovak Brigade which, side by side with the Red Army, fought its way westward, toward the border of the homeland.[100] On April 8, 1944, the Czechoslovak Government was in a position to announce that the Soviet Army and with it the

[97] *Ibid.* 97
[98] *Ibid.* 102
[99] 3 *Un. Nat. Rev.* 320
[100] *Ibid.* 59

Czechoslovak Brigade had reached the territory of the Republic and that the tricolor of Czechoslovakia had been hoisted on the tops of the Carpathian mountains.[101] A month later, on May 8, 1944, the Czechoslovak and the Soviet Governments concluded an agreement regarding the future administration of liberated Czechoslovak areas.[102] The agreement provided that

(1) After the entry, as the result of military operations, of Soviet and Allied troops on Czechoslovak territory, the sovereign power and all responsibility in all matters concerning the prosecution of the war will lie, as far as military operations and all measures necessary for their execution are concerned, in the hands of the Supreme Commander of the Soviet and Allied troops.

(2) A Czechoslovak Government Commissioner is to be appointed for the liberated territories whose duties will be as follows: (a) to establish and conduct, according to Czechoslovak laws, the administration of the territory liberated from the enemy. (b). . . .

. . . .

(6) As soon as any part of the liberated territory ceases to be a zone of direct military operations, the Czechoslovak Government takes over completely the power of administration of public affairs and will give the Soviet and Allied Commander, through its civil and military organs, every assistance and help. . . .

These provisions implied the determination, on the part of the Soviet Government, to treat the dismemberment of the Czechoslovak Republic as null and void and to respect the jurisdictional rights of the returning sovereign.

Thus both from the Czechoslovak and from the Soviet standpoint the Republic was legally in existence within her pre-1938 borders. From the German and Hungarian standpoint, however, large parts of her territory now formed part of the German Reich and the Hungarian Kingdom, and their male inhabitants were in large numbers drafted into the German and Hungarian armies. The status of such soldiers was clarified in the following announcement of the Czechoslovak Government, broadcast from London on June 12, 1944:

The Government of the Czechoslovak Republic is fully acquainted with the fact that certain Czechs, Slovaks, and Carpathian Russians have been forced or inveigled into the German or Hun-

[101] 21 *Bull. Int. News* 313
[102] 4 *Un. Nat. Rev.* 185

garian army. It is essential for you to evade this service because it is service against your country and against the interests of your nation. Take the earliest opportunity to join Allied soldiers. Armed service against the Czechoslovak Republic is one of the most heinous crimes which citizens of the Republic can commit. Do not fight against our Allies. Go over to the Allied armies and immediately join service in the Czechoslovak units. . . .

Those who fail to take advantage of an opportunity to desert from the enemy's army will be regarded as citizens voluntarily serving the enemy and will bear the consequences.[103]

The position of the Czechoslovak Government regarding the nullity of the Munich Agreement had already been endorsed by the French National Committee in September, 1942. The successful landing of the Anglo-Saxon Allies in North Africa in November of that year had enabled the transfer of the said Committee to Algiers, where it constituted itself on June 3, 1943, as the "French Committee of National Liberation." [104] On November 3, 1943, a French Provisional Consultative Assembly was opened in the capital of Algeria,[105] and on June 2, 1944, a few days before the western Allies landed on the shores of Normandy, the Committee adopted the name "Provisional Government of the French Republic." [106] The Great Powers withheld recognition for many months (it was not accorded by the United States, Great Britain, and the Soviet Union until October 23, 1944 [107]), but some governments granted it in one form or another, among them the Czechoslovak Government by signing, on August 22, 1944, jointly with the French Government the following statement:

While again declaring that they consider the Munich Treaty with all its consequences as null and void, the Government of the Czechoslovak Republic and the Provisional Government of the French Republic state that the relations between the two States have been reestablished to the same extent as they existed before the signature of that treaty. . . .

Today's declaration is a reaffirmation of a similar declaration made by General de Gaulle in the autumn of 1942. . . .[108]

103 *Ibid.* 186
104 3 *Un. Nat. Rev.* 289
105 *Ibid.* 488
106 4 *Un. Nat. Rev.* 189
107 21 *Bull. Int. News* 894; 11 *D. S. Bull.* 83
108 4 *Un. Nat. Rev.* 228

Among the consequences of the Munich Treaty was not only the cession of the so-called Sudeten area to Germany, but also the transfer of portions of Slovakia and Ruthenia to Hungary under the Vienna Award of November 2, 1938, and the transfer of the Těšin area to Poland as a consequence of the Polish ultimatum of September 30, 1938. While Poland herself had succumbed to the German aggressor within less than a year of her assault on the Slavic sister nation, Hungary had joined the Axis in the war against Great Britain, the Soviet Union, and the United States. In the fall of 1944 the Red Army advanced through Rumania into the Hungarian plain, and in January, 1945, Hungary surrendered. On January 21, 1945, a newly formed Hungarian Government signed an armistice with the Soviet Commander in Chief, the latter also acting as duly authorized representative of the Governments of the United States and Great Britain.[109] Article 19 of the instrument provided that "the Vienna Award of November 2, 1938, is declared null and void." This clause restored with retroactive force Czechoslovak sovereignty over the areas of Slovakia and Ruthenia, transferred under that award to Hungary.

The months of February and March, 1945, witnessed the conquest of western Hungary and the liberation of western Slovakia by the Red Army. For the Czechoslovak Government in London the time had come to return to the homeland. On April 3, 1945, President Beneš arrived in Košice, the main city of central Slovakia. The following day a new government was formed, headed by the former Czechoslovak envoy to Moscow, Mr. Zdeněk Fierlinger. It issued on April 5, 1945, a programmatic proclamation which contained for the first time a hint that the Carpatho-Ukraine might be transferred to the Soviet Union.[110]

During April, 1945, the Red Army advanced from the east and southeast into Moravia and Bohemia; at the same time American forces entered the Sudeten area of the latter

[109] 12 D. S. Bull. 83

[110] 5 Un. Nat. Rev. 128 ("The Government will take care that the Carpatho-Russian question raised by the inhabitants of that country will be settled as soon as possible. The Government will wish the question solved according to the democratically expressed will of the Carpathian and Ukrainian people in complete friendship between Czechoslovakia and the USSR.")

province from the west and southwest. On May 8, 1945, Germany surrendered unconditionally,[111] although certain portions of the German army in Bohemia continued to resist for a few days. Finally they, too, surrendered. But now two foreign, though Allied, armies were on the territory of the Republic. Apparently some of their commanders tended to apply the rules of military occupation to the liberated territory of their Ally. This, of course, was bound to be felt by the population as an encroachment upon their restored national sovereignty. The situation was further complicated by the question whether and how far assets of the German army located on Czechoslovak territory could be claimed as war booty by the Allied armed forces.

At the same time another problem arose. The Provisional Government of Poland advanced claims to the Těšin area which Polish troops even tried to seize by force. To discuss all these issues, Prime Minister Fierlinger went in June, 1945, to Moscow where he had conversations with the leading statesmen of the Soviet Union and the Polish Republic. On June 29, 1945, he signed on behalf of the Czechoslovak Republic a treaty with the Soviet Union [112] by which the Carpatho-Ukraine was, "according to the wish manifested by the population . . . and on the basis of the friendly agreement of both high contracting parties" united "with its long-standing motherland, the Ukraine," and included in the Ukrainian Soviet Socialist Republic. The announcement of the treaty was followed on July 2, 1945, by a broadcast of Prime Minister Fierlinger on the results of the Moscow Conference.[113] Regarding the Těšin dispute he stated the following:

We received from the most responsible Soviet source the assurance that, in the solution of the frontier problems after this war, Czechoslovakia has the right to insist on her pre-Munich frontiers and that, whatever solution might be reached with Poland, it could be effected only by mutual agreement. Consequently we must reject any solution by force or any agitation detrimental to the mutual relations of the two States. . . .

111 Above, 127
112 5 *Un. Nat. Rev.* 157
113 *Ibid.* 211

As to the attempts at setting up foreign military governments on the territory of the Republic and regarding the booty question he said:

Another important point in our negotiations was the problem of the war booty which the Red Army justifiably claims. In the spirit of our original negotiations with the Soviet Government, we have asked that the competence of the Soviet military organizations in our territory should be precisely defined in this respect, so that no misunderstanding can arise. Stalin assured us that the export of all kinds of material from Czechoslovakia shall be immediately stopped, except when such material belongs to the Red Army or when an agreement has been reached with the Czechoslovak authorities in individual cases.

For this reason all stores and works hitherto in the custody of the Red Army will be immediately released, except where the property concerned can definitely be described as war booty. . . . Marshal Stalin . . . also informed us that during the next few days he intended to concentrate all Soviet units in the frontier regions adjoining the German border and the U. S. demarcation line. Thus, there will, in due course, be no more Soviet garrison commands in the interior of our country. Only at some of the railway junctions will Soviet control organizations remain to safeguard the transport necessary for the Soviet Army. From this it logically follows that the U. S. Army, too, is to withdraw to the demarcation line originally laid down—behind our western frontiers—and that Plzno, Budějovice and Krumlov will again be completely controlled by us as behooves an independent Allied State.

Along the same lines the United States Department of State announced on November 9, 1945, that the United States military authorities were planning to withdraw United States forces from Czechoslovakia by December 1, 1945, and that the United States Government had learned from the Soviet Government that its plans provided for the withdrawal of Soviet forces from Czechoslovakia by the same date.[114] The announcement also undertook to explain the continuing presence of foreign forces on the territory of a liberated Ally as follows:

Allied forces, which have remained on Czechoslovak territory to assist the Czech people in the elimination of the remnants of the Nazi forces, are no longer needed to protect the Czechoslovak people against Nazi depredations. Furthermore, the continued pres-

[114] 13 *D. S. Bull.* 766

ence in Czechoslovakia of the Allied forces undoubtedly constitutes a drain on Czechoslovak economy and resources and delays normal recovery and rehabilitation.

At this writing, the Allied forces are gone, and the full sovereignty of the Republic is restored, in fact as well as in law, over her entire pre-Munich territory with the exception of Ruthenia.

CHAPTER XXIV

ALBANIA

O_N April 6-7, 1939, the Kingdom of Albania, a Member State of the League of Nations, was invaded by the troops of King Victor Emmanuel III. The native ruler, King Zog I, attempted to resist, yet after a few days the Albanian forces were crushed and Zog left the country. On April 9, 1939, he sent to the Secretary General of the League of Nations, Mr. Avenol, a letter in which he informed him of the aggression and added:

While protesting . . . against this violence on the part of Italy, and against the disappearance of the independence of Albania, a Member of the League of Nations, I request Your Excellency to bring these facts to the knowledge of the Members of the League of Nations, at the same time inviting them not to recognize a state of things accomplished by Italy with blood and iron, and to take steps for the re-establishment of the Albanian people in the possession of their former rights.[1]

Mr. Avenol subsequently stated that he had not received this letter until May 13, 1939; but he admitted that he had received on April 12 from the Albanian Chargé d'Affaires in Paris the following communication, dated April 8, 1939:

Acting on instructions from my Government, in the presence of the unspeakable aggression on the part of Fascist Italy against my country, I have the honour to request the immediate meeting of the Council of the League of Nations to decide with regard to the aid to be given to Albania in the present violation of her independence and the integrity of her territory.

The circumstances of this ignoble assault on all rules of law and humanity call for an immediate meeting of the Council and the utmost rigour in the steps taken in conformity with Article 10, and incidentally Article 11 and Article 17, of the Covenant of the League of Nations.[2]

Mr. Avenol answered on April 12:

I venture to draw your attention to the fact that on April 8 the Albanian Government was in a position to communicate with me

[1] *LNOJ* 1939, 246
[2] *Ibid.*

either directly or through its accredited representative in Geneva.

I regret that I am today unable to regard your letter as constituting an appeal under the Covenant.[3]

Within five days of the invasion, on April 12, 1939, that is, at a time when the country was hardly pacified, the Italian authorities managed to convene a puppet constituent assembly which declared King Zog I deposed, appointed a government, and offered the crown to King Victor Emmanuel III of Italy. One of the first acts of the new puppet government was to send on April 13, 1939, the following communication to the Secretary General of the League:

> The Albanian Government set up by the Constituent Assembly has unanimously decided in favor of the withdrawal of the Albanian State from the League of Nations. I have the honor to request you to give effect to this decision, and to send me acknowledgment of the receipt of the present communication.[4]

The Secretary General gave the following reply:

> Not being competent to decide as to the validity of this communication, I am transmitting it with the present reply to the Members of the League of Nations for their information.

This answer was correct as far as it went. But it did not go very far; Mr. Avenol did not cause the Albanian question to be placed on the agenda of the meeting of the League Council that was scheduled for May, 1939.

On April 16, 1939, the King of Italy accepted the crown. A few days later, in order to uphold the pretence of an Albanian State and Government, a "treaty" was concluded between Italy and her puppet, concerning economic, monetary, and customs matters.[5]

The Government of the United States had already, on April 8, 1939, issued a statement denouncing in strong terms the "forcible and violent invasion of Albania."[6]

In Great Britain several Members of the House of Commons raised the issue of the change of status of Albania, and tried to commit the Government to a policy of non-

---

[3] *Ibid.*
[4] *Ibid.*
[5] A summary of the treaty was printed in the *Czechoslovak Monitor* (published in London) of May 3, 1939.
[6] 20 *D. S. Press Rel.* 261

recognition.[7] Their efforts were as unsuccessful as those regarding Czechoslovakia.

On May 22, 1939, the Council of the League of Nations met under the Presidency of Mr. Maisky (U.S.S.R.). Although the Albanian question had not been put on the agenda, it was hardly possible to withold the Albanian correspondence from the knowledge of the Council members, and Mr. Avenol submitted the communications of April 8, 9 and 13.[8] In the ensuing debate the President was of the opinion that the Council was faced with an undoubted aggression by a Great Power against a small Power, and that King Zog's letter as well as the rest of the correspondence should be considered, not by the Council, but by the Assembly. His proposal to refer the entire correspondence to the latter was finally adopted,[9] but when the Assembly met in December, 1939, the Albanian case was not taken up again. As in the cases of Ethiopia and Czechoslovakia, however, Albania was not dropped from the roster of the Member States of the League; it still appeared on the document fixing the contributions of the League Members for 1945.[10]

On June 3, 1939, the Albanian puppet government concluded with its Italian masters another "treaty" providing for the direction of Albania's foreign relations by Italy, and consequently for the closing of the Albanian Foreign Office and the Albanian diplomatic and consular agencies abroad.[11] The foreign representatives in Albania were informed that they would henceforth not be accorded diplomatic privileges and immunities.[12] Informing the House of Commons of these developments, Mr. Chamberlain stated that under the circumstances the British representative would cease to have

[7] 346 H. C. Deb. 790, 1111, 1483; 347 H. C. Deb. 1377
[8] LNOJ 1939, 246
[9] Ibid. 248
[10] Above, 221, n. 40. In the cases of Ethiopia and Czechoslovakia the amounts were assessed which corresponded to the unit numbers of these countries; in those of Albania, Denmark, Estonia, Latvia and Lithuania, the column listing the "units in accordance with the scale in force for 1945" shows for these countries a (1) with a mark referring to the following footnote: "Une unité pour mémoire; la contribution qu'elle représente n'est pas comptée dans le total." According to information obtained from the Chief Accountant of the League of Nations, Mr. P. G. Watterson, the agencies of the League adopted the principle that States occupied by Axis Powers were released from the payment of contributions.
[11] 16 Bull. Int. News 605
[12] 20 D. S. Press Rel. 527

the title Minister, but would continue as Consul General. Asked by Mr. Henderson whether the granting of this constitution would in no way affect the decision of His Majesty's Government not to recognize the annexation of Albania by the Italian Government, the Prime Minister replied: "We have reached no conclusion on that." [13] Yet on October 31, 1939, he announced that "it is proposed to appoint a Consulate General in Durazzo, and it will be necessary to apply in the usual way to the Italian Government for an exequatur." [14]

According to the Government's own views such an application implied de facto recognition. The British Consul General obtained his exequatur and left on November 21, 1939, for Durazzo.

Thereafter very few traces of the Albanian diplomatic situation are to be found until 1942, when both Great Britain and the United States were at war with Italy. On November 18, 1942, the British Foreign Secretary, Mr. Eden, told the House that

At the final peace settlement, in so far as the future of Albania is concerned, the British Government will not be influenced by any changes brought about by Italy's aggression.[15]

On December 17, 1942, Mr. Eden told the House: "His Majesty's Government . . . wish to see Albania freed from Italian yoke and restored to her independence." [16]

The United States Department of State issued on December 12, 1942, the following statement: [17]

. . . .

Consistent with its well established policy not to recognize territorial conquest by force, the Government of the United States has never recognized the annexation of Albania by the Italian crown.

The restoration of a free Albania is inherent in that statement of principles.[18]

13 348 *H. C. Deb.* 875
14 352 *H. C. Deb.* 1755
15 385 *H. C. Deb.* 321
16 *Ibid.* 2114
17 7 *D. S. Bull.* 998
18 I.e. the Atlantic Charter (above, 83)

On September 3, 1943, Italy surrendered to the Allies.[19]
Under the terms of the armistice the Italians had also to
evacuate Albania. Germany, however, continued the war, and
her armies replaced the Italian troops who had been in control of the country. The Germans were able to enlist the
support of a certain number of natives who established
themselves as a German puppet government. Yet the col-
laborationists met with ever increasing resistance from Albanian partisans. The situation in Albania prompted the
United States Government to make on April 6, 1944—the
anniversary of the Italian invasion of 1939—the following
statement:

On April 6, 1939—Good Friday—the forces of Fascism struck at
Albania in sudden and shameless aggression, and Mussolini proclaimed its incorporation into Fascism's so-called Empire. Although
the fall of Mussolini and the lifting of the Fascist yoke brought not
freedom, but Nazi occupation, the Albanian people have not, since
that Good Friday five years ago, abandoned their struggle to throw
out the invader and regain their freedom.

As is well known, the Government of the United States never
recognized the Fascist annexation of Albania. Today it looks to the
Albanian people to unite their efforts against the Nazi enemy, thus
hastening the restoration to their country of the freedom they so
ardently desire.[20]

The activities of the Albanian partisans elicited also the
praise of Mr. Attlee in the British House of Commons.
Speaking for the Government he said on May 23, 1944, in
reply to a question of Wing Commander Hulbert:

Guerilla activity is fairly widespread throughout Albania and,
with the exception of a few Quisling politicians who have formed
a government in collaboration with the Germans, the Albanian
people as a whole are resolutely opposed to the Axis invaders of
their country. . . .[21]

A few weeks later, on June 2, 1944, the United States
Department of State reiterated its declaration of non-
recognition of the Italian annexation of Albania by the
following statement:

[19] The signature of the armistice was announced on September 8, 1943, by
a proclamation of Gen. Eisenhower (3 *Un. Nat. Rev.* 373); its terms, however, were not disclosed until November 6, 1945 (13 *D. S. Bull.* 748).
[20] 10 *D. S. Bull.* 315
[21] 400 *H. C. Deb.* 572

Five years ago today, on June 3, 1939, a Fascist constitution was imposed upon the Albanian people by the Mussolini regime of Italy. The Albanian people never accepted this constitution nor the series of puppet governments set up to administer it.

The United States, of course, never recognized the Fascist annexation of Albania which followed the unprovoked aggression of April 7, 1939, and considers that the right to freedom under institutions of their own choosing resides in the people of Albania.

Albanian patriots have fought, and continue to fight to drive the Nazis from their country. This is a part of the common struggle to which these sturdy people can make a precious contribution if they can achieve unity in the efforts of their arms. Thus they can hasten the day of their liberation.[22]

By October, 1944, the general military situation in the Balkans had already caused the slow but constant withdrawal of the German forces in southeastern Europe toward the inner portions of Central Europe. The retreat was accompanied by increased activities of the Albanian and Yugoslav partisans. On October 28, 1944, the Albanian Quisling government resigned.[23] On November 15, 1944, the United States Department of State commented on the new situation as follows:

There are two or three resistance groups now fighting in Albania, and the Germans have been driven out of a major part of the country. . . .

This Government has not recognized any single one of the groups as an Albanian authority. However, we have repeatedly emphasized our traditional friendship for the Albanian people and our desire that their full independence shall be achieved.[24]

On November 21, 1944, the national capital, Tirana, and the seaport of Durazzo were liberated by the newly formed Albanian National Army,[25] and a national government headed by Colonel General Enver Hoxha established control over the country. No recognition, however, was granted to this government by the Great Powers. The issue was raised in the House of Commons by the Member, Mr. Price, who asked the Foreign Secretary on March 14, 1945,

whether he has yet received a request for the recognition of the Albanian Government, set up in Tirana under General Enver

22 10 *D. S. Bull.* 510
23 21 *Bull. Int. News* 966
24 11 *D. S. Bull.* 591
25 21 *Bull. Int. News* 1063

Hoxha; and whether it is proposed to invite this government to send a representative to the Conference at San Francisco.[26]

Mr. Eden answered that

His Majesty's Government have recently received such a request. They consider, however, that the situation in Albania is at present too obscure to justify recognition of the present administration as a Government. The answer to the second part of the question is "No, Sir."

To Mr. Price's further question, "Do we recognize any authority, de facto, in Albania?" Mr. Eden replied: "A British Military Mission is shortly to arrive in Albania which will keep His Majesty's Government informed." In fact, shortly thereafter a British as well as an American military mission arrived at Tirana. Yet throughout the year 1945 the policies of non-recognition adopted with regard to the Government of Colonel General Enver Hoxha remained unchanged. The latter, however, was at least able to win for its country economic aid. On August 2, 1945, an agreement was signed at Rome between the United Nations Relief and Rehabilitation Administration and "the Democratic Government of Albania.[27] It provided for the extension of the UNRRA activities to the latter country. The agreement, of course, could not possibly be construed as implied recognition of the Albanian Government by the governments participating in the UNRRA organization.

Toward the end of 1945 the situation in the Balkans was complicated by a flare-up of the old dispute between Greeks and Albanians over the so-called "Northern Epirus," that is, the regions around Sarande, Argyrokastro, and Korcha. These regions contain a more or less strong admixture of Greeks; after the First World War they were finally assigned to Albania; now a section of Greek public opinion demanded the reconsideration of that border settlement. According to unofficial reports, the Greek Government submitted a memorandum to the major Allied Powers expressing a "very strong desire" for Allied military occupation of all of Albania, and emphasizing that Albania "is in reality an

[26] 409 *H. C. Deb.* 213
[27] 13 *D. S. Bull.* 179

enemy country" and the "Allied attitude towards Albania is inexplicable." [28]

The statement that "Albania is in reality an enemy country" is certainly indefensible as far as the United States is concerned. For the latter never recognized the Italian annexation of Albania, and consequently from the American standpoint Albania could not be regarded as an enemy country on the ground that she was an integral part of Italy; nor did a state of war ever come into being between Albania herself and the United States. Regarding Great Britain the situation may appear more uncertain. The British Government doubtless granted de facto recognition to the Italian annexation,[29] and so far never withdrew that recognition in any form, but only uttered pious wishes for the restoration of Albanian independence.[30] In particular, no declaration after the pattern of the Moscow Declaration on Austria [31] was ever issued regarding Albania.

The efforts of certain Greek circles to deter the Great Powers from recognizing the status and government of Albania increased in intensity in subsequent weeks. On November 10, 1945, however, the United States Government announced its readiness to enter into diplomatic relations with the existing regime in Albania "as the provisional Government of Albania." [32] The statement added:

In establishing official relations with an Albanian Government, the United States Government desires to act in conformity with the obligations and principles to which it subscribed in the Crimea Declaration on Liberated Europe and accordingly requests assurances that the forthcoming elections for a Constituent Assembly shall be held on a genuinely free basis, with secret ballot and without threats or intimidation; that all democratic individuals and groups in Albania shall enjoy freedom of speech and the right lawfully to present and support their candidates; and that foreign press correspondents shall be permitted to enter Albania to observe and report freely on the elections and the work of the Constituent Assembly.

The Government of the United States also desires that the Al-

28 *New York Times* of October 9, 1945, p. 3
29 Above, 248
30 Above, 250
31 Above, 181
32 13 *D. S. Bull.* 766

banian authorities shall confirm that the treaties and agreements which were in force between the United States and Albania on April 7, 1939, remain valid. The United States Government, on its part, confirms the continuing validity of these instruments.

Upon receipt of the assurances requested, the Government of the United States shall be prepared to proceed with the exchange of diplomatic representatives.

This statement made it clear that the United States Government considered Albania a liberated and not an enemy country. It also shows that the theory advanced in this work regarding the effect of non-recognition on the treaties between the non-recognizing and the occupied State [33] is borne out by recent American diplomatic practice. Simultaneously with the American note the British and Soviet Governments communicated with Colonel General Enver Hoxha on the same subject.[34] Shortly thereafter, general elections were held which confirmed General Hoxha in power.

[33] Above, 103
[34] *New York Times* of November 11, 1945

CHAPTER XXV

SOVIET EXPANSION

T̲H̲E̲ outbreak of the Second World War prompted the Soviet Government to initiate a program of territorial expansion aiming predominantly at the partial restoration of the pre-1914 frontiers of Russia in the west and southwest. On September 16, 1939, the People's Commissar for Foreign Affairs, Mr. Molotov, delivered to the Polish Envoy at Moscow a note stating that

The Polish Government has disintegrated; the Polish State and its Government have ceased to exist; in the same way the agreements between the Soviet Union and Poland have come to an end. Poland has become a suitable field for all manner of hazards and surprises which might constitute a threat to the Soviet Union. The Soviet Union can, therefore, no longer preserve a neutral attitude, and the Soviet Government has ordered their troops to cross the frontier and take under their protection the life and property of the population of the Western Ukraine and Western Byelorussia.[1]

On September 17, 1939, the Red Army entered Polish territory and within a few days occupied the eastern part of the Polish State; on September 23, 1939, a demarcation line was agreed upon between Germany and the Soviet Union. Shortly thereafter, however, this agreement was superseded by a treaty, concluded at Moscow on September 29, 1939. Its preamble stated that

The German and Soviet Governments, after the dissolution of the former State of Poland, consider it as their exclusive task to re-establish peace and order in these territories. . . .[2]

The territorial settlement was contained in the following articles:

Art. 1. The German and Soviet Governments fix as the frontier of their imperial interests in the former territory of Poland the line marked in the attached map. This line will be defined again in a complementary protocol.

[1] 16 *Bull. Int. News* 986; see also 351 *H. C. Deb.* 975 ff.
[2] 16 *Bull. Int. News* 1041

Art. 2. The two parties recognize as final the frontier of their imperial interests fixed in Article 1. They will refuse all interference by third Powers in this settlement.

Art. 3. The new political settlement necessary in the territories west of the line fixed in Article 1 will be established by the German Government and the territories east of this line by the Soviet Government.

On the day of the signature of the foregoing treaty, a Pact of Mutual Assistance was signed between the Soviet Union and Estonia.[3] It provided for mutual military assistance in the case of aggression by a third Power, and placed at the disposal of the Soviet Union a certain number of leased bases. Similar pacts were concluded by the Soviet Government with Latvia (on October 5, 1939),[4] and with Lithuania (on October 10, 1939).[5] Article 1 of the latter also provided for the transfer of the city and district of Vilna to Lithuania.

In the meantime the President of the Polish Republic, Mr. Mościcki, and members of his Government had reached Paris. There Mr. Mościcki resigned. In conformity with Article 19 of the Polish Constitution of April 23, 1935, he was succeeded in office by Mr. Raczkiewicz, former President of the Senate. The latter presently established a government-in-exile. This government was explicitly recognized by a number of States,[6] among them the United States. To this effect Secretary Hull issued on October 2, 1939, the following statement:

More than 20 years ago the United States recognized and has since maintained diplomatic relations with the Polish Government. Poland is now the victim of force used as an instrument of national policy. Its territory has been taken over and its government has had to seek refuge abroad. Mere seizure of territory, however, does not extinguish the legal existence of a government. The United States therefore continues to regard the Government of Poland in existence and continues to recognize Count Jerzy Potocki as its Ambassador in Washington.[7]

On October 19, 1939, the new Polish Government presented to the Government of Lithuania a formal protest

[3] *Ibid.* 1042
[4] *Ibid.* 1129
[5] *Ibid.* 1130
[6] 34 *AJIL* 134
[7] 1 *D. S. Bull.* 342

"against the acceptance by that Government of any territory ceded by the U.S.S.R. which does not belong to the said Union," and notified of this protest the Powers which recognized the Polish Government [8] and also the Secretary General of the League of Nations.[9] The American Government published the protest with a formal acknowledgment of receipt, yet without any further statement. Simultaneously, the Polish Government addressed to the Powers a protest against the German-Soviet Agreement of September 29, 1939, and notified of this step the Secretary General of the League by the following note:

> The Governments of Germany and of the U.S.S.R. recently published an Agreement concerning the delimitation of the "imperial interests" of their States in the territory of the Republic of Poland.
>
> The Polish Government duly addressed, through the diplomatic channel, an energetic protest to all States against this Agreement, declaring that it can have no legal effect whatever, being absolutely contrary to the fundamental principles of international law in force. The Agreement, in fact, contains stipulations disposing of the territory of a State Member of the League of Nations which has been the victim of an unprovoked aggression.
>
> I am instructed by my Government to reiterate before the League of Nations a solemn protest against the Agreement in question and to declare that it will always be regarded by the Polish nation and by the Polish Government null and void.
>
> I have the honor to request you to be good enough to bring the present communication to the knowledge of all the States Members of the League of Nations.[10]

The statement that "disposing of the territory of a State Member of the League of Nations which has been victim of unprovoked aggression" is "absolutely contrary to the fundamental principles of international law in force" would appear to refer to Article 10 of the League Covenant, since it stressed the League Membership of the victim. If this is admitted, it would further appear that the draftsmen of the statement had no doubt of the binding force of Article 10, since they called it "a fundamental principle of international law in force."

The Soviet Government organized the parts of Poland

[8] *Ibid.* 403
[9] *LNOJ* 1939, 386
[10] *Ibid.*

taken over under the treaty of September 29, 1939, into two areas under the names of Western Byelorussia and the Western Ukraine. In both areas, in the second half of October, Constituent Assemblies were elected, which passed on October 26 and 29 respectively resolutions requesting admission into the Soviet Union as parts of the Byelorussian and Ukrainian Soviet Socialist Republics. On November 1, 1939, the request was granted by the Supreme Soviet of the U.S.S.R. and the incorporation took place.

Meanwhile, the Soviet Government had taken action in another direction, namely regarding Finland. On October 5, 1939, it invited the Finns to enter into negotiations. The latter decided to dispatch a delegation to Moscow. On arrival the delegation was presented with the following demands: Lease of the Port of Hankoe; cession of five islands in the Gulf of Finland and 2,761 square kilometres of territory in the Karelian Isthmus, demilitarization of the Finnish-Soviet border, mutual pledge not to enter into any alliance hostile to the other party. In return the Soviet Union offered 5,529 square kilometres of territory in the north and its assent to the fortification by Finland of the Aland Islands. The negotiations broke down over Finland's refusal to lease Hankoe, to demilitarize the border, and to cede an adequate area in the Karelian Isthmus. The Finns started to mobilize. Hostilities broke out on November 29, yet war was not declared. The Soviet Government tried to solve the dispute by recognizing a new Finnish Government headed by Mr. Kuusinen, who had been member of a Finnish Communist government in 1918, but was forced to take refuge in Moscow after the anti-Communist Finns had been victorious. The Kuusinen Government, however, was unable to assert itself in Finland, and real war ensued.[11]

The Finns hastened to bring the dispute before the League of Nations. On December 3, 1939, the permanent delegate of Finland asked the Secretary General of the League, Mr. Avenol, by virtue of Article 11 and Article 15 of the Covenant, to summon forthwith a meeting of the Council and the Assembly and to propose to them to take the steps necessary

[11] Dallin, *Soviet Russia's Foreign Policy 1939–1942*, 120

to put an end to aggression.[12] On the same day, Mr. Avenol invited the Council Members to meet at Geneva on December 9, and submitted to the President of the Assembly the proposal to convoke the latter on December 11.

For the Soviet Government, Mr. Molotov replied on December 5 to the summons by the following telegram:

In accordance with instructions from the U.S.S.R. Government, I have the honor to inform you that Government considers unjustified proposal to convene December 9 Council League of Nations and December 11 Assembly League of Nations on the initiative of M. Rodolphe Holsti and in virtue of Article 11, paragraph 1, of the League Covenant.

The U.S.S.R. is not at war with Finland and does not threaten the Finnish nation with war. Consequently, reference to Article 11, paragraph 1, is unjustified. Soviet Union maintains peaceful relations with the Democratic Republic of Finland, whose Government signed with the U.S.S.R. on December 2nd Pact of Assistance and Friendship. This Pact settled all the questions which the Soviet Government has fruitlessly discussed with delegates former Finnish Government now divested of its power.

By its declaration of December 1st, the Government of the Democratic Republic of Finland requested the Soviet Government to lend assistance to that Republic by armed forces with a view to the joint liquidation at the earliest possible moment of the very dangerous seat of war created in Finland by its former rulers. In these circumstances, appeal by M. Rodolphe Holsti to the League cannot justify convocation of the Council and the Assembly, especially as the persons on whose behalf M. Rodolphe Holsti has approached the League cannot be regarded as mandatories of the Finnish people.

If, notwithstanding considerations set out above, Council and Assembly are convened to consider the appeal of M. Rodolphe Holsti, U.S.S.R. Government would be unable to take part in these meetings. This decision is also based on the fact that the communication from the Secretary-General of the League concerning convocation Council and Assembly reproduces the text of the letter from M. Rodolphe Holsti, which is full of insults and calumnies against the Soviet Government, this being incompatible with the respect due to the U.S.S.R.[13]

When the Council met on December 9, Mr. Holsti proposed to refer the dispute to the Assembly. His proposal was adopted without discussion.[14] The session of the As-

12 *LNOJ* 1939, 509
13 *Ibid.* 512
14 *Ibid.* 497

sembly was opened on December 11; the League Members
which had fallen victims to Axis aggression—Ethiopia, Austria, Czechoslovakia, and Albania—were not represented,
nor was the U.S.S.R. Mr. Hambro (Norway) was elected
President, and the Finnish-Soviet dispute taken up at once.
At the proposal of the General Committee of the Assembly
a Special Committee of thirteen members was appointed and
the meeting adjourned.[15] On the same day the Chairman of
the Special Committee sent by wire to the Soviet Government
an appeal to cease hostilities and open immediate negotiations under the mediation of the Assembly with a view to
restoring peace, adding that the same appeal had been addressed to Finland and accepted by her.[16]

The next day, December 12, the Soviet Government replied that it was not able to accept the invitation for reasons
set out in the telegram of December 4 to the Secretary General.[17] The Special Committee submitted to the Assembly
a report [18] culminating in the following resolution:

The Assembly

I

. . . .

Solemnly condemns the action taken by the U.S.S.R. against the
State of Finland;
Urgently appeals to every Member of the League to provide
Finland with such material and humanitarian assistance as may be
in its power and to refrain from any action which might weaken
Finland's power of resistance.
Authorizes the Secretary-General to lend the aid of his technical
services on the organization of the aforesaid assistance to Finland;
And likewise authorizes the Secretary-General, in view of the
Assembly resolution of October 4, 1931, to consult non-member
States with a view to possible co-operation.

II

Whereas, notwithstanding an invitation extended to it on two
occasions, the U.S.S.R. has refused to be present at the examination
of its dispute with Finland before the Council and the Assembly;
And whereas, by thus refusing to recognize the duty of the

15 LNOJ, Records of the Twentieth Assembly (1939), 11
16 LNOJ 1939, 529
17 Ibid.
18 Ibid. 531

Council and the Assembly as regards the execution of Article 15 of the Covenant, it has failed to observe one of the League's most essential covenants for the safeguarding of peace and the security of nations;

And whereas it has vainly attempted to justify its refusal on the ground of the relations which it has established with an alleged Government which is neither de jure nor de facto the Government recognized by the people of Finland in accordance with the free working of their institutions;

And whereas the U.S.S.R. has not merely violated the Covenant of the League, but has by its own action placed itself outside the Covenant;

And whereas the Council is competent under Article 16 of the Covenant to consider what consequences should follow from this situation;

Recommends the Council to pronounce upon the question.[19]

The resolution of the Special Committee was adopted.

In the ensuing debate the delegates unanimously denounced the action of the Soviet Government. The Mexican delegate, however, while declaring in favor of the draft resolution, strongly advised the Council against the exclusion of the Soviet Union. Said Mr. Tello:

Although the question which has been raised by several delegations has not been submitted to us for consideration, and although Mexico is not a Member of the Council, my Government considers that, since exclusion was not even contemplated in previous cases, it could not, for its part, approve this extreme sanction, which, moreover, would put an end to all possibility of reaching, within the framework of the League, a pacific settlement favorable to Finland.[20]

Mr. Wellington Koo limited himself to the following statement:

I have a very brief declaration to make. Under the circumstances which you know, the Chinese delegation will abstain from taking part in the vote on any part of the report.[21]

Not without interest is the comment made on the draft resolution by Mr. Butler (United Kingdom):

The latter part of the resolution reveals the attitude of the Soviet Government and invites the Council to draw the obvious conclusions which result from the declarations made in the report. We in this

[19] *Ibid.* 540
[20] *LNOJ, Records of the Twentieth Assembly* (1939), 27
[21] *Ibid.* 36

Assembly are signatories of the Covenant devised for certain purposes, set out in the Preamble, which have all been openly and deliberately flouted. It is true that the absence and withdrawal of important States have rendered difficult in practice the integral fulfillment of the obligations of the Covenant; the fact was formally recognized by most of the delegations represented here last year. But we still remain the guardians of the principles of the Covenant and we are obliged to maintain its standards to the fullest extent of our power. His Majesty's Government in the United Kingdom have always stood for those very principles and standards and do not intend to depart from them.[22]

The draft resolution was unanimously adopted.[23] Immediately thereafter the Council of the League met under the chairmanship of Mr. Costa du Rels (Bolivia). The latter read out the foregoing Assembly Resolution as well as the text of Article 16, paragraph 4, of the Covenant,[24] and submitted the following draft resolution:

The Council
Having taken cognizance of the resolution adopted by the Assembly on December 14th, 1939, regarding the appeal of the Finnish Government;
1, Associates itself with the condemnation by the Assembly of the action of the U.S.S.R. against the Finnish State; and
2. For the reasons set forth in the Resolution of the Assembly, in virtue of Article 16, paragraph 4, of the Covenant,
Finds, that, by its act, the U.S.S.R. has placed itself outside the League of Nations. It follows that the U.S.S.R. is no longer a Member of the League.[25]

After a short debate, in which Mr. Paul-Boncour (France) mentioned in passing the names of Austria and Czechoslovakia, the resolution was adopted with the votes of the Union of South Africa, Belgium, Bolivia, the United Kingdom, the Dominican Republic, Egypt, and France, while the delegates of China, Finland, Greece, and Yugoslavia abstained from voting, and two Council Members, the representatives of Iran and Peru, were absent from the meeting.

The vote of the League Council ended the membership of

22 *Ibid.* 34
23 *Ibid.* 36
24 "Any Member of the League which has violated any covenant of the League may be declared no longer a Member of the League by a vote of the Council concurred in by the representatives of all the other Members of the League represented therein."
25 *LNOJ* 1939, 506-8

the Soviet Union in the League,[26] but it did not stop the war. The Finns were finally defeated and peace was concluded at Moscow on March 12, 1940.[27] Under the terms of the peace treaty, the Finns had to cede more territory than had been originally demanded; yet their national independence was preserved. This cession gave no rise to any statements of non-recognition on the part of third Powers or on the part of the agencies of the League, whose Member Finland continued to be.

Further action of the Soviet Government in other areas was foreshadowed by a speech which Mr. Molotov delivered on March 29, 1940, and in which he said:

Of the neighboring States to the South Rumania is one with which we have no pact of non-aggression. This is due to the existence of an unsettled dispute, the question of Bessarabia, whose seizure by Rumania the Soviet Union has never recognized.[28]

Yet action was first taken in the Baltic. On June 14, 1940, the Government of the U.S.S.R. dispatched to the Lithuanian Republic a note, calling, within a short time limit, for the formation of a new Lithuanian Government "able to carry out the treaty of October, 1939," and for the grant of additional military bases. The Lithuanian Government accepted. Similar notes were dispatched to Estonia and Latvia on June 16, 1940, and immediately accepted.[29] In all three countries new governments were formed, which dissolved the existing legislatures and set elections for mid-July, 1940.

While the preparations to these elections were in progress, the Soviet Government took action against Rumania. On June 26, 1940, the People's Commissar for Foreign Affairs handed the Rumanian Minister in Moscow a note demanding the immediate return to the U.S.S.R. of Bessarabia and the cession of the northern Bukovina, and calling for a reply by June 27, 1940.[30] The Rumanian Government accepted the

---

26 In an article "Was the Soviet Union Expelled from the League of Nations?" (39 *AJIL* 35) Leo Gross claims that the vote of the Council was unable to effect the exclusion of the Soviet Union on the ground that paragraph 4 of Article 16 required the concurring vote of the representatives of all the Council Members except the violator, and not only of those participating in the meeting and voting.

27 Text, 2 *D. S. Bull.* 453

28 Dallin, *op. cit.* 201

29 *Ibid.* 250

30 *Ibid.;* text, 17 *Bull. Int. News* 854

Soviet demands, and on June 28, 1940, the evacuation by the Rumanian and occupation by the Red Army began and was carried out within a few days. From no quarters were any declarations of non-recognition issued. Northern Bukovina and the northern part of Bessarabia were incorporated into the Ukrainian Soviet Socialist Republic, the southern part of Bessarabia attached to the Moldavian Autonomous Soviet Socialist Republic, and the latter transformed on August 2, 1940, into a constituent republic of the Union under the name of Moldavian Soviet Socialist Republic.

In the meantime elections were held in the three Baltic States. The legislative bodies which emerged were in favor of joining the Soviet Union. Resolutions to this effect were passed on July 21, 1940, and in the first half of August Lithuania, Latvia, and Estonia were admitted as constituent republics into the Soviet Union. While, however, the Soviet-Rumanian settlement had been passed over in silence, the American and the British Governments refused to recognize the change of status of the Baltic republics. On July 23, 1940, the following statement of the Acting United States Secretary of State, Mr. Sumner Welles, was released:

During these past few days the devious processes whereunder the political independence and territorial integrity of the three small Baltic republics—Estonia, Latvia, and Lithuania—were to be deliberately annihilated by one of their more powerful neighbors, have been rapidly drawing to their conclusion. . . .

The policy of this Government is universally known. The people of the United States are opposed to predatory activities no matter whether they are carried on by the use of force or by the threat of force. They are likewise opposed to any form of intervention, on the part of one state, however powerful, in the domestic concerns of any other sovereign state, however weak.

These principles constitute the very foundations upon which the existing republics of the New World rest.

The United States will continue to stand by these principles, because of the conviction of the American people that unless the doctrine in which these principles are inherent once again governs the relations between nations, the rule of reason, of justice and of law—in other words, the basis of modern civilization itself—cannot be preserved.[31]

This statement was unmistakably a declaration of non-

[31] 3 *D. S. Bull.* 48

recognition. It did not use that term explicitly; but the "doctrine in which these principles are inherent" is obviously the Stimson Doctrine.

The practical measures taken by the American Government were in keeping with this interpretation. The diplomatic and consular agencies of the Baltic republics were allowed to continue their activities as representatives of the Baltic States, although the governments which had appointed them were no longer in existence. Thus the same state of affairs prevailed—and at this writing still prevails—which had obtained in the case of Czechoslovakia between March, 1939, and the recognition of the Government of President Beneš. The American legations in the Baltic States, of course, had to be closed, since, as had been the case in Czechoslovakia, the new local authorities no longer recognized their status. The Baltic representatives in the United States, however, are still carried with their status of precedence on the official diplomatic list.[32]

The British Government issued at first no declaration of non-recognition, but it took presently measures clearly revealing the intention not to recognize the change of status of the Baltic republics. The British legations in the Baltic capitals could not be maintained since the new authorities in control would not recognize their diplomatic status; but the Baltic legations in Great Britain were further recognized as such; the Baltic vessels in British ports were interned, the Baltic assets located in Great Britain frozen.[33]

[32] Under date March 14, 1942, the Department of State executed a series of documents (No. 1228, 1229, 1230, 1242), signed by Mr. Sumner Welles, with the following texts: (1) "I certify that the absorption of Latvia by either Germany or the U.S.S.R. is not recognized by the Government of the United States." (2) "I certify that the legality of the so-called 'nationalization' laws and decrees, or of any of the acts of either the Soviet regime which functioned in Latvia or of the regime now functioning in that country is not recognized by the Government of the United States." (3) "I certify that the legal existence of the treaty of Friendship, Commerce and Consular Rights, as well as of all other treaties between the United States and the Republic of Latvia has not been affected by the occupation of Latvia by foreign military forces." (4) "I certify that Dr. Alfred Bilmanis is duly accredited to this Government as Envoy Extraordinary and Minister Plenipotentiary of Latvia." The documents listed under (2) and (3) form an important contribution to the theory of non-recognition and bear out the views advanced in Part II of this work regarding the validity of acts of the non-recognized occupant and the continuing legal existence of the treaties between the non-recognizing and the dispossessed sovereign.

[33] Dallin, *op. cit.* 323

On October 22, 1940, Sir Stafford Cripps offered on behalf of the British Government to the Soviet Government a compromise on the basis of de facto recognition of Soviet sovereignty in the Baltic States, yet nothing came of it.[34] At a later stage, in connection with the signature of the Anglo-Soviet Treaty of Alliance of May 26, 1942, the British Government decreed a change of status of the Baltic envoys: They were removed from the official diplomatic list on which they had hitherto figured, and only granted "diplomatic privileges on a personal basis." [35] That this, however, did not imply recognition of Soviet sovereignty over their countries results from a statement made by a spokesman of the Government in the House of Commons as late as December 21, 1944. On that day Sir Henry Williams asked the Foreign Secretary "whether His Majesty's Government still recognize the Governments of the Republics of Latvia, Estonia, and Lithuania?" [36]

Answering for Mr. Eden, Mr. George Hall said: "His Majesty's Government have not recognized any Governments in the Republics of Latvia, Estonia, and Lithuania, since the changes which occurred in June, 1940."

Not satisfied with this answer, Sir Henry Williams continued: "As these changes are in conflict with the prinples of the Atlantic Charter and our agreement with the U.S.S.R.,[37] why have we left these people in the lurch?"

Mr. Hall answered: "I do not know that it can be said that they have been left in the lurch as, since 1940, no government in these territories has sought, or indeed been granted, recognition."

It might have been better had Mr. Hall not spoken of the recognition of governments, but of the recognition of the sovereignty of the U.S.S.R. in the Baltic territories, since this was the real issue. His answer, however, is clear enough in that, by refusing to recognize "any Governments" in those areas, the British Government refused to recognize the

[34] *Ibid.* 324
[35] According to information obtained from the British Information Library in New York, the first issue of the Diplomatic List on which the names of the Baltic envoys did not appear was that of August 1, 1942.
[36] 406 *H. C. Deb.* 1953
[37] The Treaty of Alliance of May 26, 1942 (below, 269)

incorporation, for the only existing bodies were, and are, the All-Union Government of the U.S.S.R. and the governments formed under the Soviet Constitution as Governments of the Estonian, Latvian, and Lithuanian Soviet Socialist Republics. It is not so clear, on the other hand, whether Mr. Hall's statement was to mean that Great Britain recognized the continued legal existence of the Baltic States, although for the time being without any recognized government. Since, however, he used the term "in the Republics of . . ." and not "in the former Republics of . . ." it is fair to assume that the answer to the above question should be in the affirmative.

The incorporation of the Baltic republics in the U.S.S.R. gave rise to a number of cases in American courts, mostly involving the issue of the nationalization of Baltic shipping. These cases are not uninteresting inasmuch as they reflect recent judicial opinion regarding the controversial question of the legal effects of non-recognition of a territorial change. In three cases, namely, (1) the *Kotkas*,[38] (2) the *Regent*,[39] (3) the *Signe* (later renamed the *Florida*),[40] libels of persons acting on behalf of the Soviet Government had been filed in order to obtain possession of Baltic ships which their masters refused to surrender. The district courts had first to decide on motions of the libelants for letters rogatory to be issued to a competent court of the Soviet Union for the purpose of procuring testimony of parties residing in the respective Baltic countries. All these motions were denied on the ground that since the United States did not recognize the incorporation of the Baltic republics in the Soviet Union, no court of the latter could issue effective process to residents of those republics. Thereupon the libels were dismissed for failure on the part of the libelants to prove their right of possession. It is noteworthy that in the (Estonian) *Signe* case both the district court and the court of review [41]

[38] 35 *Fed. Suppl.* 983 ff., District Court, E. D. New York, November 22, 1940; 37 *Fed. Suppl.* 835 ff., do. March 31, 1941
[39] 35 *Fed. Suppl.* 985 ff., District Court, E. D. New York, November 22, 1940
[40] 37 *Fed. Suppl.* 819 ff., District Court E. D. Louisiana, New Orleans Div., March 4, 1941; 39 *Fed. Suppl.* 810 ff., do. July 22, 1941
[41] 133 F. (2d) 719 ff., Circuit Court of Appeals, Fifth Circuit, February 20, 1943

emphasized that as a consequence of the non-recognition of the incorporation, the treaties concluded between the American Government and the former Estonian Government continued in force and that the American Government continued to recognize the Acting Consul General of Estonia as being in charge of the legation for the "temporarily supplanted government of the Republic of Estonia."

The question of the validity of the acts of a non-recognized occupant was also at issue in a more recent case, the *Maret*, decided by the U. S. Court of Appeals for the Third Circuit on October 17, 1944.[42] The *Maret* was a ship of Estonian registry which, at the time of the incorporation of Estonia into the Soviet Union happened to be in the territorial waters of the Virgin Islands. By an order published in the State Gazette of the Estonian S.S.R. the ship was nationalized and the captain ordered to proceed to Murmansk. He was willing to comply with the order, but asked for certain advances to purchase necessary supplies, and the Amtorg Trading Company in New York, an agency of the Soviet Government, provided him with funds. Thereafter, however, the ship, while still at St. Thomas, Virgin Islands, was requisitioned by the U. S. Maritime Commission, and the latter deposited with the Treasurer of the United States an amount of $25,000 "on account of just compensation" for the *Maret*. The Amtorg brought suit in the U. S. District Court of the Virgin Islands, seeking payment of a portion of the above amount. Its action was opposed by the Consul General of the Estonian Republic, Mr. Kaiv, acting for some of the co-owners of the ship. He produced a certificate issued by the United States Secretary of State under date April 15, 1941, to the effect that "the legality of the so-called 'nationalization' laws and decrees, or of any of the acts of the regime now functioning in Estonia, is not recognized by the Government of the United States." The district court, however, decided in favor of the Amtorg. Mr. Kaiv appealed. The circuit court reversed the decision of the lower court, and stated in its opinion that not only the question of the recognition or non-recognition of the Soviet Republic of Estonia was a political question to be determined by the

[42] 145 F. (2d) 431

Executive branch of the Government, but that the same applied also to the issue of the validity or non-validity of the decrees of the non-recognized Power.[43]

A similar position was taken by the Irish courts in a case also concerning Baltic ships claimed by representatives of the Soviet Government under the nationalization decrees.[44] Informed by the Government of Eire that it did not recognize the U.S.S.R. as a sovereign independent State either de facto or de jure in Latvia or Estonia, the courts reached the following conclusions:

(1) That the Government of Eire having stated their opinion that the States of Latvia and Estonia were not under the sovereign independent authority of the U.S.S.R. the court must treat as nullities the various transactions and documents alleged to have culminated in the alleged sovereignty and purporting to pass the property in those ships.

(2) Inasmuch as the sovereignty of the U.S.S.R. over Latvia and Estonia had not been established, the vessels were not the property of the U.S.S.R. . . . [45]

A few weeks after Germany had launched her attack on the Soviet Union, an agreement was concluded on July 30, 1941, between the Soviet Government and the Polish Government-in-Exile, aimed at the establishment of friendly relations between their countries.[46] Article I of this Agreement provided that

The Soviet Government of the U.S.S.R. recognizes the Soviet-German treaties of 1939 as to territorial changes in Poland as having lost their validity.

[43] *Ibid.* at 442: "Nonrecognition of a foreign sovereign and nonrecognition of its decrees are to be deemed to be as essential a part of the power confided by the Constitution to the Executive for the conduct of foreign affairs as recognition." "When the fact of nonrecognition of a foreign sovereign and nonrecognition of its decrees by our Executive is demonstrated as in the case at bar, the courts of this country may not examine the effect of decrees of the unrecognized foreign sovereign and determine rights in property, subject to the examining court, upon the basis of those decrees. A policy of nonrecognition when demonstrated by the Executive must be deemed to be as affirmative and positive in effect as a policy of recognition." In reaching these conclusions the court extensively discussed and rejected the views advanced by Dickinson and Borchard and underlying the decisions in Sokoloff v. National City Bank and Russian Reinsurance Company v. Stoddard (above, 105, n. 10).

[44] Zarine v. Owners, etc., Eire High Court, April 29 and 30, and May 1 and 10, 1941; Eire Supreme Court, July 3, 1941 (36 *AJIL* 490)

[45] 36 *AJIL* 504

[46] 18 *Bull. Int. News* 1016

It will be remembered that the Soviet-German Treaty of September 29, 1939, had fixed a line as the "frontier of the imperial interests" of either Government in the "former" territory of Poland, that the Contracting Parties "recognized as final" that frontier, and committed themselves "to refuse all interference by third Powers in this settlement." After the conclusion of the Polish-Soviet Agreement of July 30, 1941, the British Foreign Secretary, Mr. Eden, handed the Polish Prime Minister a note informing him that the British Government did not recognize any territorial changes which had been effected in Poland since August, 1939.[47] Did Article I of the Soviet-Polish Treaty mean that the Soviet Union no longer claimed to be the sovereign of that part of Poland which she had incorporated in the fall, 1939, and that the Soviet Government was now willing to tolerate "interference by third Powers" in the settlement of the border question? The answer is to be found in the history of the subsequent Soviet-Polish dispute.

On May 26, 1942, a Treaty of Alliance was concluded between Great Britain and the Soviet Union.[48] In Article III the Contracting Parties declared their desire to unite with other like-minded States in adopting proposals for common action to preserve peace and resist aggression in the postwar period. Article V provided that

The High Contracting Parties, having regard to the interests of the security of each of them, agree to work together in close and friendly collaboration after the reestablishment of peace for the organization of security and economic prosperity in Europe. They will take into account the interests of the United Nations in these objects, and they will act in accordance with the two principles of not seeking territorial aggrandizement for themselves and of non-interference in the internal affairs of other States.

Nothing was said in the treaty about whether Great Britain now accorded recognition to the territorial expansion of the Soviet Union effected in 1939 and 1940. It has been argued[49] that the omission from the treaty of any reservation on the part of Great Britain regarding these changes must be regarded as recognition by implication.

[47] *Ibid.*
[48] Text, 36 *AJIL*, Suppl., 216
[49] By A. Kerensky in the *New York Times* of January 13, 1945

This assertion, however, does not seem conclusive, nor is it borne out by the subsequent attitude of the British Government in the question of the Polish-Soviet border.

On New Year's Day, 1943, Stalingrad was still under siege; but a few weeks later the world was shaken by the announcement that the Red Army had forged a ring of steel around the German forces that besieged the Volga stronghold, and, not much later, that the German field marshal had surrendered with all his troops. It was from that moment on that the Soviet armies began their slow but irresistible trek westward, toward the heartland of the enemy. Since their ultimate destination was the German Reichskanzlei in Berlin, they would have to cross the Soviet border of 1938, and the question would arise whether they were entering just another portion of the Soviet land or the territory of a foreign State.

The Polish Government-in-Exile in London was quick in realizing the implications of Stalingrad for the Polish border question. On February 4, 1943, the Polish Prime Minister, General Sikorski, made a report to the Polish National Council (Polska Rada Narodowa) in London.[50] He stressed the necessity of ensuring for Poland a broad and really secure access to the sea as the basis of Poland's closer co-operation with the maritime democracies; in the matter of Poland's eastern frontiers he declared a firm stand on the principles of the Atlantic Charter. His report revealed a certain moderation; but the Polish Government-in-Exile adopted on February 25, 1943, a resolution of a somewhat different character. It read:

The Polish Government affirms that neither before the outbreak of this war, nor during it, has the Polish nation ever agreed to any cooperation with the Germans against the Soviet Union.

In her relations with the U.S.S.R., Poland has not ceased to be ready to cooperate with the Soviet Union in the prosecution of the war and in maintaining friendly and neighborly relations after victory.

The Polish Government repudiates most definitely the malicious propaganda which accuses Poland of indirect or direct inimical tendencies towards Soviet Russia. It is absolutely absurd to suspect Poland of intentions to base the eastern boundaries of the Polish

Republic on the Dnieper or Black Sea or to impute to Poland any tendencies to move her frontiers further to the East.

The Polish Government which represents Poland in the boundaries in which Poland, first among the Allied nations, took up the fight imposed on her, has from the moment of the conclusion of the Polish-Soviet Treaty of July 30, 1941, maintained unchangeable the attitude that as far as the question of frontiers between Poland and Russia is concerned, the status quo previous to September 1, 1939, is in force, and considers undermining of this attitude which is in conformity with the Atlantic Charter, as detrimental to the unity of the Allied nations. . . .[51]

This resolution was supported by the following resolution, passed the same day by the Polish National Council:

The Polish National Council, maintaining—in unanimous agreement with the Government—its attitude that the difficulties existing in creating mutual trust in collaboration between United Nations must be removed, declares that the integrity of the Polish Republic's territory in her frontiers of September 1, 1939, and her sovereignty are inviolable and indivisible. No unilateral acts or illegal activities from any quarter whatsoever directed against either the territory or the sovereignty of the Polish Republic or the rights of her citizens in Poland or outside her territorial boundaries can in any way alter this state of affairs.[52]

Although the Soviet Government did not officially take issue with these statements, it was obvious that Polish-Soviet relations were deteriorating. The breaking point was reached in April, 1943. The German propaganda had spread news of the discovery near Smolensk (at that time still German-occupied) in a common grave of the massacred bodies of about 10,000 Polish officers, allegedly killed while being prisoners of war in Soviet camps. The Polish Government-in-Exile instructed its representative in Switzerland to request the International Red Cross at Geneva to send a delegation to investigate on the spot the true state of affairs, and issued on April 16 and 17, 1943, statements which could hardly be construed otherwise than as charging by innuendo the Soviet authorities with the assassination of those officers.[53] The Soviet Government replied by severing diplomatic relations with the Polish Government-in-Exile. On April 26,

[51] *Ibid.* 125
[52] *Ibid.*
[53] *Ibid.* 212

1943, it dispatched the following note to the Polish Ambassador in Moscow:

The Soviet Government considers the recent behavior of the Polish Government with regard to the U.S.S.R. as entirely abnormal, violating all regulations and standards of relations between two allied states.

The slanderous campaign hostile to the Soviet Union launched by German Fascists in connection with the murder of Polish officers, which they themselves committed in the Smolensk area on territory occupied by German troops, was at once taken up by the Polish Government and is being fanned in every way by the Polish official press. Far from offering rebuff to the vile Fascist slander on the U.S.S.R., the Polish Government did not even find it necessary to address the Soviet Government with an inquiry or explanation on this subject. . . .

The Soviet Government is aware that this hostile campaign against the Soviet Union was undertaken by the Polish Government in order to exert pressure upon the Soviet Government by making use of the Hitlerite slanderous fake for the purpose of wresting from it territorial concessions at the expense of interests of the Soviet Ukraine, Soviet Byelorussia and Soviet Lithuania.

All these circumstances compel the Soviet Government to recognize that the present government of Poland, having slid to the path of accord with Hitler's government, actually has discontinued allied relations with the U.S.S.R. and has adopted a hostile attitude toward the Soviet Union.

On the strength of all the above, the Soviet Government has decided to sever relations with the Polish Government.[54]

The paragraph of this statement which dealt with the territorial aspect of the dispute left no doubt that in spite of the treaty of July 30, 1941, the Soviet Government considered Soviet sovereignty over the territories acquired in 1939 and 1940 as continuing. Thus, issue on the border question was officially and explicitly joined. In the meantime, the Red Army continued to drive the invader from the Soviet territory. On the last day of 1943, Zhitomir was liberated, and in the first days of the new year the battlefront was nearing the Volhynian sector of the Polish-Soviet border as fixed by the Treaty of Riga.[55] At this juncture the Polish Government-in-Exile handed to those of the United Nations with which it maintained diplomatic relations the following Declaration, dated January 5, 1944:

[54] *Ibid.* 222
[55] Above, 27

In their victorious struggle against the German invader, Soviet forces are reported to have crossed the frontier of Poland. . . .

The Polish Government . . . is responsible for the fate of the nation. It affirms its indestructible right to independence, confirmed by . . . binding international treaties.

The provisions of these treaties, based on the free agreement of the parties, not on the enforcement of the will of one side to the detriment of the other, cannot be reversed by accomplished facts. The conduct of the Polish nation in the course of the present war has proved that it has never recognized and will not recognize solutions imposed by force.

The Polish Government expects that the Soviet Union . . . will not fail to respect the rights and interests of the Polish Republic and its citizens.[56]

The Soviet Government retorted immediately by the following broadcast:

On January 5, a declaration of the exiled Polish Government on the question of Soviet-Polish relations was published in London. It contained a number of erroneous affirmations, including an erroneous affirmation concerning the Soviet-Polish frontier.

As is known, the Soviet Constitution established a Soviet-Polish frontier corresponding with the desires of the population of the western Ukraine and western Byelorussia, expressed in a plebiscite carried out on broad democratic principles in the year 1939. The territories of the western Ukraine, populated in an overwhelming majority by Ukrainians, were incorporated into the Soviet Ukraine, while the territories of western Byelorussia, populated in an overwhelming majority by Byelorussians, were incorporated into Soviet Byelorussia. . . .

The injustice caused by the Riga Treaty in the year 1921, which was forced on the Soviet Union with regard to Ukrainians inhabiting the western Ukraine and Byelorussians inhabiting western Byelorussia, was thus rectified. The entry of the western Ukraine and western Byelorussia into the Soviet Union did not interfere with the interests of Poland, but, on the contrary, created a reliable basis for a firm and permanent friendship between the Polish people and the neighboring Ukrainian, Byelorussian, and Russian peoples. . . .

The Soviet Government does not consider the frontiers of 1939 unchangeable. The borders can be corrected in favor of Poland on such lines that districts in which the Polish population predominates be handed over to Poland. In such case the Soviet-Polish border could approximately follow the so-called Curzon Line, which was adopted in the year 1919 by the Supreme Council of the Allied Powers and which provided for the incorporation of the western Ukraine and western Byelorussia into the Soviet Union.

[56] 4 *Un. Nat. Rev.* 79

Poland's western borders must be extended through the joining to Poland of age-old Polish lands taken away from Poland by Germany, without which it is impossible to unite the whole of the Polish people in its own state, which thus will acquire the necessary outlet to the Baltic Sea. . . .[57]

The reply of the Polish Government-in-Exile, published on January 14, 1944, was this:

The Polish Government have taken cognizance of the declaration of the Soviet Government contained in a Tass communiqué of January 11th, 1944, which was issued as a reply to a declaration of the Polish Government of January 5th. . . .

While the Polish Government cannot recognize unilateral decisions or accomplished facts which have taken place on the territory of the Polish Republic, they have repeatedly expressed their sincere desire for a Polish-Soviet agreement on terms which would be just and acceptable to both sides. . . .

To this end the Polish Government are approaching the British and United States Governments with a view to securing through their intermediary discussion by the Polish and Soviet Governments, with participation of the British and American Governments, of all outstanding questions the settlement of which should lead to friendly and permanent cooperation between Poland and the Soviet Union.

The Polish Government believe this to be desirable in the interest of victory of the United Nations and harmonious relations in post-war Europe.[58]

On February 28, 1944, the British Prime Minister attempted to bridge the gulf between his two Allies. Addressing the House of Commons, he said with reference to the Teheran Conference:

It was with great pleasure that I heard from Marshal Stalin that he, too, was resolved upon the creation and maintenance of a strong, integral, independent Poland as one of the leading Powers in Europe. . . . I am convinced that that represents the settled policy of the Soviet Union.

Here I may remind the House that we ourselves have never in the past guaranteed on behalf of the British Government any particular frontier line to Poland. We did not approve the Polish occupation of Vilna in 1920, and the British view in 1919 stands expressed in the so-called Curzon line. . . .

I have always held the view that all questions of territorial settlement and adjustment should stand until the end of the war and that

57 *Ibid.* 91
58 *Ibid.* 80

the victorious Powers should then arrive at a formal and final agreement governing the articulation of Europe as a whole.

However, the advance of Russian armies in the Polish regions in which the Polish underground army is active makes it indispensable that some kind of friendly working agreement should be arrived at to govern wartime conditions and to enable all anti-Hitlerite forces to work together against the common foe.[59]

Mr. Churchill's efforts were of no avail, and the crisis dragged on. Meanwhile a "Union of Polish Patriots" had been formed in Moscow under the aegis of the Soviet Government, and on July 23, 1944, it announced that the "National Council of the Homeland" had decided to form in Chelm a Polish Committee of National Liberation, which would be the supreme authority in the liberated area of Poland and would act on the basis of the constitution of March 17, 1921, the only one legally voted; the frontiers would be settled by mutual agreement, in accordance with the principle of "Polish territory for Poland, Byelorussian, Ukrainian, and Lithuanian territory for Soviet Byelorussia, Soviet Ukraine, and Soviet Lithuania." [60] On July 27, 1943, Radio Moscow broadcast that the day before an agreement had been signed by the Government and the Polish Committee of National Liberation on the relations between the Soviet High Command and the Polish administration in liberated Poland whereby the supreme power in the areas of fighting was to be vested in the Soviet Commander in Chief until the operations would end, while the Polish Committee of National Liberation was to establish an administration in accordance with the above constitution.[61]

The situation remained unchanged until the end of the year, causing considerable concern in Allied circles. On December 15, 1944, Mr. Churchill again made a plea on behalf of a settlement of the dispute, recalling on that occasion his statement of February 22, 1944.[62] On December 18, the new United States Secretary of State, Mr. Stettinius, issued the following statement:

It has been the consistently held policy of the United States Government that questions relating to boundaries should be left in

[59] 397 H. C. Deb. 697
[60] 21 Bull. Int. News 651
[61] Ibid. 656
[62] 406 H. C. Deb. 1478 ff.

abeyance until the termination of hostilities. As Secretary Hull stated in his address of April 9, 1944, "this does not mean that certain questions may not and should not in the meantime be settled by friendly conference and agreement." In the case of the future frontiers of Poland, if a mutual agreement is reached by the United Nations directly concerned, this Government would have no objection to such an agreement which could make an essential contribution to the prosecution of the war against the common enemy. . . .

The United States Government continues to adhere to its traditional policy of declining to give guarantees for any specific frontiers. The United States Government is working for the establishment of a world security organization through which the United States, together with other member states, would assume responsibility for the preservation of general security.[63]

This statement proved that the Government of the United States still persisted in not recognizing the state of affairs created in 1939, since Mr. Stettinius spoke of the future frontiers of Poland. The London Poles persisted in an intransigent attitude. At this point the Soviet Government recognized on January 5, 1945, the Polish Committee of National Liberation, which the victorious advance of the Red Army including the newly created Polish divisions fighting in its ranks had enabled to transfer its seat to Lublin, as the Provisional National Government of Poland.[64] The western Allies refused to follow suit, and continued to recognize the Polish Government-in-Exile in London. The situation was apt to endanger inter-Allied unity. To find a way out of the impasse was one of the main objectives of the Crimea Conference, held at Yalta between February 4 and 11, 1945.[65] On February 12, 1945, its decisions regarding Poland were disclosed as follows:

A new situation has been created in Poland as a result of her complete liberation by the Red Army. This calls for the establishment of a Polish provisional government which can be more broadly based than was possible before the recent liberation of western Poland. The provisional government which is now functioning in Poland should be therefore reorganized on a broader democratic basis with the inclusion of democratic leaders from Poland itself and from Poles abroad. This new government should then be called the Polish Provisional Government of National Unity. . . .

[63] 11 D. S. Bull. 836
[64] 22 Bull. Int. News 92
[65] Above, 187

When a Polish Provisional Government of National Unity has been properly formed in conformity with the above, the Government of the U.S.S.R., which now maintains diplomatic relations with the present provisional government of Poland, and the Government of the United Kingdom and the Government of the United States of America, will establish diplomatic relations with the new Polish Provisional Government of National Unity. . . .

The three heads of government consider that the eastern frontier of Poland should follow the Curzon line, with digressions from it in some regions of five to eight kilometers in favor of Poland. They recognize that Poland must receive substantial accessions of territory in the north and west. They feel that the opinion of the new Polish Provisional Government of National Unity should be sought in due course on the extent of these accessions and that the final delimitation of the western frontiers of Poland should thereafter await the peace conference.[66]

This statement seems to indicate that the Soviet Government was willing to recede from its position that the settlement of the Soviet-Polish border dispute was not the concern of third Powers. On the other hand, the Government of the United States expressed its readiness to accept the solution devised by the Soviet Government and the British Government. Doubtless, however, the text implied no recognition, on the part of Great Britain and the United States, of the sovereignty of the Soviet Union over eastern Poland.

On March 1, 1945, President Roosevelt reported to Congress on the conference; concerning the Polish border issue he stated the following:

The decision with respect to the boundaries of Poland was a compromise, under which, however, the Poles will receive compensation in territory in the north and west in exchange for what they lose by the Curzon line. The limits of the western boundaries will be permanently fixed in the final peace conference. It was agreed that a large coastline should be included.

It is well known that the people east of the Curzon line are predominantly White Russians and Ukrainians, and that the people west of the line are predominantly Polish. As far back as 1919, the representatives of the Allies agreed that the Curzon line represented a fair boundary between the two peoples.

I am convinced that the agreement on Poland, under the circumstances, is the most hopeful agreement possible for a free, independent and prosperous Polish State.[67]

[66] 12 *D. S. Bull.* 215
[67] *Ibid.* 321 at 325

The Polish Government-in-Exile felt differently. On February 13, 1945, it dispatched to the Allied Chancelleries the following note:

On February 12 . . . the British Foreign Office handed to the Polish Ambassador in London the text of a resolution concerning Poland, adopted by President Roosevelt, Premier Churchill and Marshal Stalin at the Yalta Conference between February 4 and 11. . . .

The method adopted in the case of Poland is a contradiction of the elementary principles binding the Allies and constitutes a violation of the letter and the spirit of the Atlantic Charter and the right of every nation to defend its own interest.

The Polish Government declares that the decision of the Three Power Conference concerning Poland cannot be recognized by the Polish Government and cannot bind the Polish nation.

The Polish Government will consider the severance of the eastern half of the territory of Poland through the imposition of a Polish-Soviet frontier following along the so-called Curzon Line as the fifth partition of Poland now accomplished by her Allies.[68]

The diatribes of the London Poles were answered by the British Prime Minister in the House of Commons on February 27, 1945. Said Mr. Churchill:

The House is well aware from the speeches I have made to them that the freedom, independence, integrity and sovereignty of Poland have always seemed to His Majesty's Government more important than actual frontiers. . . . The Russian claim, first advanced in Tehran in November, 1943, has always been unchanged for the Curzon line in the East, and the Russian offer has always been that ample compensation should be gained for Poland at the expense of Germany in the north and in the west. . . . I have never concealed from the House, that personally, I think that Russia's claim is just and right. If I champion this frontier for Russia, it is not because I bow to force. It is because I believe it is the fairest division of territory that can in all the circumstances be made between the two countries whose history has been so chequered and intermingled.

The Curzon line was drawn in 1919 by an expert Commission. . . . It was drawn at a time when Russia had few friends among the Allies. . . . One cannot feel that either the circumstances or the personalities concerned would have given undue favor to Soviet Russia. . . . They just tried to find out what was the right and proper line to draw. The British Government in those days approved this line including, of course, the exclusion of Lvov from Poland.

In supporting the Russian claim to the Curzon line, I repudiate and repulse any suggestion that we are making a questionable compromise or yielding to force or fear, and I assert with the utmost conviction the broad justice of the policy upon which, for the first time, all the three great Allies have now taken their stand. Moreover, the three Powers have now agreed that Poland shall receive substantial accessions in the north and in the west.

The published Crimea Agreement is not a ready-made plan, imposed by the Great Powers on the Polish people. . . . The three Powers are agreed that acceptance by the Poles of the provisions on the eastern frontiers and, so far as can now be ascertained, on the western frontiers, is an essential condition of the establishment and future welfare and security of a strong, independent, homogeneous Polish State. . . .[69]

The hoped-for reconstruction of the Polish Provisional Government and, following this, the final settlement of the eastern border of Poland, was delayed due to the rise of divergencies in the construction of the Yalta text by the Conference Powers. The stalemate was not overcome until June, 1945. On June 12 it was announced that the various Polish democratic groups, among them representatives of the London emigration, had been invited to Moscow;[70] and on June 28, that a new Provisional Government of National Unity had been formed.[71] On July 5 the Governments of the United States and Great Britain granted recognition to that government and withdrew their recognition from the London Government-in-Exile which ceased to exist.[72] The American announcement was made by the President of the United States who added that "the new Government has informed me in a written communication that it has recognized in their entirety the decisions of the Crimean Conference on the Polish question."[73]

The Polish statement, of course, also included the acceptance of the Yalta terms regarding the eastern borders of the restored Polish Republic. Accordingly, no further mention was made of this issue in the Potsdam Declaration of August 2, 1945.[74] Yet in accordance with the Yalta de-

[69] 408 *H. C. Deb.* 1275
[70] 12 *D. S. Bull.* 1095
[71] 1 *Chron.* 9
[72] *Ibid.*
[73] 13 *D. S. Bull.* 47
[74] Above, 128

cisions the border settlement, to be final, had to be incorporated into a treaty between the new Polish Provisional Government of National Unity and the Soviet Government. A
treaty to this effect was in fact signed at Moscow on August
17, 1945,[75] and is now in force, the ratifications having been
exchanged at Warsaw on February 5, 1946. The preamble
and main provisions of the treaty read as follows:

The President of the Supreme Soviet of the U.S.S.R. and the
President of the Polish Republic, desirous to settle the problem of
the state frontier between the Soviet Union and Poland in the
spirit of friendship and accord, have decided to conclude for this
purpose the present Treaty. . . .

Article 1   In accordance with the decision of the Crimean Conference, to establish the state frontier between the U.S.S.R. and
the Polish Republic along the "Curzon Line," deviating from the
line in Poland's favor in some districts from 5 to 8 km. . . . , con-
ceding additionally to Poland . . . :

Article 2   In accordance with the provisions of Article 1, the
state frontier between the U.S.S.R. and the Polish Republic passes
along the following line:
        [Follows the description of the line]

Article 3   Pending final decisions on territorial questions at the
peace settlement, part of the Soviet-Polish frontier adjoining the
Baltic Sea will pass, in conformity with the decisions of the Berlin
conference, along the line leading from the point situated on the
eastern shore of Danzig Bay and indicated on the map annexed
hereto, eastward to the north of Braunsberg-Goldap up to the point
where this line meets the frontier line described in Article 2 of the
present treaty.

The wording of the preamble, which speaks of the border
in terms of a problem yet to be settled, and of Article 1,
which refers to the decision of the Crimea Conference "to establish" that border, would appear to indicate the willing-
ness of the Soviet Government to base its claim to the frontiers of western Byelorussia and the western Ukraine no
longer on the unilateral annexation of 1939, but on multilateral international agreements concluded with other Great
Powers and, following this, the assent of the Power directly
concerned.

*   *   *

Among the neighbors of the Soviet Union, two, namely
Rumania and Finland, entered the war on the Axis side.

75 14 *D. S. Bull.* 341

Rumania became an enemy not only of the Soviet Union and Great Britain, but also of the United States. During the war she succeeded in recovering temporarily the areas which she had surrendered to the Soviet Union in June, 1940—Bessarabia and the northern Bukovina. But by September, 1944, the Red Army had forced her to give up. On September 12, 1944, an armistice was signed at Moscow between the Governments of the United States of America, the Soviet Union, and the United Kingdom on the one hand, and the Government of Rumania on the other hand.[76] Article 4 of the instrument provided that

> The State frontier between the Union of Soviet Socialist Republics and Rumania, established by the Soviet-Rumanian Agreement of June 8, 1940, is restored.

It stands to reason that by becoming co-signatories of the armistice, the United States and Great Britain implicitly granted full recognition to Soviet sovereignty over the above-mentioned areas. This is also borne out by the following statement, released by the American State Department on October 19, 1945:

> The terms of surrender for Rumania were in the form of an armistice agreement in which this government participated at all stages. . . . The settlement with regard to Bessarabia merely restores the frontier between the two states as established by the Soviet-Rumanian agreement of June 8, 1940.[77]

Regarding Finland the situation was somewhat different. This country joined Germany in her attack on the Soviet Union, and subsequently a state of war ensued between the Finns and Great Britain, but the United States, although entering the war against Germany on the side of the Soviet Union, remained at peace with Finland. By September, 1944, Finland realized that Germany's cause was lost and that the only way of salvation was to come to terms with the Allies. On September 19, 1944, an armistice was concluded between the U.S.S.R. and the United Kingdom on the one, and Finland on the other hand.[78] Its main territorial clauses were the following:

[76] 11 *D. S. Bull.* 289
[77] *Ibid.* 453
[78] *Cmd.* 6586

The Government of the U.S.S.R. and His Majesty's Government in the United Kingdom of Great Britain and Northern Ireland, acting on behalf of all the United Nations at war with Finland, on the one hand, and the Government of Finland on the other hand, have decided to conclude the present agreement for armistice:

. . . .

Article 6. The effect of the Peace Treaty between the Soviet Union and Finland concluded in Moscow on March 12, 1940, is restored, subject to the changes which follow from the present agreement.

Article 7. Finland returns to the Soviet Union the Oblast of Petsamo (Pechenga), voluntarily ceded to Finland by the Soviet State in accordance with the peace treaties of October 12, 1920 [79] and March 12, 1940.[80]

As in the Rumanian case, these clauses are believed to imply British recognition of Soviet sovereignty over the areas ceded or retroceded by the Finns.

As to the Baltic republics, the Soviet Government continued to consider and treat them as constituent republics of the Soviet Union, while neither Great Britain nor the United States issued any official statement that could be construed as explicit or implied abandonment of the policy of non-recognition of their incorporation into the Soviet Union. The League of Nations, too, continued to list Estonia, Latvia, and Lithuania on the roster of the League Members, in the same way, however, as Albania and Denmark, that is, by recording their contributions with only one unit *pour mémoire*.[81] The situation regarding the Baltic legations is at this writing still unchanged as far as the United States is concerned. As stated before, in Great Britain they had been tacitly suppressed in 1942. Accordingly, when on January 31, 1945, the Member of the House of Commons, Sir A. Beit, asked the Foreign Secretary whether His Majesty's Government was represented in Finland, the Baltic States, Bulgaria, Rumania, and Hungary, Mr. Law, speaking for the Government, answered that "His Majesty's Government is not in diplomatic relations with any of the countries mentioned."[82]

[79] 3 *LNTS* 6
[80] 2 *D. S. Bull.* 453
[81] Above, 247, n. 10
[82] 407 *H. C. Deb.* 1464

The Yalta Declaration was silent on the fate of the Baltic States, nor did the Foreign Offices of the United States and Great Britain mention the issue in their reports on the Crimea Conference. Their position, however, was outlined in the following directive of the Supreme Headquarters of the Allied (British and American) Expeditionary Forces (SHAEF), issued on May 12, 1945:

Up to the present the United States and British Governments have not formally recognized any territorial changes brought about by the present war. Latvians, Estonians and Lithuanians . . . will not be returned to their native districts, repatriated to the Soviet Union or transferred to the U.S.S.R. zone in Germany unless they specifically claim Soviet citizenship. Those claiming Soviet citizenship will not be transferred until a declaration as to the method of disposal has been made.[83]

The Potsdam Declaration made no mention of the Baltic question either, yet from its Section VI certain inferences regarding the matter would appear to be warranted. The section reads:

VI. City of Koenigsberg and the Adjacent Area

The Conference examined a proposal by the Soviet Government that pending the final determination of territorial questions at the peace settlement the section of the western frontier of the Union of Soviet Socialist Republics which is adjacent to the Baltic Sea should pass from a point on the eastern shore of the Bay of Danzig to the east, north of Braunsberg-Goldap, to the meeting point of the frontiers of Lithuania, the Polish Republic and East Prussia.

The Conference has agreed in principle to the proposal of the Soviet Government concerning the ultimate transfer to the Soviet Union of the city of Koenigsberg and the area adjacent to it as described above, subject to expert examination of the actual frontier.

The President of the United States and the British Prime Minister have declared that they will support the proposal of the Conference at the forthcoming peace settlement.[84]

This text would appear to indicate that ultimately ("at the forthcoming peace settlement") the American and British Governments intend to assent to the incorporation of the Baltic republics into the Soviet Union. For it is hard to see how the city of Koenigsberg and its adjacent area could be

[83] *New York Times* of October 19, 1945 (Report Drew Middleton)
[84] 13 *D. S. Bull.* 158

transferred to the U.S.S.R. unless Lithuania, too, belongs to the latter. On the other hand, the text makes it clear that the territorial questions will have to remain open until the final settlement at the peace conference.

The latter principle, and consequently the continuing non-recognition of the incorporation of the Baltic republics into the Soviet Union, was once more emphasized by the American and British Governments in the fall of 1945. On October 6, 1945, the indictment of the major German war criminals before the International Military Tribunal was signed by the representatives of the American, French, British, and Soviet Governments.[85] Among the war crimes listed under count three thereof were charges of atrocities committed in the "Estonian Soviet Socialist Republic," the "Lithuanian Soviet Socialist Republic," and the "Latvian Soviet Socialist Republic." According to press reports,[86] the United States prosecutor, Supreme Court Justice Robert H. Jackson, in signing the indictment, made the following reservation, laid down in a letter filed the same day with the Secretary of the Tribunal:

In the indictment of German war criminals signed today reference is made to Estonia, Latvia, Lithuania and certain other territories as being within the area of the U.S.S.R. This language is proposed by Russia and is accepted to avoid delay which would have been occasioned by the insistence on an alteration in the text. The indictment is signed subject to this reservation and understanding:

I have no authority either to admit or to challenge, on behalf of the United States, the Soviet claims to sovereignty over such territories. Nothing, therefore, in this indictment is to be construed as a recognition by the United States of such sovereignty or as indicating any attitude, either on the part of the United States or on the part of the undersigned, toward any claim to redisposition of such sovereignty.

Likewise, the British Foreign Office stated on October 19, 1945, that the British signature on the indictment of the German war criminals did not imply recognition of the Baltic States as Soviet territory, as they are called in the document.[87]

85 *New York Times* of October 19, 1945
86 Do. of October 20, 1945
87 *Ibid.*

CONCLUSION

I<small>T</small> is the object of this last chapter to draw such conclusions as may be derived from the foregoing material. To this effect, two questions will have to be answered: How far was the idea of non-recognition of territorial changes brought about by force able to stand the test of the strenuous years which elapsed since Mr. Stimson dispatched his epoch-making notes to China and Japan? And is it desirable that the doctrine, hitherto only based on a policy of the United States, on certain inter-American compacts, and implied in the Covenant of the now defunct League of Nations, receive an extended application in the international law of the future?

The analysis of the diplomatic practice of the last decade shows that only the United States, although not bound by any legal commitments except the Saavedra Lamas Anti-War Treaty [1] and the Montevideo Convention on the Rights and Duties of States,[2] was fairly consistent in the application of the principle not to recognize territorial changes effected by force. It is true that the American Government did not always refrain from steps not entirely fitting into the pattern of non-recognition, and on the other hand at times failed to go full length in taking such measures as would appear to be the logical consequences of a consistent non-recognition policy. By and large, however, the practice of the United States remained true to the principles proclaimed by Secretary Stimson in his notes of January 7, 1932.

Quite different is the picture resulting from the practice of the States which had assumed the commitments of the League Covenant. Only in the Manchurian case was the non-recognition principle able to assert itself. It failed miserably in the cases of Ethiopia, Austria, Czechoslovakia, and Albania, when, subject to very few exceptions such as, in certain instances, China, the Soviet Union and New Zealand, one League Member after the other granted recognition to

[1] Above, 75
[2] Above, 77

285

territorial changes effected by external aggression. What were the reasons for such conduct? Was it the conviction that neither Article 10 of the Covenant implied, nor the Assembly Resolution of March 11, 1932,[3] expressed, a generally binding obligation not to recognize the forcible seizure of territory of the League Members? The reader who has attentively scrutinized the material presented in this work, in particular the utterances of government representatives regarding the non-recognition commitments as well as the story of the Council session of May, 1938, will hardly feel inclined to answer this question in the affirmative. What happened was no doubt exclusively due to extralegal considerations, or, to put it in other words, the fixation of appeasement developed in the statesmen of the League Members a mental process which caused the sense of a legal duty of non-recognition to wither away. This was almost explicitly admitted by Prime Minister Chamberlain when he told the House of Commons on February 21, 1938, that formal recognition of Italian sovereignty in Ethiopia could only be morally justified if it was found to be a factor, and an essential factor, in "general appeasement." [4] At any rate, in the end the Member States of the League showed general unwillingness to admit a binding obligation of non-recognition, and it was in the first place the disregard of the duties under Article 10 of the Covenant that undermined the structure of the League of Nations until the outbreak of the Second World War and the exclusion of the Soviet Union caused its final collapse.

In the place of the League, a new international organization of global scope has been erected whose constitution does not prescribe a legal duty of the members to respect and preserve as against external aggression the political independence and territorial integrity of their fellow-members,[5] nor, consequently, the legal duty, implied in the former, not to recognize territorial changes resulting from such aggression. But does this mean that the Stimson Doctrine has proved a failure, that it has no future in international law?

[3] Above, 62
[4] Above, 139
[5] Above, Ch. XIV

In trying to find an answer to this question, we have to weigh the positive aspects of the Doctrine against its short-comings, but also to look at the state of affairs prevailing after the United Nations Charter has come into force.

That shortcomings and limitations attach to the non-recognition principle cannot be denied. In the first place, non-recognition alone is not enough to prevent invasion, nor to end occupation by the invader. Then, non-recognition of a territorial transfer does not in itself end all intercourse between the non-recognizing State and the seized area. The nationals of the former will normally continue, and be allowed to continue, personal and business relations with the latter. This entails for their sovereign the necessity of safeguarding their interests. Moreover, in case the dispossessing Power establishes in the seized area a system of oppression or extermination of whole groups of the population, a non-recognizing State may desire to help the victims by granting them access to its own territory. In either case, in spite of non-recognition, certain official contacts will be imperative. Sometimes it may be possible to effect them by means of special agents, or through a third Power. In other cases, however, the dispatch of officers of consular status will prove unavoidable. This, of course, will normally force the non-recognizing Power to apply to the occupant for an exequatur. That such a request implies de facto recognition, is accepted theory.[6] Sometimes important political considerations may even prompt a State committed to non-recognition to send diplomatic representatives into the seized area, may it only be to secure a vantage point for observation or even for underground work against the occupant. Also, in certain instances non-recognition may not be advisable because the occupant may take umbrage at it, even use it as a pretext for military action against the non-recognizing State, while the latter cannot afford to precipitate a premature clash. Thus, frequently a foreign office may find itself in a dilemma between its legal commitments or settled policy on the one, and considerations of the raison d'État on the other hand.

As to the positive aspects of non-recognition, they mani-

6 Above, 102

fest themselves in the political, juridical, and ethical sphere.

Politically, the non-recognition of a forcible seizure of territory is of considerable value for upholding the morale of the population of the seized area, for strengthening their spirit of resistance, not only for their own benefit, but often also for the ultimate benefit of the non-recognizing State, as many recent instances have shown.[7]

Juridically, non-recognition acts during the occupation on behalf of the nationals of the seized State who find themselves within the jurisdiction of the non-recognizing State, in particular in case war breaks out between the latter and the occupant. After the end of the occupation, non-recognition affords the returning sovereign a clearer legal position regarding the rescission of measures of the dispossessing Power. The questions that arose during and at the end of the Second World War with respect to the personal status and the assets of nationals of occupied countries clearly show the great importance of the Stimson Doctrine in the administrative and judicial fields.

Ethically, non-recognition is the most pertinent manifestation of the postulate that a unilateral tour de force should not be allowed to bring about a valid change in the existing territorial order.

These positive aspects of the non-recognition idea, it is believed, decidedly outweigh its undeniable shortcomings and limitations, and would appear to warrant the expectation that in spite of having been barred from the United Nations Charter, the principle embodied in the Stimson Doctrine is bound to play an important role in the international law of the future. In fact, looking at recent diplomatic happenings, we see that many months after the Dumbarton Oaks proposals were announced, the republics of the Americas solemnly re-emphasized the non-recognition principle in the Act of Chapultepec, which proclaimed it part of the international law of the Americas.[8] The inter-American treaties which have raised non-recognition to the rank of a legal duty are in force today as they were when the United

[7] See Mr. Litvinov's speech of May 12, 1938, at the League Council (above, 145 ff.)
[8] Above, 83

Nations Charter was adopted and when it came into force, and it is hardly likely that they will be abrogated, in particular in view of the latent threat of aggression inherent in certain Latin-American developments. Nor has the coming into force of the United Nations Charter hitherto affected the non-recognition policy of the United States. This is evidenced by a series of official statements made in the very last months and weeks. To these belong the reservations attached to the American signature on the indictment of the German war criminals,[9] and also President Truman's speech of October 27, 1945 (Navy Day)[10] when he said:

Let me restate the fundamentals of that foreign policy of the United States:

. . . .

6. We shall refuse to recognize any government imposed upon any nation by the force of any foreign power. In some cases it may be impossible to prevent forceful imposition of such government. But the United States will not recognize any such government.

In keeping with these words of the President are subsequent official utterances, thus the release of the Department of State of January 9, 1946, which emphasized that "the United States did not recognize the German annexation of Austria," [11] and a report, dated January 16, 1946,[12] to the effect that

It was in May, 1941, that Siam took part of Cambodja in the south and part of Laos, west of the Mekong river, in the north.

The State Department has informed the French, Siamese, and British Governments that we do not recognize the validity of the transfer of the Indo-Chinese territories acquired by Siam at that time on the ground that they were acquired in the course of Japanese aggression and we consider that those territories should be restored by Siam.

It was explained at the Department that this view was not to be considered as supporting or opposing the merits of the pre-1941 Indo-Chinese-Siamese border and that the position of this government was without prejudice to any border readjustments that might be effected by orderly, peaceful processes subsequent to the restoration of the territories.

[9] Above, 284
[10] 13 *D. S. Bull.* 654
[11] Above, 201
[12] *New York Times* of January 17, 1946

Thus, it may well be anticipated that the principle of the Stimson Doctrine will stay as a fundamental principle of the international law of the Americas. But even within the orbit of the United Nations organization, it may again come to the fore some day. In the first place, it should not be forgotten that the proposals to amend the San Francisco draft of the United Nations Charter by inserting provisions which would have reproduced the essence of Article 10 of the Covenant, and consequently by implication the non-recognition principle, were able to command a simple majority, although not the required two-thirds majority. Furthermore, sooner or later cases may arise in which the protection of the political independence and territorial integrity of a Member State may be thwarted through the technicalities of the voting procedure, and it is quite thinkable that in such an instance the States whose desire to protect the victim of aggression by collective action has been blocked by a *liberum veto*, may fall back on the device of non-recognition as offering to the victim at least a certain measure of encouragement and support. Such a development, it is believed, should be welcomed since it would end the discrepancy which now exists between the United Nations constitution and the legal concepts of the Americas regarding the law of territorial change, a discrepancy hardly conducive to the growth of general international law. Not only for this reason, but above all for the intrinsic value of the Stimson Doctrine it should be hoped and wished that it will be able to reassert itself in new agreements of a global scope. The rebirth of the obligations which were implied in Article 10 of the League Covenant, the transformation of the non-recognition principle into world-wide law, would be a signal service to civilization, for it would mean the realization of the moral goal for which the United Nations have fought and won the Second World War: That the world be not ruled by the Prusso-Teutonic slogan, *Macht geht vor Recht*, but by the maxim of the Pax Romana,

Ex iniuria ius non oritur.

BIBLIOGRAPHY

I. GENERAL TREATISES

Hyde, Charles C. *International Law as Chiefly Interpreted and Applied by the United States*. 2d ed. Boston: Little, Brown & Co., 1945.

Oppenheim, Lassa Francis L. *International Law*. 6th ed. by H. Lauterpacht. London: Longmans, Green & Company, 1938.

II. OTHER BOOKS

Alvarez, Alejandro. *Le Droit International Américain*. Paris, 1910.

————. *Considérations Générales sur la Codification du Droit International Américain*. Rio de Janeiro, 1927.

————. *Le Continent Américain et la Codification du Droit International*. Paris, 1938.

Bustamante y Sirven, Antonio Sanchez de. *La Commission des Jurisconsultes de Rio et le Droit International*. Rio de Janeiro, 1928.

Boldur, Alexandre. *La Bessarabie et les Relations Russo-Roumaines*. Paris, 1927.

Buell, Raymond L. *Poland, Key to Europe*. New York: Knopf, 1939.

Dallin, David J. *Soviet Russia's Foreign Policy 1939–1942*. New Haven: Yale University Press, 1942.

Dell, Robert E. *The Geneva Racket*. London: Hale, 1941.

Dennis, Alfred L. *The Foreign Policies of Soviet Russia*. New York: Dutton & Company, 1924.

Eagleton, Clyde. *International Government*. New York: Roland Press, 1932.

Feilchenfeld, Ernst H. *The International Economic Law of Belligerent Occupation*. Washington: Carnegie Endowment for International Peace, 1942.

Goebel, Julius L. *The Recognition Policy of the United States*. New York: Columbia University Press, 1915.

Graham, Malbone W. *In Quest of a Law of Recognition*. Berkeley: University of California Press, 1933.

————. *The League of Nations and the Recognition of States*. Berkeley: University of California Press, 1933.

————. *The Diplomatic Recognition of the Border States*. Berkeley: University of California Press, 1935.

Hill, Chesney. *Recent Policies of Non-Recognition (International Conciliation No. 293)*. New York: Carnegie Endowment for International Peace, 1933.

Komarnicki, Titus. *La Question de l'Intégrité Territoriale dans le Pacte de la Société des Nations.* Paris: Presse Universitaire, 1923.

Lagarde, Ernest. *La Reconnaissance du Gouvernement des Soviets.* Paris: Payot, 1924.

Lecharny, Louis. *La Validité des Actes Internes des Gouvernements de Fait a l'égard des Etrangers.* Paris: Rousseau, 1929.

Le Normand, René. *La Reconnaissance Internationale.* Paris: Camis et Cie, 1899.

Lindley, Mark F. *The Acquisition and Government of Backward Territories.* London and New York: Longmans, Green & Company, 1926.

McMahon, John L. *Recent Changes in the Recognition Policies of the United States.* Washington: The Catholic University of America Press, 1933.

McMahon, Matthew M. *Conquest and Modern International Law.* Washington: The Catholic University of America Press, 1940.

McNair, Sir Arnold D. *Legal Effects of War.* 2d ed. Cambridge: The Cambridge University Press, 1944.

Milioukov, Paul. *La Politique Extérieure des Soviets.* Paris, 1936.

Noël-Henry. *Le Gouvernement de Fait devant le Juge.* Paris: Guillon, 1927.

Phillipson, Coleman. *Termination of War and Treaties of Peace.* London: Fisher Unwin Ltd., 1916.

Robin, Raymond. *Des Occupations Militaires en dehors des Occupations de Guerre.* Paris: Recueil Sirey, 1913.

Schindler, Dietrich. *Die Verbindlichkeit der Beschlüsse des Völkerbundes.* Zuerich: Orell-Fuessli, 1927.

Schücking, Walther. *Die Satzung des Völkerbundes,* 3d ed. Berlin: Vahlen, 1931.

Sharp, Roland Hall. *Duties of Non-Recognition in Practice, 1775–1934 (Geneva Special Studies,* Vol. V, No. 4). Geneva: Geneva Research Center, 1934.

———. *Non-Recognition as a Legal Obligation, 1775–1934.* Liège: Thone, 1934.

Shotwell, James T. *On the Rim of the Abyss.* New York: Macmillan, 1936.

Stimson, Henry L. *The Far Eastern Crisis.* New York: Harper and Bros., 1936.

Taracouzio, Timothy. *The Soviet Union and International Law.* New York: Macmillan, 1935.

Temperley, Harold W. *A History of the Peace Conference of Paris.* London: Frowde, 1920–4.

Wheeler-Bennett, John W. *The Forgotten Peace.* New York: Morrow and Company, 1939.

Williams, Sir John Fischer. *Some Aspects of the Covenant of the League of Nations.* London: Oxford University Press, 1934.

Wright, Herbert F. *The Attitude of the United States towards*

Austria (House Document No. 477, 78th Congress, 2d Session). Washington: U. S. Government Printing Office, 1944.

III. ACADÉMIE DE DROIT INTERNATIONAL, LA HAYE, RECUEIL DES COURS

Gemma, Scipione. "Les Gouvernements de Fait" (V. 14, 1924, p. 297).

Erich, Rafael. "La Naissance et la Reconnaissance des États" (V. 13, 1926, p. 430).

Schücking, Walther. "Le Développement du Pacte de la Société des Nations" (V. 20, 1927, p. 353).

Williams, Sir John Fischer. "La Doctrine de la Reconnaissance en Droit International et ses Développements Récents" (V. 44, 1933, p. 203).

Lauterpacht, H. "Règles Générales du Droit de la Paix" (V. 62, 1937, p. 99).

IV. PROCEEDINGS OF THE AMERICAN SOCIETY OF INTERNATIONAL LAW

Middlebush, Frederick A. "Non-Recognition as Sanction in International Law" (V. 27, 1933, p. 40).

Briggs, Herbert. "Non-Recognition of Title by Conquest and Its Limitations" (V. 34, 1940, p. 72).

V. TRANSACTIONS OF THE GROTIUS SOCIETY

Williams, Sir John Fischer. "Recognition" (V. 15, 1929, p. 53).

———. "The New Doctrine of Recognition" (V. 18, 1932, p. 109).

Lauterpacht, H. "The Pact of Paris and the Budapest Articles of Interpretation" (V. 20, 1934, p. 178).

VI. ARTICLES IN LAW JOURNALS, LAW REVIEWS, YEARBOOKS, ETC.

1. AMERICAN JOURNAL OF INTERNATIONAL LAW

(In Chronological Order)

Hyde, Charles C. "Recognition of New Governments by the United States" (V. 13, 1919, p. 306).

Hershey, Amos. "The Status of Mr. Bakhmetiev" (V. 16, 1922, p. 426).

Dickinson, Edwin D. "Recognition Cases 1925–1930" (V. 25, 1931, p. 214).

Jessup, Philip C. "The Estrada Doctrine" (V. 25, 1931, p. 719).

Hyde, Charles C. "Termination of Treaties in Case of Absorption of States" (V. 26, 1932, p. 133).

Borchard, Edwin H. "Unrecognized Governments in American Courts" (V. 26, 1932, p. 261).

Wright, Quincy. "The Stimson Note" (V. 26, 1932, p. 342).

Woolsey, H. L. "The Chaco Dispute" (V. 26, 1932, p. 796).

Wright, Quincy. "The Meaning of the Pact of Paris" (V. 27, 1933, p. 39).

Jessup, Philip C. "The Saavedra Lamas Anti-War Draft Treaty" (V. 27, 1933, p. 109).

Moore, John B. "The New Isolation" (V. 27, 1933, p. 607).

Jessup, Philip C. "The Argentine Anti-War Pact" (V. 28, 1934, p. 538).

Woolsey, H. L. "The Chaco Dispute" (V. 28, 1934, p. 724).

Hudson, Manley. "The Budapest Resolutions on the Briand-Kellogg Pact" (V. 29, 1935, p. 92).

Baty, Thomas. "Abuse of the Terms Recognition and War" (V. 30, 1936, p. 377).

Hyde, Charles C. "Conquest Today" (V. 30, 1936, p. 471).

Garner, James W. "Non-Recognition of Illegal Territorial Annexations" (V. 30, 1936, p. 679).

Brown, Philip M. "The Recognition of New States and New Governments" (V. 30, 1936, p. 689).

Wright, Quincy. "The British Courts and Ethiopian Recognition" (V. 31, 1937, p. 683).

Fenwick, G. G. "Fuit Austria" (V. 32, 1938, p. 313).

Garner, James W. "Problems of State Succession Raised by the German Annexation of Austria" (V. 32, 1938, p. 421).

———. "Germany's Responsibility for Austrian Debts" (V. 32, 1938, p. 766).

Wright, Quincy. "The Munich Settlement and International Law" (V. 33, 1939, p. 12).

Briggs, Herbert. "De Facto and De Jure Recognition. The Arantzazu Mendi" (V. 33, 1939, p. 681).

Kelsen, Hans. "Recognition in International Law" (V. 35, 1941, p. 605).

Brown, Philip M. "Sovereignty in Exile" (V. 35, 1941, p. 666).

———. "The Effects of Recognition" (V. 36, 1942, p. 106).

Borchard, Edwin H. "Recognition and Non-Recognition" (V. 36, 1942, p. 108).

Oppenheimer, F. E. "Governments and Authorities in Exile" (V. 36, 1942, p. 568).

Woolsey, L. H. "Forced Transfer of Property in Enemy Occupied Territory" (V. 37, 1943, p. 282).

Pergler, Charles. "The Munich Repudiation" (V. 37, 1943, p. 308).

Borchard, Edwin H. "Flaws in Post-War Plans" (V. 38, 1944, p. 284).

Jessup, Philip C. "A Belligerent Occupant's Power" (V. 38, 1944, p. 457).

Wright, Herbert F. "The Legality of the Annexation of Austria" (V. 38, 1944, p. 621).

Graham, Malbone W. "The Legal Status of the Bukovina and Bessarabia" (V. 38, 1944, p. 667).

Gross, Leo. "Was the Soviet Union Expelled from the League of Nations?" (V. 39, 1945, p. 35).

2. BRITISH YEAR BOOK OF INTERNATIONAL LAW

(In Chronological Order)

McNair, Sir Arnold D. "Judicial Recognition of States and Governments" (V. 2, 1921, p. 57).

Williams, Sir John Fischer. "Sovereignty, Seisin and the League" (V. 7, 1926, p. 24).

McNair, Sir Arnold D. "The Stimson Doctrine of Non-Recognition" (V. 14, 1933, p. 65).

Brierly, J. L. "The Meaning and Legal Effect of the Resolution of the League of Nations of March 11, 1932" (V. 16, 1935, p. 159).

Williams, Sir John Fischer. "Sanctions and the Covenant" (V. 17, 1936, p. 130).

3. REVUE DE DROIT INTERNATIONAL ET DE LÉGISLATION COMPARÉE

Lorimer, James. "La Doctrine de la Reconnaissance" (S. 1, V. 16, 1884, p. 333).

Raestad, Arnold. "La Reconnaissance Internationale de Nouveaux États" (S. 3, V. 17, 1936, p. 257).

4. REVUE GÉNÉRALE DU DROIT INTERNATIONAL PUBLIC

Larnaude, F. "Les Gouvernements de Fait" (V. 28, 1921, p. 457).

5. VARIOUS AMERICAN AND ENGLISH LAW REVIEWS

Baty, Thomas. "So-Called De Facto Recognition," 31 *Yale L. J.* (1922), 469.

Dickinson, Edwin D. "International Recognition in National Courts," 18 *Mich. L. Rev.* (1920), 531.

———. "Unrecognized Governments and States in English and American Courts," 22 *Mich. L. Rev.* (1923–4), 39 and 118.

Lauterpacht, H. "Recognition of States in International Law," 53 *Yale L. J.* (1944), 385.

McNair, Sir Arnold D. "Municipal Effect of Belligerent Occupation," 57 *L. Q. Rev.* (1941), 331.

Moore, John B. "Fifty Years of International Law," 50 *Harv. L. Rev.* (1937), 395.

Westlake, John. "The Nature and Extent of Title by Conquest," 17 *L. Q. Rev.* (1901), 392.

Williams, Sir John Fischer. "Some Thoughts on Recognition," 47 *Harv. L. Rev.* (1934), 776.

VII. SOURCES AND DIGESTS

Angeborg, Comte de. *Le Congrès de Vienne et les Traités de 1815.* Paris: Amyot, 1864.

De Clercq, Edouard. *Recueil des Traités de la France.* Paris: Durant et Pedone, 1880.

Hertslet, Sir Edward. *The Map of Europe by Treaties.* London: Butterworth and Company, 1875–1891.

League of Nations, Treaty Series, Geneva.

Martens, George Fred. de, et Continuateurs. *Recueil des Traités.* Goettingen: Dieterich, 1791–1835.

————. *Nouveau Recueil des Traités.* Goettingen: Dieterich, 1817–1842.

————. *Nouveau Recueil Général des Traités.* Goettingen: Dieterich, 1845–1875.

————. *Nouveau Recueil Général des Traités, 2me Série.* Goettingen and Leipzig: Dieterich, 1876–1908.

————. *Nouveau Recueil Général des Traités, 3me Série.* Leipzig: Dieterich and Others, 1909–1939.

Martin, Lawrence. *The Treaties of Peace 1919–1923.* New York: Carnegie Endowment for International Peace, 1924.

Status of the Pan American Treaties and Conventions, revised by the Juridical Division of the Pan American Union. Washington: U. S. Government Printing Office, 1945.

Treaties, Conventions between the United States and Other Powers. Washington: U. S. Government Printing Office.

United States, Treaty Series. Washington: U. S. Government Printing Office.

The Hague Conventions and Declarations of 1889 and 1907, ed. by James B. Scott. New York: Carnegie Endowment for International Peace, Oxford University Press, 1915.

British and Foreign State Papers. London.

Papers Presented by the Secretary of State for Foreign Affairs to Parliament by Command of His Majesty. London: His Majesty's Stationery Office.

Parliamentary Debates (Hansard), Fifth Series. London: His Majesty's Stationery Office.

United States, Congressional Record. Washington: U. S. Government Printing Office.

U. S. Department of State, Papers Relating to the Foreign Relations of the United States. Washington: U. S. Government Printing Office.

————. *Press Releases,* do.

————. *Bulletin,* do.

Annual Report, Office of the Alien Property Custodian, Fiscal Year Ending June 1945.

Statutory Rules and Orders. London: His Majesty's Stationery Office.

Federal Register. Washington: U. S. Government Printing Office.

United States Code Annotated. St. Paul, Minn.: West Publishing Company.

Reichsgesetzblatt. Berlin: Reichsverlagsamt.

Staatsgesetzblatt für die Republik Österreich, Wien.

Gooch, George P., and Temperley, Harold W. *British Documents on the Origin of the World War, 1898–1914.* London: His Majesty's Stationery Office.

Bulletin of International News. London: Royal Institute of International Affairs.

Chronology of International Events and Documents, New Series. London: Royal Institute of International Affairs.

Survey of International Affairs. London: Oxford University Press.

Documents on International Affairs. London: Oxford University Press.

International Conciliation. New York: Carnegie Endowment for International Peace.

League of Nations, Official Journal. Geneva: League of Nations.

League of Nations, Conference for the Reduction and Limitation of Armaments, Minutes and Documents. Geneva: League of Nations.

Second Pan-American Conference, Minutes and Documents. Mexico, 1902.

Third International American Conference: Minutes, Resolutions, Documents. Rio de Janeiro, 1907.

International Commission of Jurists, Rio de Janeiro, 1927. Rio de Janeiro: Imprensa Nacional, 1927.

Report of the Delegates to the Sixth International Conference of American States. Washington: U. S. Government Printing Office, 1928.

Draft of an Anti-War Treaty, translated and published by the Argentine Embassy. Washington: 1932.

The Argentine Anti-War Treaty. Buenos Aires: Ministerio de Relaciones Exteriores, 1932.

Minutes and Antecedents of the Seventh International Conference of American States. Montevideo, 1933.

Report of the Delegation of the United States of America to the Inter-American Conference for the Maintenance of Peace. Washington: U. S. Government Printing Office, 1936.

Draft of a Convention for the Maintenance of Peace. Washington, 1936.

Draft Convention on the Rights and Duties of States in Case of Aggression, Research in International Law of the Harvard Law School, 33 *AJIL* (1939), Suppl., p. 823.

The United Nations Review, New York.

United Nations Conference on International Organization, Documents. London and New York, 1945.

The United Nations Conference. Report on the Conference Held at San Francisco 25 April–26 June 1945 by the Right Hon. Peter Fraser, Chairman of the New Zealand Delegation. Wellington: Department of External Affairs, 1945.

Hackworth, Green H. *Digest of International Law.* Washington: U. S. Government Printing Office.

Jones, S. Shepard, and Myers, Denys. *Documents on American Foreign Relations.* Boston: World Peace Foundation.

Hudson, Manley. *International Legislation.* Washington: Carnegie Endowment for International Peace.

Moore, John B. *A Digest of International Law.* Washington: U.S. Government Printing Office, 1906.

————. *History and Digest of International Arbitrations.* Washington: U. S. Government Printing Office, 1898.

Lauterpacht, H. *Annual Digest of Public Law Cases.* London: Butterworth and Company.

Recueil des Actes Diplomatiques, Traités et Documents concernant la Pologne. Paris: Comité National Polonais, 1920.

Czechoslovak Sources and Documents. New York: The Czechoslovak Information Service, 1943.

Czechoslovak Yearbook of International Law. London: 1942.

Treaties and Conventions with or concerning China and Korea, published by William W. Rockhill. Washington: U. S. Government Printing Office, 1904.

Treaties, Conventions, etc., between China and Foreign States, published by order of the Inspector General of Customs, Shanghai, 1908.

Treaties and Agreements with or concerning China 1894–1919, compiled and edited by John V. A. MacMurray. New York: Oxford University Press, 1921.

AJIL *American Journal of International Law*

Angeborg Angeborg, Comte de, *Le Congrès de Vienne et les Traités de 1815*

Ann. Dig. Lauterpacht, H., *Annual Digest of Public Law Cases*

ASIL Proceedings of the American Society of International Law

BFSP British and Foreign State Papers

Br. Y. Bk. British Year Book of International Law

Bull. Int. News Bulletin of International News

China Treaties Treaties, Conventions, etc., between China and Foreign States, published by order of the Inspector General of Customs

Chron. Chronology of International Events and Documents, New Series

Cmd. Papers Presented by the Secretary of State for Foreign Affairs to Parliament by Command of His Majesty

Cz. S. & D. Czechoslovak Sources and Documents

Cz. Y. Bk. Czechoslovak Yearbook of International Law

De Clercq De Clercq, Edouard, *Recueil des Traités de la France*

D. S. Bull. United States Department of State, Bulletin

D. S. Press Rel. United States Department of State, Press Releases

Doc. Am. For. Rel. Jones, S. Shepard, and Myers, Denys, Documents on American Foreign Relations

Doc. Int. Aff. Documents on International Affairs

Fed. Reg. Federal Register

For. Rel. U. S. Department of State, Papers Relating to the Foreign Relations of the United States

Gen., Gén. General, Général

Gooch-Temperley Gooch, George P., and Temperley, Harold W., *British Documents on the Origin of the World War 1898–1914*

Hackworth Hackworth, Green H., *Digest of International Law*

Hague Rec. Académie de Droit International, La Haye, *Recueil des Cours*

H. C. Deb. Parliamentary Debates (Hansard), Fifth Series, House of Commons

H. L. Deb. Parliamentary Debates (Hansard), Fifth Series, House of Lords

Int. Conc. International Conciliation

Journ. Dr. Int. Journal du Droit International

LNOJ League of Nations, Official Journal

LNTS League of Nations, Treaty Series

MacMurray *Treaties and Agreements with and concerning China 1894–1919*, compiled and edited by John V. A. MacMurray

Moore, *Arb.* Moore, John B., *History and Digest of International Arbitrations*

Moore, *Dig.* Moore, John B., *A Digest of International Law*

Nouv. Nouveau

Polish Doc. Recueil des Actes Diplomatiques, Traités et Documents concernant la Pologne

Rec. Recueil

Rev. Dr. Int. Revue de Droit International et de Législation Comparée

Rockhill *Treaties and Conventions with or concerning China and Korea*, edited by William W. Rockhill

S. Series, Série

Spec. Special

S. R. & O. Statutory Rules and Orders

Suppl. Supplement

Temperley Temperley, Harold W., *A History of the Peace Conference of Paris*

Un. Nat. Rev. The United Nations Review

USCA United States Code Annotated

U. S. Treaties Treaties, Conventions between the United States and Other Powers

USTS United States Department of State, Treaty Series

INDEX

Abyssinia, *see* Ethiopia
Adams, John Quincy, 4
Adams, M.P., 224
Addis Ababa, 133, 136, 153, 154
Adrianople, Tr. of (1829), 9 [22]
Aehrenthal, Count, 13 [5]
Afghanistan, 73
Africa, 153, 240
Aggression, 30, 39-43, 46, 47, 48,[55]
58,[38] 59, 62-65, 74-76, 81, 82, 86, 87,
89, 90, 96, 100, 110,[18] 118, 119, 125,
143-148, 153, 158, 159, 165, 176, 208,
215, 217, 226, 228, 255, 256, 258,
269, 288-290; definition of (Litvinov Conventions), 31,[20] 73, 74;
definition of (Act of Chapultepec), 83; Harvard Draft Convention, 81; Havana Declaration, 82;
San Francisco Conference, 89, 90;
United Nations Charter, 91, 92;
Axis, 86, 259; Japanese against
China, 61, 84, 124, 126, 128, 289;
Italian against Ethiopia, 132, 134,
136, 137, 139, 148, 165; Italian
against Albania, 245, 248-250; German against Austria, 155, 159, 165,
177, 181, 188, 202, 203; German
against Czechoslovakia, 224
Aggressor, 16, 41, 46-48, 57, 59,[38]
73, 74, 81, 82, 90, 100, 110,[18] 124,
132, 134, 145, 146, 158, 159, 165,
188, 214, 241
Aland Islands, 257
Albania, 66,[55] 100, 103,[8] 135, 169,
245-253, 259, 282, 285
Albanian, 168, 245-252; State, 13;
Government, 245, 246, 250, 252
Alexander I, Tsar, 8
Alexander, M.P., 118,[3] 227-229
Alexander, Sir H., 192
Algeria, Algiers, 240
Alien Enemies, *see* Enemy Aliens
Alien Registration (U. S.), 126, 168,
170
Aliens of Enemy Nationality, *see*
Enemy Aliens
Aliens Order (Brit.), 74-176, 185
Allied Powers, Principal, 24, 29, 31
Allied and Associated Powers, 26,
119 [4]
Allies, Principal, 28; Western, 193
Alsace-Lorraine, 9
Alvarez, 37, 38
American (U. S.), *see* United States

(Inter-) American, 37-39, 76, 78,
92;[14] Nations, Republics, States,
34, 37-39, 68, 75-78; 82, 83, 135,
141, 229
American Institute of International
Law, 37, 38
American Society of International
Law, 150 [51]
Americas, The, 39, 82, 289, 290
Amiens, Tr. of (1802), 3
Amtorg Trading Co., 267
Anderson, 37
Anderson, Sir J., 175, 176
Anglo-French, 211-215; Anglo-Ital-
ian, 140, 141, 151; Anglo-Soviet
(Tr. of Alliance, 1942), 84, 265,
269
Annexation, 9, 12, 14, 15, 17, 18, 31,
46, 53,[16] 100, 106, 111, 116,[2] 117,
135, 138, 146, 169; premature, 17;
in southeastern Europe, 15; Ru-
manian, of Bessarabia, 29, 30;
Polish, of Vilna, 31; Japanese, of
Korea, 53;[16] Japanese, of Man-
churia, 132; Italian, of Ethiopia,
132-137, 146, 150-152, 155, 174;
Italian, of Albania, 248-252; Ger-
man, of Austria, 100, 155-159, 163-
169, 171, 174, 181-183, 186, 189,
192, 201, 203, 208, 289; German, of
Bohemia-Moravia, 223-229; Hun-
garian, of Carpatho-Ukraine, 209;
Soviet, of eastern Poland, 280.
See also Non-Recognition
Anschluss, 165, 171,[46] 186, 195
Anti-Comintern Pact, 124
Anti-War Treaty (Saavedra Lamas),
75-80, 95, 117,[2] 218, 228, 285
Appeasement, 90, 139, 150-152, 286
Argentine, The, 66,[55] 68,[2, 3] 75-78,
134. *See also* Anti-War Treaty
Argyrokastro, 251
Asia, vi, 90
Askwith, Ld., 80 [1]
Athens, 14; Tr. of (1913), 13 [7]
Atlantic Charter, 83, 84, 188, 203,
265, 270, 271, 278
Attlee, P.M., 128, 249, 283
Australia, 66,[55] 109
Australian, 89, 91
Austria (Empire), 5-9; (Republic)
32, 66,[55] 100, 114,[7] 135, 155-209,
217, 221, 252, 259, 261, 285-289
Austria-Hungary, 12,[2] 13 [5]

For List of Cases see end of Index.

301

Saavedra Lamas, 9, 75, 78, 95. *See also* Anti-War Treaty
Salvador, El, 66,[55] 77, 123
Sandler, 221
Sandys, M.P., 225-227
San Francisco, Cal., Conference of, 88, 90, 92, 251, 290
Sankey, Viscount, 80 [1]
San Stefano, Tr. of, 10
Santiago de Chile, 34, 37; Tr. of (1904), 35 [6]
Sarande, 251
Sardinia, Sardinian, 9
Schindler, 97 [7]
Schleswig-Holstein, 9
Schmidt, Guido, 156
Schücking, 97 [7]
Schuschnigg, Chanc., 155, 156, 182
Schwarzkopf, 172 [46]
Scialoja, 43, 44
Self-Defense, 41, 62, 76
Self-Determination, 18, 20, 22, 23, 40, 62, 76, 210-212
Sempill, Ld., 180, 181
Serbia, 10, 13,[6, 7] 15
Serbian, 14
Seoul, 53
Seyss-Inquart, 156, 157
Sfatul Tzearii, 28, 29
Shanghai, 61, 62
Sharp, 97 [7]
Shikoku, 128
Shimonoseki, Tr. of, 50
Siam, 66,[55] 69, 289
Siamese, 289
Siberia, 50, 55
Sicily, 5, 9
Sidor, P.M., 218
Sikorski, P.M., 270
Silesia, 209
Silverman, M.P., 180
Simon, Sir J., 64, 65, 99, 229, 230
Sinclair, Sir A., M.P., 141, 225, 226
Sinkiang, 130
Sino-Japanese, 67, 69, 98, 124, 267
Slavic, 241
Slovak(s), 214-224, 233, 234, 239; Government, 218, 224
Slovakia, 100, 102,[6] 209, 216, 218, 222-224, 227, 229-233, 241
Slovenia, 182
Smolensk, 271, 272
Snell, Ld., 160
Sokolnikov, 20
Sorensen, M.P., 176
South African Republic, 17 [2]
South America, 90, 185 [74]
South American Republics, 90
South Manchuria, 52, 55-57
South Manchuria Railway, 52, 56, 131

Sovereignty, 6, 17, 19, 30, 31, 44, 46, 48, 52, 53,[16] 55, 58, 59, 63, 69, 81-83, 96, 100-102, 104,[9] 106, 107, 115, 117, 128, 130, 131, 133, 137-140, 149-152, 166, 182, 197, 225, 229, 235, 236, 238, 241, 242, 265, 268, 271, 272, 277, 278, 281, 282, 284, 286
Soviet, 26-31, 47, 73, 84, 125, 129-131, 191-193, 239-243, 256-259, 263-266, 270-275, 281-284; Soviet-German, 268, 269; Soviet-Polish, 269, 273, 277, 280; Soviet-Rumanian, 263, 281; Soviet Russian, 19; Soviet-Turkish Treaty (1921), 47, 117;[2] Soviet-Japanese Non-Aggression Treaty (1941), 175, 177; Soviet-British Treaty of Alliance (1942), 84, 265, 269; Soviet-Chinese Treaty (1945), 129, 130
Soviet Byelorussia, 272, 273, 275
Soviet Government, 20-23, 26-31, 55, 56, 84, 86, 105,[10] 123-130, 158, 165, 188-191, 198, 199, 222, 233-236, 239, 242, 243, 253-262, 265-277, 280-284
Soviet Lithuania, 272, 275
Soviet Russia, 20, 26, 28, 151, 270, 278
Soviet Ukraine, 272, 273, 275
Soviet Union, 31, 33,[5] 84, 86, 123-131, 139, 145, 151, 155, 181, 198, 199, 214, 218, 238-242, 254-257, 260-263, 266, 267, 274, 280-286
Spain, 5, 64, 66,[55] 77, 124, 160, 164,[19] 233
Spanish, 164, 165
Šrámek, Mgr., P.M., 235, 238
Stalin, 127, 187, 243, 274, 278
Stalingrad, 270
Status quo, v, 8, 24,[9] 40, 49, 53, 69, 88, 117, 118, 160, 271
Stettinius, 275
Stimson, Secr., 58-61, 66, 228, 285; Doctrine, v, 75, 76, 106, 110,[18] 117, 264, 286-290; Notes, 58-61, 95, 117, 123
Strauss, M.P., 185, 187, 188, 190, 193
St. Germain, Tr. of, 157, 160, 177
St. Petersburg, 9,[22] 51,[5] 53
St. Thomas, V.I., 267
Sub-Carpathian Russia, 238
Sublime Porte, 9
Sudeten, 216; area, 100, 214, 218, 241; Germans, 209-212; Sudetenland, 205, 218
Suifenho, 131
Sultan, 14
Supreme Council of Allied Powers (1919), 15, 23, 24,[11] 27
Supreme Headquarters, Allied Expeditionary Forces (1944), 283
Sweden, 5, 66 [55]

LIST OF CASES